Diplomatic
MISSIONS

The Ambassador
in Canadian
Foreign Policy

Diplomatic MISSIONS

The Ambassador in Canadian Foreign Policy

Edited by
Robert Wolfe

School of Policy Studies
Queen's University

Canadian Centre for Foreign
Policy Development

Canadian Cataloguing in Publication Data

Main entry under title:

Diplomatic missions

Papers presented at a workshop held in Ottawa, June 25-26, 1997.
Includes bibliographical references.
ISBN 0-88911-803-5 (bound)   0-88911-801-9 (pbk.)

1. Diplomats – Canada – Congresses. 2. Diplomatic and consular service,
Canadian – Congresses. 3. Canada – Foreign relations – Congresses.
I. Wolfe, Robert David, 1950–   . II. Queen's University (Kingston, Ont.).
School of Policy Studies.

FC602.D56 1998   327.71   C98-931672-6

Contents

PART III: DIPLOMATIC PARTNERS

PART IV: APPENDICES

Preface

Heads of mission represent Canada to the world, but what do they actually do? The diverse participants in this collective search for answers included men and women who joined the foreign service in the 1960s and 1970s. They have served in Africa, Asia, Latin America, Europe, the United States, and resident missions to international organizations. They have experience in advanced economies, countries in transition, and developing countries and they have worked in the domains of trade, political relations, public affairs, development assistance, and management. These authors do not represent all perspectives on the foreign service — every reader will see gaps — but I think that their collective portrait of the Canadian ambassador is a fair likeness.

This book is the outcome of the Workshop on the Role of Canadian Heads of Mission held in the Norman Robertson conference room of the Lester B. Pearson Building in Ottawa, June 25-26, 1997 — a happy choice of site, as both Pearson and Robertson had been distinguished heads of mission. The workshop and the book resulted from the collaboration of the Canadian Foreign Service Institute (CFSI) and the Canadian Centre for Foreign Policy Development (CCFPD) in the Department of Foreign Affairs and International Trade, and the Centre for International Relations at Queen's University.

I am grateful that so many colleagues, both academics and foreign service officers, attended the workshop and made comments. We were fortunate to have the active participation of the late John Halstead. I especially appreciate the contribution of those who chaired sessions — Ingrid Hall, Maureen Molot, Allan Sullivan, and J.H. Taylor.

Conferences are labour intensive. This one depended on the commitment and hard work of Doug Fogerty of CFSI, a former ambassador dedicated to the education of future foreign service officers; and of Graham Mitchell, another former ambassador and then Dean of CFSI. He saw the potential in the project and was determined to overcome all obstacles to bring it to a successful conclusion.

The idea for this project began in conversations at Queen's University with Louis Delvoie, who helped generate support for it and provided counsel and encouragement. The project also depended on the enthusiasm, support, and suggestions of Andrew Cooper, Lucie Edwards, Rob McRae, and Kim Nossal. Andrew Cooper, Louis Delvoie, Kim Nossal, and David Black reviewed various chapters.

I relied for administrative help on the staff of the Centre for International Relations, in particular Nicole Evans. Research assistance was provided by Yasemin Heinbecker and John Manning. Publication was supported by the Canadian Centre for Foreign Policy Development. Hazel Fotheringham and Marilyn Banting copyedited the manuscript. The professionalism of the staff of the Publications Unit of the School of Policy Studies made my task as editor much easier: Valerie Jarus and Mark Howes managed the production process. Mark Howes designed the cover, using photographs taken by John Sloan in Tokyo.

Robert Wolfe

1

The Many Diplomatic Missions of Canada's Ambassadors

Robert Wolfe

Why does Canada have so many ambassadors? What do they do? The answers may seem obvious to anyone who has ever served abroad, but it is surprisingly difficult to find anything in writing. The traditional ambassadorial tasks are *representing, protecting, reporting, negotiating*, and *promoting friendly relations*.[1] Canadian ambassadors still talk to other governments but they also engage in public diplomacy, whether promoting Canada (culture or trade) or attempting to influence local opinion, for example, on human rights. As managers, responsible for program delivery, notably development assistance, ambassadors are exemplars of the latest trends in public management — missions abroad deliver a full range of government services out of integrated offices whose size has been shrinking steadily. This book attempts to situate the many diplomatic missions of Canada's ambassadors in the context of a changing foreign ministry, a changing state, a new world order, and rapidly evolving technologies of transportation and communications.

For a small country, Canada has a great many officials who occupy the roles of ambassador, high commissioner, consul general, or consul — heads of mission, for short.[2] Canadian representation abroad began to increase prior to the First World War, grew considerably during the 1920s, but then expanded more rapidly than that of any other advanced industrial economy after the Second World War. The most intense period of growth was in the late 1940s, but the number of posts rose steadily until the mid-1970s (Canada 1981, pp. 89, 106). Growth has been slower since, though it still continues, even in the era of cutbacks. Canada had 120 missions and 29 offices in 107 countries in February 1997 (see Appendix A), an increase from 110 missions in 78 countries in 1981 and 38 missions, of which only 7 were "diplomatic," in 1945.[3] Over 1,700 Canadians and over 4,000 locally engaged staff work at these missions, and over half of the program staff do not work for the foreign ministry. This diplomatic establishment uses billions of dollars in Canadian-owned assets abroad and costs hundreds of millions of dollars a year to run.[4]

Canada is not alone in having a great many missions, although it has a relatively high number. The general explanation for the persistence and proliferation of the resident ambassador as an institution is its apparent importance both to the conduct of international affairs and to the work of governments. Ambassadors are one of the institutions on which states depend to help sustain order and stability in the world. At one level, they are the concrete, day-by-day reproduction of the society of states. At another level, they act on behalf of the members of their community, helping that community to maintain its strength and cohesion by doing what needs to be done abroad. Globalization is associated with an increase in the intensity of interactions among states, and with an increase in diplomatic representation. Ambassadors are still "lying abroad," it seems, because the new technologies of transportation and communications have brought "abroad" much closer to home and because the myriad effects of globalization have made "abroad" much more relevant to people and their governments. Far from being in decline, the resident ambassador is flourishing.[5]

The role of the ambassador may be of continuing importance, and the practice of diplomacy is central to an understanding of foreign policy, but most foreign ministries do not seem to have an explicit modern doctrine on the role of an embassy, and scholars largely ignore ambassadors. The literature on contemporary world order is enormous, but the ambassador is scarcely visible in theoretical discussions of foreign policy, in the literature on leaders as diplomats (Dunn 1996), or in the analysis of conference diplomacy (Kaufman 1988; Winham 1993). Many ambassadors have written their memoirs, but the scholarly literature is largely concerned with the great powers. Practitioners and scholars alike implicitly know what an ambassador is, but when asked to be explicit, most tend to reply, in effect, that an ambassador is what an ambassador does.

The first purpose of this book is to attempt to delineate the place of ambassadors in foreign policy, without trying to suggest that they are the only diplomatic actors, or that what they do is all of foreign relations. It may seem odd to speak of the ambassador *in* foreign policy. "Policy" refers to actions a government chooses to take on behalf of a public rather than a private purpose. "Foreign policy" at a minimum refers to actions that the government takes outside the country. Harold Nicolson, one of the classic writers on diplomacy, tried to separate policy and negotiation, or the legislative and executive aspects of diplomacy, arguing that Cabinet decides but professionals should negotiate (Nicolson 1939, p. 3). Such thinking was once common among students of public administration. It has been superseded in practice by peripatetic ministers; it has been superseded in theory by a rejection of the radical separation of subject and object. One 1960s study on the roles and responsibilities of the then Department of External Affairs thought that headquarters should be responsible for providing advice and formulating recommendations to ministers and to Cabinet while posts carried out negotiations, looked after Canadian interests, and sent information to Ottawa (Hilliker and Barry 1995, p. 303). Life is rarely so tidy. In 1996, an internal review concluded that the re-named Department of Foreign Affairs and International Trade (DFAIT) has four basic roles, which flow from its legal mandate: (i) developing and coordinating the government's international policy; (ii) advocating Canadian interests and values overseas; (iii) providing services to Canadians (promoting trade and investment, securing and improving market access, providing consular assistance and passports); and (iv) supporting other government departments and agencies abroad (including provincial governments). All of these roles are shared between posts and headquarters, with no tidy division — though in some sense the more headquarters is interested in events in a country, the more Canada needs a local contact to make arrangements and follow-up. Formulating and executing foreign policy are inextricably linked. Reporting on local developments by an ambassador is part of policy formulation; a statement in the House of Commons by the prime minister can be part of execution, if it is seen as one way to communicate a policy to other governments. The presence or absence of the ambassador can in itself be a statement of policy, as Canada demonstrated in May 1998 by publicly recalling its high commissioner from India in protest against that country's nuclear tests.

The second purpose of this book is to delineate the role of *Canadian* ambassadors. Such an inquiry will have particular interest to students of Canadian foreign policy, but the Canadian experience may also be generally relevant to the circumstances of other small countries. The American literature on diplomacy is extensive, as is the British literature, but the role of the ambassador is shaped both by the nature of international society and by the nature of the state. States respond to comparable international circumstances — not only embassies but foreign ministries come to have similar characteristics — but differently placed states might have different diplomatic needs and responsibilities (Steiner 1982, p. 365; compare "Types of European Diplomacy" in Nicolson 1939). The experiences of a superpower's ambassadors will not be the same as those of a small country, though being a superpower does not ensure that governments or analysts have a clear idea of what an embassy should do (Eagleburger and Barry 1996; for an example of the American inferential genre, see Miller 1992). American ambassadors are in a different group for two reasons. First, their country's size and wealth means that they generally have a much larger staff than their counterparts. Second, the role of the United States in the world makes the US ambassador as the representative of the president an important figure in any country, whether that person is an experienced professional or a political nonentity. Diplomatic skill matters more for Canadian ambassadors, who are never of such importance.

This book is part of what Andrew F. Cooper (chapter 2) calls a revival of interest in diplomacy. It is also part of the continuing interest in the study of foreign policy in general, Canada's in particular. The book is not, however, directly concerned with either foreign policy or diplomacy writ large, nor is it about the role of the foreign ministry in the bureaucratic politics of making foreign policy. The chapters illustrate many of the "puzzles" about contemporary diplomacy that Cooper identifies as being at the heart of emergent diplomatic practice. We live in an era of great apparent change of a kind that might have profound implications for diplomacy. Globalization seems to alter the responsibilities and internal organization of the state, while the end of the Cold War may have signalled change in the nature of the international system. The ambassador may still be "lying abroad," but new technological and political entities might reshape the role of the head of mission. By asking questions about *what* ambassadors do and *where* they do it, we may learn a good deal about how the Canadian state sees itself in relation to the international system, and about how the Canadian government pursues the interests of its citizens abroad.

The idea of a "diplomatic mission" implies action taken for a public purpose as part of foreign policy. The notion of policy further implies that the action is not arbitrary, that thought has been given to the purposes served by the ambassador. The Canadian government has many policies that it pursues abroad with all sorts of people, organizations, and countries, but they are not necessarily a consistent or coherent "foreign policy," nor are all policies pursued through each ambassador. It is for this reason that the title refers to the many diplomatic missions of Canada's ambassadors. I have not been able to find any single explicit doctrine that governs what they do, though I have looked in official reports, government statements, and the memoirs of practitioners. In the next section, therefore, I attempt to discern the implicit doctrine that has affected change in the number, location, and size of Canadian missions.

EXPANDING CANADA'S DIPLOMATIC MISSIONS

Change in the nature of the Canadian state and of the international system has affected the pattern of this country's diplomatic representation. Canada has many more missions now than it did 60 years ago in part because there are many more sovereign countries in the world, and because of how Canadians see the purpose of diplomacy. At the time of Confederation, the diplomatic unity of the empire rendered the question of colonial diplomatic representation moot. The sovereign existence of the Canadian state dates to 1867, and as a signatory of the Treaty of Versailles, Canada was a member of the League of Nations from its beginning in 1919, but full diplomatic sovereignty came only with the Statute of Westminster in 1931. Canada already had 35 missions abroad by then, but none were embassies. A handful were called legations (a lesser species of diplomatic mission that has now disappeared); the rest were trade commissions or immigration offices (Canada 1981, Table FST-2).

Prior to the Second World War, Canada's diplomatic establishment had been small because it was scarcely needed. Even with the United States, Canadians did not waste much time in exchanges on the state of the world, as opposed to the problems faced by Americans trucking in bond across southern Ontario. "The war unleashed Canadian diplomacy," according to John Holmes (1979, p. 188). Canadians were no longer content to sit on the sidelines waiting for others to drag them into war, nor as citizens of one of the world's wealthiest and strongest powers in the era of reconstruction, were Canadians prepared to pay for decisions made by others. The most famous articulation of the orientations and principles of Canada's postwar foreign policy was the speech given by Louis St. Laurent, then secretary of state for external affairs, at the University of Toronto in January 1947. St. Laurent confirmed that Canada had learned during the war that an active engagement with the world was essential for our prosperity and security. Seen in the light of this historic change, he said, "… the recent expansion of the diplomatic service of this country is a natural development. We are preparing ourselves to fulfil the growing responsibilities in world affairs which we have accepted as a modern state. We wish the Commonwealth to be an effective instrument of co-operation, and we have, therefore, appointed High Commissioners in the capitals of every Commonwealth country." He continued

> We have also multiplied rapidly our diplomatic representation in foreign countries. Before very long, we shall have provided ourselves with diplomatic representation in the capitals of every major country in the world. We have not taken this step merely through a desire to follow a conventional practice, or to advertise ourselves abroad. We have done so because our geography, our climate, our natural resources, have so conditioned our economy that the continued prosperity and well-being of our people can best be served by the prosperity and well being of the whole world. We have thus a useful part to play in world affairs, useful to ourselves through being useful to others, and to play that part we must have our own spokesmen among our neighbours (St. Laurent 1947, pp. 32-33).

St. Laurent's speech set the stage for the rapid expansion of Canada's diplomatic missions, but countries typically do not exchange embassies with every other country. What is surprising is that Canada participates in a relatively high number of exchanges of ambassadors. For the world as a whole in 1991, less than a quarter of all potential diplomatic missions were established. Potential diplomatic missions exist between every country and every other country. Using Nierop's (1994) calculations, there were 167 countries in 1991. The number of potential diplomatic connections (one or both states sending an ambassador to the other) was 167, therefore, and the number of potential diplomatic missions was 167 x 167.

The United States was first on the list in 1950, with 70 of a possible 81 connections, and Canada was 23rd on the list, with 34 connections. The number of possible connections increased from 81 in 1950 to 167 in 1991. The United States was first or second in all those years, as its number of diplomatic connections more than doubled — but Canada's connections more than tripled (324 percent). The United States still led the list of diplomatic connections in 1991, exchanging at least one resident emissary with 150 of the 167 countries listed in the *Europa World Year Book* for 1992, but Canada had jumped to the eleventh spot, with 110 connections. Three-quarters of countries on the list exchange at least one resident ambassador with fewer than half of the other countries. With the exception of Australia, the other countries that have shown comparable upward mobility would have been considered developing countries during this period, and Australia with only 77 missions in 1991 (up 350 percent from 22 in 1950), was thirty-fourth on the list. Another measure is asymmetry between the number of diplomats a country sends abroad, and the number it receives in its capital. In 1985-86, the United States led this list too: it sent 4,129 diplomatic personnel abroad in 109 embassies, and received only 2,461 diplomatic personnel in 110 embassies. Canada was eighth on this list, sending 1,116 in 76 embassies and receiving 736 diplomats in 79 missions. Australia was twelfth, sending 870 diplomats in 67 embassies, and receiving 441 in 61 embassies. (Nierop 1994, p. 66, Tables A1, A2 and A3).

Canada's diplomatic representation, it seems, is relatively larger and has expanded more rapidly than that of other advanced industrial countries. This expansion seems to have been anticipated in St. Laurent's speech, where diplomatic missions were seen as an integral part of an active foreign policy in a changed world order. St. Laurent and his advisors were hard-headed pragmatists who pursued Canadian interests based on what came to be called the functional principle. Not surprisingly, the number and distribution of posts does not easily correspond to the traditional hypotheses in theories of international relations. Senior officials in External Affairs did not see the world as a hierarchy. Had they done so, they might have made do with only one embassy, located in Washington. Similarly, their view of *diplomacy* was not defined by contrast to *war* — representation was not concentrated either among allies or in areas of actual or potential threat to Canada. They were as interested in the so-called "low politics" issues of economic and social affairs as in the "high politics" questions of war and peace, and they thought Canada should be represented in all major countries as well as in all Commonwealth countries. Posts could be created because of a perception of commercial possibilities, or based on a country's apparent regional political importance. Sometimes maintaining "Western influence" was thought important as part of Cold War calculations about the management of East-West relations. Other stated reasons to create posts were the need to manage and deliver burgeoning development assistance programs and the need to balance representation in Commonwealth and francophone countries (Hilliker and Barry 1995, pp. 318-21). Having security interests on two oceans, extensive peacekeeping commitments, and large immigrant populations no doubt were also factors.

Given the preponderance of the United States in Canadian affairs, it might be argued that Canada opened a great many embassies in order to prove to itself, through the recognition of others, that its sovereignty was real, despite the American presence. Canadians would not be alone in assigning a symbolic role to ambassadors. The exchange of ambassadors is a vital act of mutual recognition of states as states. New states created since the Second World War have been constituted by the conventional understandings of sovereignty — they are all thought to have similar responsibilities within an established territory. States acknowledge each other's existence by extending diplomatic recognition, which implies legitimacy as a state and membership in the society of states, but not necessarily approval of the government. Leaving aside whether new states have like capabilities to exercise those responsibilities, by establishing an embassy other states recognize them as actors in world politics and begin the process of shaping the nature of their participation in international relations. The ambassador as an institution is a key part of the process of integration, and in itself is central to Canadian foreign policy. The converse might also hold. In *not* dispatching ambassadors to many newly independent states, we do not contribute to their integration; if a large number of significant countries fail to establish missions, they convey the message that the new states are outside international society.

Even the location of an ambassador is significant. When Canada was unable to open a resident mission, Peter Hancock recalled, the newly independent states of the former Soviet Union preferred that its non-resident ambassadors be accredited from anywhere but Moscow (Hancock 1997). A different problem had earlier arisen in Israel, whose claim to Jerusalem is not internationally recognized. During the 1979 Canadian election campaign, Joe Clark, then leader of an opposition party, promised to move Canada's embassy from Tel Aviv to Jerusalem. Weeks later, as a newly-elected prime minister, he confirmed the promise in a press conference, despite advice to the contrary from officials. The move was expected to please Jewish voters at home; it certainly pleased the prime minister of Israel who telephoned Clark to express his appreciation. But the planned move infuriated

Arab leaders, and less than five months later, it was cancelled (Takach 1989). The location of the embassy was foreign policy. It signified a recognition of Israel's claims to land captured in war. Israelis welcomed such recognition by a G7 country, Arabs did not.

The status of the head of mission is also significant. During the 1950s and early 1960s, when Canada established posts in Africa, Asia, and Latin America in the new countries created as colonial powers retreated, posts earlier established as "legations" were raised to embassy status. Canada ceased to make this sort of distinction in the relative importance of sovereign states, and by the early 1960s no further legations were established. (For an account of this period, see Hilliker and Barry 1995, pp. 172-78). A *downgrading* of status can therefore be a useful signal. Janet Graham (chapter 4) was sent to Lagos to be *acting* high commissioner as a political signal during a difficult period in Canada's relations with Nigeria. The signal was understood, she reports, although it limited her effectiveness in managing an already small mission. In contrast, the words of an ambassador can carry particular weight because of, rather than in spite of, the symbolism of the role. When Marc Perron, as Canada's ambassador to Mexico, made strong comments about official corruption in a magazine interview in the fall of 1997, his message was understood by the host government. His personal effectiveness at an end, Canada withdrew him, but the embassy carried on, and the Mexican government no doubt assumed that Perron had acted with approval (if not instructions) from the highest levels in Ottawa.

Unlike the Australians, who had a philosophical commitment to concentrating resources in particular geographical areas, Canadians held a more global conception of their nation's role, but they began to create the modern foreign service based on the expansive principles enunciated in St. Laurent's speech rather than a coherent operational plan. The new diplomatic era began in 1947 with the independence of India and Pakistan — moving quickly to establish relationships with them was a self-evident step. J.H. Taylor (1997) doubted that Canadian officials considered then what would happen when the whole of the British Empire gained independence; implicitly they committed the country to the creation of new high commissions to the end of the disposition of the empire. At some stage, Canada might have had to admit that some countries were too small or too unimportant to merit a resident mission; when the French empire began to dissolve after 1960, however, the same process was repeated. For domestic reasons at the outset of the Quiet Revolution, a time when the Royal Commission on Bilingualism and Biculturalism had begun its work, Canada obviously could not fail to treat the countries of what came to be called *la francophonie* as it had the Commonwealth. Expansion of francophone missions, notably in Africa, was part of asking for recognition of Canada as a francophone state.[6] Taylor also argues that this expansion often had nothing to do with narrowly understood Canadian interests in many of the colonial territories in Africa once ruled by the British and French, because it had none. The interests were synthesized and developed after the relationship was established. At the end of the process of decolonization, he recalled, Mozambique asked if Canada discriminated against it simply because it did not have the misfortune to have been ruled by the French or the British. The same complaint could have been made by Spanish-speaking countries in the Americas, where Canadian resident representation was also limited.

Diplomatic competition with the provinces, especially Quebec, only added to the pressure to open new missions. In recent decades provincial governments have opened and closed dozens of offices in foreign countries. Kim Richard Nossal (chapter 12) shows that the establishment of provincial missions abroad has been tied to worries about representation — for example, when Alberta did not trust federal management of energy matters — or to legitimation, especially in the case of Quebec. The head of a provincial office does not enjoy the same formal status as the head of a diplomatic mission. If an ambassador is the act of mutual recognition by two sovereigns, then provincial representatives are of a different order. For Quebec, however, the fact of a mission abroad helps justify the province as a semi-sovereign entity. The value that provinces place on their offices abroad is a reminder that "diplomacy" has a practical as well as a symbolic meaning. The effort to manage bilateral relations, Nossal notes, is one provincial representatives share with the "external" representatives of all organizations, including firms. He found that the functions of provincial offices are relatively constant — like embassies, they depend on the broad needs of capitalist economies in the era of globalization — but the need for a province to have its own representative on the spot varies with trends in Canadian politics.

Once posts have been opened, decisions on the subsequent adjustment of Canadian representation are not easy. As early as 1949, the then Department of External Affairs tried without success to rank the importance of posts based on political reporting, economic reporting, consular work, information activities, representational importance, and assistance to other departments (Hilliker and Barry 1995, p. 60). A difficulty with attributing significance to the size of any bureaucratic unit, or the relative difficulty of closing the unit, is the extent to which its existence or size is thought to depend on vested "departmental" interests as opposed to a "state" or even "public" interest. Some analysts, sceptical of the utility of diplomatic missions, would claim that the proliferation of diplomatic posts is really the product of the desire of the foreign ministry and its bureaucratic leadership to expand in order to provide opportunities for professional advancement and to serve other bureaucratic interests (e.g., salience in the budget process, a sense of self-esteem, an enhanced presence in the policy process, a greater visibility among attentive publics, and so on). This diplomatic expansion may have been driven by institutional factors similar to those affecting universities in the same period: without a bottom line imposed by the market, institutions tend to grow. Not until the late 1980s and early 1990s, were limits imposed.

This bureaucratic explanation does not explain why fewer staff now work at posts abroad, but it might explain why the number of posts increases, and why few posts are closed. Nossal describes the frequent opening and closing of provincial offices, a phenomenon that is rare with respect to embassies, except in Quito, Ecuador, which is the exceptional federal "banging door" — most federal cost-cutting is done by slimming rather than closing missions. Taylor (1997) recalled that both Liberal and Conservative governments have tried to reverse the expansionist tide over the past 25 years. Each new minister starts from square one by asking for a list of the least important posts; the same names always appear. Almost all existing posts have a domestic constituency even if they had none at the outset. Closing a post usually offends somebody, not least another government; posts that disappear, therefore, tend to be consulates rather than embassies. The very instability in provincial offices that Nossal describes, compared to the much lesser instability in federal offices, suggests that the diplomatic need for provincial offices is not well-founded. One consequence of the banging door, Nossal argues, is a loss of expertise, except in the case of Quebec. Offices of other provinces are sometimes understaffed, or lack senior people with international experience. Many do not cultivate relations, or try to compete, with the Canadian embassy, nor do they fully exploit its assets by ensuring that the embassy understands their province's needs.

In this section I attempted to discern the implicit doctrine that has affected change in the number, location, and size of Canadian missions. It is evident that the considerable size of the diplomatic establishment reflects an expansive view of the scope of Canadian foreign policy. The comparison with the more volatile pattern of provincial representation suggests that ambassadors do perform a "diplomatic" role, but that tells us little about their responsibilities. I now turn, therefore, to a consideration of what ambassadors *do*.

DIPLOMATIC FUNCTIONS

St. Laurent said nothing in the speech quoted above on the role of an ambassador or of a post abroad. The closest to an official public statement of a Canadian doctrine is a book by one of Canada's great practitioners, Marcel Cadieux (1963), who tried to describe the Canadian diplomat, probably to encourage foreign service recruitment. Cadieux's generic descriptions of a diplomat's duties, of a diplomatic mission and of a "despatch" are useful, but could hardly have been definitive even at the time he wrote. At most his defence of diplomatic social life and the diplomat as generalist shows the extent to which a new foreign service had been shaped by prevailing institutional norms of diplomacy.

A foreign service is an ever-changing community. As an institution, it does not work on the basis of formulaic injunctions, despite the many forests that have been felled to provide new administrative rules to posts. It works, rather, on the basis of the informal shared understandings of its members. A well-understood implicit doctrine, therefore, might be found in memoirs. Canadian foreign ministers have played prominent roles in domestic and world politics — one even won the Nobel Prize for Peace — but their memoirs and biographies have little to say about the role of ambassadors, or about whether or not it was altered by technological change. Ministers have been going abroad to *negotiate* for over a century, since it was always easy for a minister to travel from Ottawa to Washington to ensure that the British ambassador represented Canada's interest properly (Eayrs 1961, p. 168). The arrival of jet airplanes in the 1960s allowed the secretary of state for external affairs (SSEA) (as the minister of foreign affairs was then known) to make official visits to a great many countries, often the first by any Canadian foreign minister, but such novelties only happen once, and goodwill soon ceased to be a good reason for leaving Ottawa. Mitchell Sharp recalls travelling hundreds of thousands of miles as SSEA, mostly to attend international conferences of one sort or another (Sharp 1994, p. 218). Most of the time in most countries, ministers leave *representation* to ambassadors, and seem to see little need to ask themselves why.

Memoirs of former ambassadors also shed little light on the shared understandings of their era about the role of the ambassador. Retired diplomats tend to assume that the reader will know what an "ambassador" is. Their memoirs are interesting descriptions of events in which they were engaged rather than analytic speculations on the nature of diplomacy.[7] Robert Ford, one of Canada's best known diplomats and ambassador in Moscow for 16 years, devoted his memoirs (Ford 1989) to commentary on Soviet politics. Though he served long enough to become dean of the Moscow diplomatic corps (an unusual occurrence in any capital since Canadian postings rarely exceed four years) Ford did not reflect explicitly on the role. The major exception to this approach was the unusually analytic memoir Allan Gotlieb (1991) wrote of his time in one the world's major diplomatic assignments as Canada's ambassador in Washington. Perhaps members of the generation that joined the old External Affairs prior to the war focused their memoirs, understandably, on the enormous expansion of Canadian diplomacy that they led. This focus on the great enterprise may have influenced the memoirs of their successors, the immediate postwar generation who joined External during the supposed "golden age" of Canadian diplomacy.

One of the few places where Canadians seem to have systematically recorded their shared understanding of the role of the head of mission is in the letter of instructions from the minister of foreign affairs that, in theory, every ambassador receives in addition to the commission issued by Order-in-Council. The letter of instructions is drafted by the country desk officer in Ottawa, if that junior official remembers; many ambassadors claim never to have received such a letter, or not to have received one for each head of mission assignment. The letter of instructions in itself does not provide a head of mission with legitimacy: the effect of title or position is eroded by the tendency of modern communications to flatten structures and to disperse authority. When it exists, however, the letter can be a useful guide to current departmental thinking on the role and responsibilities of the head of mission. Excerpts from recent letters are reproduced in the Appendix. We can see that ambassadors are to act in accordance with stated foreign policy objectives (note the similarity to the themes of Canada 1995), they are to represent a strong, united, and bilingual Canada, and they are to be good managers of a unified mission responsible to many parts of the Canadian government. Individual letters would also have instructions on relations with the ambassador's countries of accreditation. Louis Delvoie (chapter 3) uses his own instructions, setting forth the substantive objectives he was given by the Canadian government, to outline the context of his mission to Pakistan.

Another way to look for diplomatic functions is to organize them thematically. Some relevant themes, Cooper (chapter 2) suggests, are the nature of diplomacy and its relation to the policy process, the effect of the communications revolution, diplomats and technical expertise, the broad range of apparently diplomatic problems, relations with non-state actors, and, finally, the way in which diplomats are organized or managed. These themes recur both in the literature and in the contributions to this volume.

Access and Influence

The most important fact of resident diplomacy is that it is resident. Being there is essential if a diplomat wishes access to information, to power, and to influence. Similar access can also matter for provinces, especially for concerns not shared to the same degree by the federal government. The case can be made that the status claimed by the heads of provincial missions is necessary to open doors for trade, investment, and tourism; simply having provincial officials within federal missions might not suffice.

The big questions of international relations are not necessarily what an ambassador thinks about every day, even in a G7 capital. Paul Heinbecker (chapter 5) shows that the ambassador to a major power can spend less time on traditional foreign policy than on trying to manage the public perceptions of environmental issues, or improving Canada's fortunes by promoting investment. In the introduction to his Washington memoir, Allen Gotlieb constructed a stark contrast between a traditional conception of politics and diplomacy in Washington, and the reality he found. In the days of the "Imperial Presidency," it might have made sense to do official business only with the State Department, and never "interfere" in domestic matters. Those days are gone. Fragmentation of power is not new under the US Constitution, but the assertive role of Congress in foreign relations after Vietnam and the declining power of the political parties increased the extent of the fragmentation. Even the administration was fragmented, with the State Department often being kept in the dark on such major issues as free trade (by the Office of the US Trade Representative) and international economic coordination (by the Treasury). In consequence, Gotlieb wrote "the ambassador to Washington is accredited neither to a government nor even to a system. He is accredited to an unstable mass of people, forces, and interests that are constantly shifting, aligning, and realigning in ways that can affect or damage the interests of the country he represents" (1991, pp. 30-31).

Gotlieb tried to construct typologies that help to organize thinking about the factors that affect diplomatic activity and success in Washington. His book becomes, then, a discourse on the nature of American politics as it interacts with diplomacy. He spent little time either communicating or negotiating. "As a diplomat," he wrote, "I was seen not as someone — to invoke the old refrain — sent to lie abroad for his country, but rather as someone sent abroad to twist arms for his country" (1991, p. 26). He meant that he had been sent to influence American policy, and mostly "domestic" policy, not great questions of war and peace in the world. Such influence depends on a sophisticated understanding of how decisions are made in Washington, information about the state of play on issues important to Canada, and access to people making the decisions. Louis Delvoie argues that in the absence of material weight or anything urgent on the agenda, personal skill, energy, and imagination become major diplomatic resources. Delvoie shows how the head of mission's ability to talk to ministers and senior government officials was invaluable in meeting the challenges, demands, and obstacles that he faced in Pakistan. The effort to maintain a presence, to be active and visible, paid off in access to the people who made decisions on matters of concern to Canada, from policy on nuclear proliferation to controls on illegal immigration.

Catalytic Diplomacy

Diplomacy is not limited to exchanges between foreign ministers, and it is no longer the case that ambassadors must speak to the host government through the foreign ministry. Paul Frazer (chapter 6) notes that although he was busy in Prague, he was rarely required to call on the foreign ministry. Lucie Edwards (chapter 7) recounts that she spent little time in the foreign ministry on her visits to Somalia or Rwanda. Ambassadors deal with many host-government ministries, but they also work with business, with NGOs, and with journalists. They also work with a comparable range of Canadians. The increasingly intricate relationship between the state and societal actors, both in domestic politics and in the views on international relations of citizens, is a theme brought out more explicitly by Brian Hocking's (1995) use of the term "catalytic" diplomacy.

Given the diffuse range of issues at stake and the dispersion of power in the US system, Gotlieb (1991) thought that trying to deploy as many Canadian players as possible was essential, including senior officials in domestic departments and businessmen with interests at stake. The head of mission is involved in coordinating things that may not be coordinated at home; this activity is particularly important for provincial interests because provincial governments relate more effectively to heads of mission than they might to Ottawa desk officers. Hocking, a British scholar who has studied Canadian diplomats, observes that diplomats are often called on to coordinate other bureaucrats. As facilitators or mediators, they become skilled in the "catalytic" function of building coalitions of other states and transnational interests in pursuit of state goals, especially on such new issues as human rights and the environment. Alison Van Rooy (chapter 11) argues that the ambassador may also need to engage civil society organizations (CSOs) in pursuit of Canadian objectives, because these organizations are increasingly important in comparison to the formal state apparatus both at home and in world affairs. CSOs can seek to influence the role of the ambassador as a representative of the sending state and can be *interlocuteurs valable* for the ambassador in the receiving state. Consultation is now seen as a vital component of democratic participation in policy making, abroad as much as at home. If the ambassador represents all Canadians, and not just the governor-general, and if CSOs are one way in which Canadians discover and articulate their views of the world, then ambassadors must listen to CSOs. Business leaders will always be received by ambassadors, but CSOs can help ensure that ambassadors do not have a one-sided view of events in the host country, or of Canada's "interests." Nevertheless, Taylor (1997) saw a particular challenge for heads of mission in dealing with non-governmental organizations or provinces in light of their lesser or at least different legitimacy in the context of state-to-state relationships. As domestic issues rise in importance, however, Hocking argues that diplomats must "operate effectively in a wide range of political, economic and societal arenas, to gain access to knowledge and to increasingly fragmented political arenas where the critical locus of power may well lie outside the government." Diplomacy now requires new sorts of relationships and linkages. When we look at what "diplomats" are actually doing, therefore, the institution and the machinery continue; our understanding of them, however, depends not only on rival theories about the international system, but also on our perceptions of the relations between the state and non-state actors, in the sending and the receiving countries (Hocking 1995, pp. 18, 20, 33).

Paul Frazer shows that this "public diplomacy" preoccupies Canada's ambassador to the world's only remaining superpower. When the issues are within the domain of the foreign ministry, public diplomacy is not needed. When the foreign ministry begins to lose control, or when the agenda for interstate relations becomes broader, then embassies must make contact with other actors in the decision-making process. The Mexican government had to learn how to play this game in order to build public and then Congressional support for giving the American administration "fast-track" negotiating authority for NAFTA (Bertrab 1997). And when the public in a democracy becomes a significant element in the making of policy, ambassadors must become public advocates. Hocking reported, for example, on Canada's efforts in London to counteract the Greenpeace campaign against Canadian forestry practices (Hocking 1995, p. 29ff). The campaign was based on the assumption that public opinion was an important determinant of outcomes. Glen Bailey, a Canadian diplomat, makes a similar claim for the importance of "advocacy" in the conduct of diplomacy. He presents a case study of how Canada's embassy in Chile worked for three years to ensure that the Chileans pursued their interests in trade liberalization in the context of NAFTA rather than through bilateral arrangements with the United States. That Canada and Chile signed a bilateral accord because the US is so far unprepared to expand NAFTA demonstrates the serendipitous success of Canada's efforts — Chile had come to see its own interests in broader terms (Bailey 1995).

The Ambassador and Canadian Prosperity

Canada's first missions abroad were established not long after Confederation for commercial purposes. Promoting trade and investment is now an integral part of the head of mission's job as Anthony T. Eyton (chapter 10) shows. The bureaucratic divisions of the past are gone, and the ambassador is truly a "single window" for Canadians. Why should the government be involved in business? Arthur Andrew, a former Canadian ambassador, wrote nearly 30 years ago that the ambassador must work to establish the legal and technical conditions for selling Canada's products to the world. This task can involve "reporting or negotiating about tariffs, foreign exchange controls, transportation arrangements, communications, the application of trading laws, and the interpretation of technical standards." Involvement with these government policies "is an obvious and traditional diplomatic function" (Andrew 1970, p. 75). Many ambassadors devote a large amount of their time to trade promotion. Economists cannot prove that diplomatic interventions affect trade, but the intuition is that politics affect transaction flows. Governments work to remove political impediments to increased trade; they try to improve the general tenor of transnational commercial relations; they may want to reassure actors in states where politics matters most; and they might want to help confirm the reliability of partner firms in their own country (Pollins 1989). Visits from "Team Canada" help increase the profile of Canadians in general and of specific businesses. Governments like to trumpet the number or value of contracts signed during such visits — especially for home consumption — but business requires long-term relationships. Ambassadors can help build and sustain such relations. Some sales are clearly influenced or even determined by an ambassador's intervention, for example, by a post's identification of opportunities for first-time exporters. The ambassador has to open doors and provide useful information, but not necessarily for everybody. Big companies do not need the ambassador, except in centralized economies, or for big projects. When a major Canadian firm has business in Washington, the CEO might drop in on the ambassador as a courtesy, but it is law firms and lobbyists who obtain information and set up meetings with politicians. For small companies, however, the ambassador is valuable. In March 1998, James Cameron, a Canadian director, did not need official help in drawing attention to his Oscar nominations for *Titanic*, but controversy dogged Canada's consul general in Los Angeles, Kim Campbell, when she did not hold a reception for the other Canadian film in contention, Atom Egoyan's *The Sweet Hereafter*. If only big companies can cope with international competition in the era of globalization, Canadian distinctiveness might disappear. Ambassadors help citizens stay both Canadian and engaged with the world.

The Ambassador as Manager of Resources

Cooper notes that many writers have commented on the extensive degree of administrative decentralization evident in the management of contemporary diplomacy. At the same time, fiscal constraints have made it harder to maintain expensive foreign operations. He sees two puzzles. On the one hand, has the range of diplomacy been extended, given the widening agenda of international politics? On the other hand, has this extended range also widened the gulf between diplomatic will and fiscal capabilities, a key sub-text in the debate about Canadian diplomacy?

Lucie Edwards tells newly appointed ambassadors that the head of mission is a manager, responsible for people and resources as well as policy. She develops the notion that the modern embassy could be a prototype for the "single window" delivery of government services that Jocelyne Bourgon, Canada's most senior public servant, sees as the ideal government office. Bourgon says that citizens expect that the benefits of new technology will offer them more responsive service, with work organized to suit people not departments. They expect to get what they need in one place, without knowing whose job it is. In the single-window model, government departments work together (horizontal integration) as do different levels of government (vertical integration) (Bourgon 1997, p. 13). Can the mission actually be a single window? Paul Heinbecker thought it could. The embassy in Bonn worked hard to be the face of Canada in Germany. He and his staff tried to provide one-stop shopping for anything involving the Canadian government, from immigration to trade policy to customs to Canadian policy on land mines. They tried to do the same with anything that involved the Canadian cultural community or transactions with Canadian business. Questions from the German public could not be answered directly, but the embassy website posted information on Canada and directed visitors to much more. Louis Delvoie advances the idea a step further — a mission can be more than a single window, it can be one brain. The government structure is highly compartmentalized but in the end the head of mission should have all the information and, therefore, the potential to understand Canada's bilateral relations with a country in its totality.

The letter of instructions to a head of mission as discussed above comes from the minister of foreign affairs, who has the legal obligation in the Department of Foreign Affairs and International Trade Act to *coordinate* the direction given by the Government of Canada to the heads of Canada's diplomatic and consular missions, and to manage these missions. In practice, heads of mission may report to the director general (a middle-level manager) responsible for the relevant part of the world, but consistent with the legislation, heads of mission are meant to serve all deputy ministers with programs or interests in their territory. This book ends, therefore, with the reflections of Alan Nymark, Jean-Marc Métivier, David Lee, Peter Sutherland, and Michael Pearson (chapter 13) who write from the perspectives of other government departments (Health Canada), another agency of the Foreign Affairs portfolio (CIDA), the multilateral side of Foreign Affairs, the business community, and a minister's office.

It has taken three decades to consolidate the mission into a single coherent instrument of Canadian policy. The Glassco Royal Commission on Government Organization (Canada 1962/63), which began the process of modernizing Canadian public administration, recommended that heads of mission have authority over all Canadian government staff on post in a given country; that authority was fully granted only after "integration" of the foreign service in 1970 and "consolidation" in 1980 (Nossal 1993, p. 39). The process took two steps, with "support staff" (clerks, communicators, and secretaries) being integrated into External

Affairs before "program staff" (foreign service officers) (Andrew 1974/75). This consolidation was certainly seen to have efficiency benefits, as reflected in the creation of the "Committee on Post Management" whose task was ensuring that all the programs and departments represented at a post were well served administratively, but neither integration nor consolidation reflected a view on the policy or diplomatic role of the ambassador.[8]

The Trudeau government's major review of foreign policy in 1970 has one brief section on organization. Most of the discussion of the decision to "integrate" foreign operations concerns headquarters matters, but the implication of integration for missions is spelled out: "heads of post abroad must be given clear authority over all operations at the post [and] must represent and be accountable for all departments' interests in his area of jurisdiction." This decision had clear implications for the role of the ambassador: the selection of heads of post required "increasing emphasis in future on managerial capabilities and knowledge of the full range of government activities abroad" (Canada, 1970, p. 40). A subsequent under-secretary believed that "The objective of strengthening the roles of the head of post was to enable them to see more clearly the comprehensive nature of their responsibilities for all government programs and to manage the work of their staffs with a greater measure of coherence" (Osbaldeston 1982, p. 458. See also Lee 1987). Whatever the hopes for the process, heads of post quickly came to feel that they were responsible more for management and less for policy; the more disillusioned thought that as managers, their key role was as travel agent (Canada 1981, p. 20). Notwithstanding the efforts at reorganization, and the contribution of technology to improved communication, the 1981 royal commission on the foreign service concluded that posts had become more isolated, and little progress had been made in determining or communicating objectives for the foreign service. Foreign operations consumed the larger part of the budget of the then Department of External Affairs, but the commission found little reason to believe that anyone in Ottawa knew what went on at posts on a day-to-day basis.[9]

Much has changed during the past two decades, but the current government of Prime Minister Jean Chrétien devoted similarly limited attention to posts in its review of foreign policy. Not surprisingly for a government whose dominant objective was elimination of the fiscal deficit, the foreign service was called upon to be flexible and adaptable in maintaining a widespread diplomatic presence with diminished resources; Cooper calls it "just-in-time diplomacy" by analogy to the slimmer and faster forms of modern manufacturing. Especially significant from a symbolic standpoint is the endorsement of a policy of sharing premises with like-minded countries such as Australia. Technology and increased use of local staff would allow missions to be smaller. Janet Graham (chapter 4) describes the techniques Canada uses to manage the growing number of small missions. One thing that allows such small missions to be established quickly, and assists the ambassador to be a single window, is the technology for sharing resources. The Canadian ambassador in Montivideo, for example, is the only Canada-based member of the embassy. Instructions arrive from the geographic division in Ottawa through an Internet link. When those instructions require an official demarche, translated versions come from Canadian missions in Caracas, Mexico City, and Bogota. It may be a "micro-mission" for Canada, but Canada's head of mission is received at a high level in the Ministry of Foreign Affairs, like any other ambassador. Meanwhile, the mission trade officer and immigration officer are based at other posts nearby and the mission accounts are prepared and audited in Ottawa.

Communications

The impact of new information technologies on international relations is much discussed in the 1990s. New technologies have ended the diplomat's monopoly of all but the most important kind of information. CNN carries images of war and famine in real time; NGOs and other groups trade information and develop lobbying strategies instantly (Stanbury and Vertinsky 1994/95); and important government pronouncements are available on the net as they are delivered, ready to be analyzed in the morning newspaper or included in a school project. These developments have an effect on the Canadian view of the role of the ambassador. Richard Kohler (chapter 9) reports that at the time of writing, Canada had the most advanced diplomatic communications system in the world. Does this technology herald the era of virtual diplomacy?

Claims that traditional diplomacy is in decline either because of new features of world politics or change in the technology of transportation and communications are not new — these observations were made about the advent of the telegraph and steam ships. Prime Minister Trudeau caused much consternation in a 1969 television interview when he said, as reported by *Maclean's*, that "'I think the whole concept of diplomacy today ... is a little bit outmoded.' There was a time when diplomatic despatches were the only means of receiving information about another country, but today this information is available 'in a good newspaper'" (cited in Thordarson 1972, p. 91). Trudeau's foreign minister of the time regarded the comment as "superficial and unfair" (Sharp 1994, p. 171) and long afterward foreign service officers remembered the slight, though Trudeau did not repeat it (Canada 1981, p. 61). But similar remarks about the relative value of newspapers had been made by Lloyd George's private secretary in 1917; Lester Pearson as foreign minister admitted to the value of foreign correspondents in the 1950s; and a paper had been written on the topic as part of a program for reforming the American State Department for the 1970s (Eayrs 1971, pp. 6-7). Advances in communications had affected Canadian diplomacy at least as early as 1907, when a Cabinet minister negotiating limits on immigration in Tokyo was instructed by cable not to sign the agreement that had been reached. Worse, in 1935 the Canadian delegate to the League of Nations spoke in favour of oil sanctions against Mussolini only one hour before receiving a cable instructing him to do no such thing (Eayrs 1961, pp. 170-71). The theme figures in the memoirs of Hugh Keenleyside, a distinguished public servant, who after only two years in Mexico was not disappointed to return to Ottawa. As early as 1947, he saw limitations on an ambassador's role occasioned by rapid telecommunications and by the ease with which someone more senior could be sent out from the capital to handle matters of real importance (Keenleyside 1982, pp. 272-73, 275-76).

John Holmes, a distinguished diplomat and scholar, tartly observed after Trudeau's famous remark that "The assumption that diplomacy has been abolished by the invention of Telex and participatory democracy ... is widely and glibly held.... [but] The kind of information Ottawa needs to have about personalities and policies in Bogota before embarking on a trade treaty with Columbia or a joint initiative in the UN is unlikely to be carried in any one of the public media" (Holmes 1973, pp. 3-7). Similarly, Berridge draws on recent British and American memoirs to argue that there is no substitute for continuous engagement, whether in representation or "networking," in negotiation, which includes lobbying politicians, and in gathering intelligence, something any ambassador can do better than any journalist, because he or she knows what will be of interest at headquarters (Berridge 1995, pp. 32-33; see also Hamilton and Langhorne 1995, chapter 7). A recent deputy minister agrees, arguing that we can read about developments in a country in a newspaper and hear its views on major issues at a multilateral meeting, but it is our own diplomatic reporting that provides insight into local politics and the implications for Canada's approach to a problem. Delegations from headquarters can fly in for consultations or negotiations, but preparation, including shaping the agenda, "includes that indefinable — but irreplaceable — feel that only local knowledge and sensitivity can provide" (Smith 1996c). Technology cannot replace the need for people to be in physical proximity to each other. Kohler concludes, not surprisingly, that virtual diplomacy has much that is traditional.

Does technology draw traditionally separate functions of diplomacy and the policy process closer together? Do ambassadors have any role in policy formulation? A classic source of tension in any foreign service is the relations between missions and headquarters. People in the field will always resent being told *how* to do their jobs without sufficient guidance on *what* to do. Take the example of reporting. Cadieux asserted the need of the foreign office to be well-informed on developments in an ever more interdependent world; the duty of posts, therefore, was "to follow current events closely and to prepare reports on issues or upon decisions which immediately or remotely may affect Canadian interests" (Cadieux 1963, p. 20). Canadian diplomats have used a variety of strategies to cope with such vague advice (Pearson 1972). The most recent foreign policy review concluded that "Global media coverage and computer databases have changed the needs served by political, economic and trade reporting from many missions abroad. Instead, more time and effort is being devoted to securing access to decision-makers, negotiating, representing varied Canadian interests, and pursuing new approaches to promoting Canadian trade, investment, and technological interests" (Canada 1995, pp. 49-50).

Has the apparent integration of diplomacy into policy making been reinforced by the communications revolution? What has happened to relations between ambassadors and headquarters? How can we characterize the nature of ambassadors' relations with Ottawa on such dimensions as trust, information flow, scope for initiative, or the role of ministers? The general view is that Ottawa is not shy with its views, and consultation by phone is now frequent, though posts are often on their own if Ottawa has not thought much about an issue. The ambassador, the one who sees the whole picture, is the integrator, the creator of new knowledge, and often the manager of the flow of information. Officers with a field orientation see ambassadors as Canada's chief policy officer in their domain of responsibility, better able than anybody in Ottawa to see all aspects of what Canada does in a given country. Officers more oriented to a headquarters perspective observe that some policy is clearly developed at posts, especially when staff see an opportunity, identify the risks, and make recommendations to Ottawa. It remains essential, however, for people at headquarters to do the hard work of obtaining interdepartmental and sometimes federal-provincial agreement. Policy is a collective enterprise: posts are more engaged than ever, but they cannot drive the process. Moreover, much foreign policy is now multilateral, where most missions at best play a supportive role.

Diplomatic Entertaining

This overview cannot possibly conclude without a reference to the social life of the ambassador, famously slighted as "cookie pushing." How important is it for ambassadors to entertain local officials, other host-country nationals, Canadians, and other diplomats? Heinbecker and Delvoie both mention its importance. Most ambassadorial memoirs report on the uses of entertaining. (For example, see Gotlieb 1991 and Cooper 1985, p. 148). Knowing how decisions are made is central to diplomacy. All decisions are based on the available information, but the sources of information are infinite. In any government there are formal legislative and judicial processes that rely on explicitly rational advice, and informal social or political processes that can be based on discussion and consultation. Ambassadors can supply information in any of these forms. What is needed in some cases can be simply providing a government department with a scientific report, in others it is a speech to a lobby group. Like any other actor in the policy process, diplomats can achieve their objectives at any stage, from influencing how an issue is framed to trying to influence how a decision is implemented. Ambassadors must be well informed, they must have access to the people who make decisions, and entertaining the right people is one of the best ways to stay informed and seek access.

Journalists know that a hard working ambassador can be an excellent source of information, and that their dinner parties can sometimes be the best way to meet well-connected officials and politicians. A Washington columnist for London's *Financial Times* once observed that "it is a standard foreign correspondent's technique to seek out those diplomats not so consumed with bilateral crises and causes that they cannot get a grasp of what is really happening in the country in which they reside. Personal experience shows that the Canadians usually rank highly when not bothering about durum wheat" (Martin 1995).

Recruitment

Success at the various things that ambassadors do, from managing their missions to knowing who to entertain, obviously depends on their personal characteristics. Indeed if the mere presence of a Canadian ambassador in another country is in itself a statement of Canadian foreign policy, it follows that the person chosen as ambassador is foreign policy as much as any other action the state may take. Hector Mackenzie (chapter 8) recounts how some of these decisions are made. The nature of the state — its institutions, responsibilities, and political and social dogmas — will influence the choice of individuals sent abroad. Diplomats have been orators, mercantile agents, court clerks, and aristocratic representatives of one sovereign to another. Later they were said to be drawn from among the graduates of elite universities. But as governments became bureaucratized, diplomacy too became a profession (Hamilton and Langhorne 1995, p. 241). And until relatively recently, ambassadors were rarely women. Whether that fact has significance for international relations, or only for the social context of the sending state, remains to be explored, but it is hard to believe that the gendered nature of diplomacy could be without consequences.[10] Within any foreign ministry, a debate goes on unendingly about whether specialists or generalists are most needed. In the 1990s, DFAIT has moved away from generalists again, trying to find ways to ensure that it recruits more people with advanced training in such fields as economics and law. A tension sometimes develops between the divergent cultures of officers working as generalists in the field and specialists at headquarters, with field officers feeling underappreciated and underpromoted. Taylor (1997) thinks that the conscious decision to recruit specialists was based on wrong assumptions. The foreign service is not shaped by rational planning in Ottawa but by unforeseen circumstances in the world. Pressures to find the resources to meet new demands result in attempts to ensure representation at more posts, posts pared to the absolute minimum, posts so small that people have to be generalists. The ambassador who has to be a single window at a small mission had better be a generalist.

CONCLUSION

It should by now be evident that the contributors to this volume have a plural view of the head of mission. It is clearly not possible to describe *the* Canadian ambassador, as if each of the heads of Canada's 157 missions and offices in all parts of the world would conform to a single model. Each person makes the role their own based on their own experience and the circumstances they confront. The tasks of the mission have proliferated even more than their numbers: Canadian foreign policy has more diplomatic missions than ever. Economic interests, "widget-selling," some call it, now seem to predominate, though it might be better to say that the small staffs of most posts must be as adept at helping Canadian exporters as at lobbying the host foreign minister. Ambassadors must respond to a wider constituency both at home and abroad. The "low politics" of environmental matters and of commercial relations rather than "high politics" of international security now take a larger place in foreign policy, and Canada's relations with the world do not pass exclusively through the foreign ministry, or the federal government, or indeed any government. Foreign policy remains the prerogative of the state, by definition, but with many more players on the field, it is a growing challenge to make the voice of the state heard. The authors collectively, however, come to one (negative) conclusion: this diplomacy is not "new." Whether encouraging investment or building support for a land-mines treaty or countering negative perceptions of forestry practices, the diplomatic task remains one of knowing and influencing the people who make decisions in the world.

While no official doctrine explains the role of posts, or why Canada has so many, one justification is on the record. Gordon Smith, in a speech made while he was Canada's deputy minister for foreign affairs, acknowledged the charge from sceptics "that the issues that really count involve a relatively few number of countries, and yet diplomatic services maintain many dozens — occasionally hundreds — of missions abroad; surely the scale of representation vastly exceeds the substantive policy demand." His response was instructive: "Countries in the international system are analogous to citizens within democratic countries." Despite all the supposed new actors in world politics, governments are still accountable. "One way of encouraging state responsibility is to be there, to be present — even in many out of the way places. That 'act of recognition' is, in and of itself, a contribution to international stability and integrity; it is a statement by the community of nations that citizenship in that community is inclusive, and that every country has a positive part to play, even if it chooses not to. And when they choose not to, the international community is watching. That important role, abstract as it may be, is the one that diplomats serving abroad for their countries continue to fulfill — it is an important role on behalf of everyone who values order above chaos, rules above might" (Smith 1996c). Not necessarily the doctrine of a superpower, it does seem to describe an appropriate diplomatic mission for Canada.

NOTES

I am grateful for the comments and suggestions on this chapter and on earlier drafts of Michael Berry, Andrew Cooper, Louis Delvoie, Jacalyn Duffin, David Elder, David Haglund, Ted Hodgetts, Maureen Molot, Kim Nossal, Charles Pentland, Denis Stairs and J.H. Taylor; for the research assistance of Yasemin Heinbecker, John Manning and Todd Mayhew; and for financial support of this research by the Centre for International Relations of Queen's University.

1. Article 3 of the 1961 *Vienna Convention on Diplomatic Relations*. Bull's discussion of "Diplomacy and International Order" closely follows and explicates these categories. Bull 1995, chapter 7.
2. In legislation, a head of mission is defined as an ambassador, high commissioner or consul-general, but these terms are not themselves defined. Canada, *Department of Foreign Affairs and International Trade Act*, R.S. 1985 E22 s.1; 1995 c.5 s.2 . In this book "ambassador" should be understood to mean any head of post. On the significance of the term "high commissioner," see Lloyd, mimeo. In bureaucratic terms, ambassadors are drawn from the "executive" ranks of the public service. Unusually, they do not compete for the jobs. Most ambassadors are career rotational officers in the foreign service, but some come from other government departments, and a few come from outside the public service, including former politicians. The staffing process is run from the Department of Foreign Affairs and International Trade, but the appointments are made by Cabinet, usually on a decision by the prime minister. The term ambassador is also used for a variety of other officials who represent the state in some international capacity. As these officials are based at headquarters and are not resident abroad, they are outside the purview of this volume.
3. The 120 missions include embassies, high commissions, consulates-general, and consulates but not the eight missions to international organizations, or the honorary consulates. The 107 countries do not include the office in Taiwan, while Hong Kong is counted as part of China. For current data see Appendix A and Canada 1997, p. 8; for

previous years, see Canada 1981, pp. 89-90. On the quite different tasks of missions to international organizations, see Blair 1998, pp. 17-19.

4. The estimated value of Crown-owned property worldwide was between $2 billion and $3 billion in 1992-93. The annual rent for Crown-leased properties abroad was estimated at $133 million. In 1993-94, the estimated salary and related cost of maintaining 1,764 Canada-based staff abroad was $145 million. See the 1994 *Report* of the Auditor-General, paragraphs 22.84 and 22.133.

5. For a discussion of international relations theory and the ambassador, see Wolfe 1998. For an empirical analysis of the pattern of Canadian representation, see Robert Wolfe, "Changing Dynamic Density and the Distribution of Canadian Diplomats" (forthcoming).

6. Canada opened a mission in Cameroon because Howard Green, secretary of state for external affairs in the Diefenbaker government, found himself seated beside the foreign minister at international meetings and discovered that they could communicate. As a bilingual country, Cameroon was a member of the Commonwealth and later of *la francophonie*.

7. For excellent examples of this genre, see Reece 1996. These essay-length memoirs were written by members of the generation that joined the foreign service in the dozen or so years after the war. In this context, see also Halstead 1983. The larger part of the growing corpus of book-length Canadian diplomatic memoirs and biographies was written by or about people who joined the foreign service in the 1930s. See, for example, Reid 1981; Ignatieff 1985; Ritchie 1981; and Granatstein 1981.

8. On the department's less than enthusiastic response to the Glassco report, and the flurry of subsequent administrative reviews, see Hilliker and Barry 1995, chapter 8. The academic literature is thin in this domain. Swainson (1975) published one of the only articles on Canadian diplomats. For the views of a key actor on the strengthening of the ambassador, see Gotlieb 1979. American ambassadors faced the same difficulty, see "The Ambassador in U.S. Foreign Policy," a Congressional Research Service report to the Senate Committee on Foreign Relations, reprinted in Herz 1983, p. 7.

9. Canada 1981, pp. 85-86. For commentary on the report, see Jackson *et al.* 1982. The commissioner's own views of diplomacy were not especially sophisticated — see McDougall 1983.

10. An essential basis for a gendered analysis of the service as a whole is provided in the accounts of the careers of women pioneers and leaders in Weiers 1995. The empirical basis for an analysis of Canadian diplomatic spouses is in the McDougall report. See also the chapter on diplomatic spouses in Enloe 1989.

2

Diplomatic Puzzles: A Review of the Literature

Andrew F. Cooper

The study of diplomacy is beginning to enjoy a revival among students of international relations.[1] This revival in diplomatic studies has not produced any consensus on the subject. The emergent literature is marked by a highly fragmented treatment and focus, rather than by a uniform approach or general agreement. The dominant impression given by this increasingly diverse body of works is of a set of highly complex but significant puzzles about the nature and role of diplomacy in the contemporary world. At a general level, the puzzles are subsumed into a much wider debate about how diplomacy either meshes with or diverges from the overall pattern in the architecture of the international system. More specifically, these puzzles relate to the multifaceted evolution in the functions of diplomacy.

Going beyond the traditional scholarly concern with the institution of diplomacy, at least some of the academic literature has moved to examine more closely the expanding repertoire of diplomatic techniques. Instead of an exclusive concern with questions of protocol and representation, this alternative lens has shifted attention toward locating nuances of expression found in the sphere of information, communication, and negotiation. While further stretching the arena for debate, signs of a trend concentrating on the range of activities performed by diplomats fits well with the subject area central to this book. For the opening up of a discussion about how, as well as why, the machinery of diplomacy is changing serves as a necessary context for a concerted reassessment of the role of Canadian ambassadors and diplomatic missions.

Much of the resurgence of interest in diplomacy is directly linked to the larger elements of transformation in post-Cold War global conditions. Many of these elements, it must be cautioned, did not result only from the end of Soviet Union and bi-polarity. The number of actors, both state and societal, with a stake in international relations had increased considerably during the 1960s and 1970s. Concomitantly, the agenda of international politics had opened up to a large extent as the traditional dominance of the so-called "high" security agenda, relating to questions of war and peace, was successfully challenged by economic and social agendas. Furthermore, technological change, especially accelerated methods of communication and travel, had altered the practice of the debates about diplomacy in a number of ways. "Summit" and/or "personal" diplomacy, for example, were greatly facilitated by the ease with which leaders could move quickly around the world.

Without question though, the pace and impact of these changes has been surpassed in the late 1980s and the 1990s. For a start, the scope of the international relations agenda has become far more complex. Not only are the limits of the security agenda increasingly contested, but the economic and social agendas have both widened and deepened — to take in everything from rules for competition and investment; definitions of subsidies; numerous questions relating to gender; Aboriginal/indigenous and workers' rights, climate change, and the ozone layer, to name just a few items on a long list. At the same time, the space for a wider group of actors to operate has increased considerably. With the release of the "disciplines" imposed by the Cold War, the opportunities for innovative action by secondary states increased somewhat as well. But, as Kim Nossal and Alison Van Rooy indicate in this volume, so too did the room available for a variety of sub-national/non-central-government actors, and a host of other actors encompassing societal activists and non-governmental organizations (NGOs). (For one innovative account of these trends see Rosenau 1990.)

The intensity of these sorts of changes was further accelerated by the shift from particular changes in technology and methods of communication to a systemic, and, as pointed out by Richard Kohler in this volume, a "virtual" revolution ushering in a new information age. At the cutting edge of this revolution has been the much discussed "CNN effect," whereby television coverage gives faraway events considerable apparent, if transient, political immediacy, in turn introducing a great deal of volatility into public perception of a multitude of issues.

In the early stages of a developing crisis, governments are often pushed by media images "to do something." As events unfold in often dangerous and unpredictable ways, also reflected in the media, governments are pulled back from intervention. NGOs, in parallel fashion, can present their own images — and interpretations — of issues and events. (On the effect of the media in cases involving intervention see Strobel 1997 and Gowing 1997.)

In similar fashion the form of interaction at the international level has changed. While the position of the United States remains pivotal, both in terms of structural power and ideological influence or "soft power" (Nye 1990), the end of the

Cold War has not meant that the post-1945 "hegemon" alone can or will set the global agenda. On the contrary, the role of institutions and alternative forms of leadership has received a boost. Many of the issues at the fore of the policy agenda of the 1990s — especially those that are essentially global and interdependent — are not easily dealt with by a single nation state, even one as powerful as the US (Nye 1992). Rather these issues require forms of skillful management working either through established mechanisms such as multilateral, regional, or bilateral organizations, or through ad hoc forms of coalition and confidence-building; areas in which the US does not possess a decided comparative advantage over secondary powers.

Likewise, the clear boundaries between what have traditionally been considered the international and the domestic have broken down. Much of the logic of Putnam's "two-level" games, in which domestic conditions and issues must be factored into decision making at the international level (and vice versa) remains valid (1988). Nonetheless, the nuanced interaction between these two levels cannot be seen through a bifocal lens. As globalization and transnationalization have picked up momentum, interaction between the domestic and the international have become both multifaceted and intertwined.

I do not propose to explain these changes in the scope, intensity, and form of international interaction, but to indicate how they have raised new puzzles that animate revived interest in the study of diplomacy. As Hocking has shown, the traditional debate centred on whether we could see a "new" diplomacy or whether traditional diplomacy was in "decline" (1995). This debate is evident in the Canadian literature.

LOOKING BACK AT THE OLDER DEBATES ON DIPLOMACY

The nature of diplomacy (or the function of diplomats) has attracted much less attention — at least among political scientists — in Canada than in a number of other countries. In contrast to the abundant offerings from historians on a range of questions having to do with "their" diplomats, the Canadian literature on the evolving role of the diplomat from the international relations discipline is remarkably thin. Scholars of Canadian foreign policy, while not uninterested in the intricacies of policy making in Ottawa, appear to have found the subject of actual diplomatic practice less worthy of serious treatment.

In large part, the (relative) lack of any "hardening of the categories" among Canadian students of international relations and foreign policy accounts for their disinterest. Most Canadian political scientists interested in these sub-specialities (and this group was in itself a relatively small cohort) took what may be described as an eclectic approach. This broad perspective is important, for, as Hocking demonstrates, in a country such as the UK the debates about diplomacy have been generated by the wider (and continuous) controversy between the proponents of a state-centric view of international affairs and the advocates of a "world society" view (1995). The state-centric school has defended the traditional modes of diplomacy quite rigidly. Those with a "world society" perspective, more critically, have claimed that older forms of diplomacy (with the erosion of the territorial state) are outdated and irrelevant. Significantly, when some "hardening of the categories" took place in Canadian international relations it did so not over these more universal issues but over national preoccupations with Canada's place in the world — as middle power, satellite, dependent country, or principal power. (See, for example, Molot 1990.)

Standing out as the exception to this pattern of disinterest was James Eayrs. Thematically, Eayrs' writings in the 1960s and early 1970s epitomize the dual concerns with decline and newness. Almost alone among his contemporaries, Eayrs paid attention to the possible impact of wider forces on the future role of diplomacy and career diplomats. Nor, in a most uncharacteristic Canadian fashion, did he pull any punches about what the future held. Under the weight of new forces and conditions, Eayrs confidently predicted that the performance of professional diplomacy would move toward decline, or "deliquesence," melt away into nothingness, fade into limbo (1971, p. 69). To be sure, Eayrs anticipated this disappearing act on normative/subjective grounds; he did not disguise his view of the ethical and operational shortcomings of diplomats, which he claimed ranged from a lack of moral sensitivity to crass opportunism. But, just as clearly, he based his prediction on an assessment of a number of objective conditions centred on changes in the state system, new actors emerging in diplomacy, and the impact of technological innovation. Eayrs' most oft-quoted lines were, "Most of [External Affairs] postings are expendable, Much of its work is redundant. Many of its officials are unnecessary. The name is "External," not "Eternal" (ibid., p. 8).

At the time, Eayrs' critique had both a political/administrative perspective and an intellectual impact. It provided scholarly support for successive waves of bureaucratic reorganizations of the Canadian foreign service. Above all, this formidable critique played into Pierre Trudeau's dissatisfaction with the "outmoded" nature of diplomatic practices generally and the performance of the Department of External Affairs specifically (cited in Thordarson 1972, p. 91). From an intellectual perspective, the critique elicited a response from a number of those individuals instrumental in developing Canadian statecraft. Arthur Andrew, who as a Diplomat in Residence at the University of Toronto (or as he says, in the preface to a later book, "Ambassador to Jim Eayrs" (1993), wrote a book called *Defence by Other Means: Diplomacy for the Underdog* mainly to defend the profession.

Other responses came from A.W.F. Plumptre (1973) and John Holmes, who called his response a sermon on diplomacy (1973).

All of these rejoinders put the onus squarely on the "new" instead of the "decline." Pointedly, Holmes questioned whether the "function of diplomacy [could] be exorcized" as decisively as Eayrs had suggested (p. 33). What was needed, in Holmes' view, was not an outright rejection of the function of diplomacy but rather a better appreciation of how diplomacy has evolved. Achieving this meant, above all, studying more closely the way "the functions, habits, and priorities of diplomacy are mutable," being aware that the "kinds and breeds of diplomats or interlocutors are likely to multiply," and accepting the idea that "the role of the ambassador does need serious rather than captious re-examination" (ibid.).

Eayrs, in his critique of the study of diplomacy in the late 1960s and early 1970s, foresaw many of the puzzles now facing diplomacy and diplomats. The scope of diplomatic activity has opened up, much as he suggested it would. Domestically, the public — or at least some elements of the public — are no longer content to remain on the sidelines "seen and not heard." This process can be interpreted as an outgrowth of "changes in the nature of the states system" at the international level" (Eayrs 1971, p. 75) and especially the erosion of national sovereignty. Moreover, Eayrs' views of how technological change would increase the intensity and speed of diplomatic activity were remarkably prescient. Although unaware of the notion of "cyberdiplomacy," he pointed to a future in which technological advances in electronic communication and easily available information would "enable the individual to make his mark upon events by placing at his disposal resources previously monopolized by foreign offices." Forecasting some of the tactics of a variety of later societal activists, he wrote "The requirement for setting up your own department of external affairs in your basement are remarkably modest. You need only be reasonably literate, fairly persistent, moderately affluent" (p. 78).

In other respects, Eayrs' predictions were less accurate. His expectation that the profession of diplomacy would be destroyed by "overproduction" (i.e., the need to adapt to the proliferation of state entities) has not transpired. While the proliferation of states, accentuated by the break-up of some nation states into small entities, has severely complicated diplomatic practice, these trends have not de-legitimized diplomatic mechanisms (ibid., pp. 74, 75). On the contrary, the major problem associated with the proliferation of actors is finding the resources (both in terms of funding and personnel) needed to extend diplomatic links to these newer countries. In hindsight, Eayrs' interpretation of the impact of new actors seems to be misleading and/or exaggerated. For one thing, Eayrs over-emphasized the role of the city-state in international affairs. While non-central actors have become more important since the 1970s (leading to visions from some writers of a "new medievalism"; see, for example, Ruggie 1993), the prerogatives of "urban managers" have not yet transcended the powers of national leaders in North America, as Eayrs predicted they would. For another thing, Eayrs elevated too much the emergence of "the individual" in diplomacy (p. 76). True, in a wide number of capacities (whether labelled as "private" or "unofficial" diplomats), private individuals are playing an expanded role in diplomacy. But this dynamic still falls short of the paramountcy Eayrs attributed to it. Nor has this trend been as autonomous from the state as Eayrs expected (or hoped for). Much of the ascendant role of the individual as diplomat has come as leaders have more people on staff, as special advisers are used on foreign policy, and as professional diplomats become trouble-shooters. As such, this trend centralizes more than it diffuses diplomatic activity.

The expanding scope, intensity, and form of diplomacy in the globalized and interdependent context of the 1980s and 1990s has not meant that diplomacy and diplomats are any less important. On the contrary, diplomacy appears to be more important precisely because of this added complexity. In the words of one participant/observer, "The virtual mission and the virtual ministry are no longer entirely in the realms of science fiction; but, equally, abandoned missions and abolished ministries are not part of the real world either. Contemporary diplomacy shows every sign of adapting vigorously to new conditions and participants: a private world once famous for the conventionalities of its metier has become a much more public, complicated and fascinating piece of kinetic art" (Langhorne 1996, p. 12).

A good example of this paradoxical situation may be illustrated with reference to the question of sovereignty. As Eayrs predicted, the role of the nation state has receded in a variety of ways. Yet this decaying of the Westphalian system, as Mark Zacher (1992) has since phrased it, has not reduced the role of diplomacy. While territoriality and integrity of border held primacy, states could believe that self-help was a viable option. With the shift toward a world market, increasingly open borders, transnational actors, around-the-clock access to money markets, stock exchanges and information, and some move toward globalization of values, however, a multifaceted bargaining dynamic has emerged at the state level. This complex dynamic, in turn, encourages the diplomatic function. Following writers such as Jackson (1990) and Keohane (1995, pp. 165-86), an important distinction must be made here between "formal" (or "negative") sovereignty and "operational" (or "positive") sovereignty. Formal sovereignty continues to provide legal authority. But a strong argument may be made that the major contemporary tests of sovereignty relate to its "operational" component, that is, how a state chooses to limit its own legal freedom as part of diplomatic/negotiating exercises.

LOOKING AT THE PUZZLES OF CONTEMPORARY DIPLOMACY

The contemporary literature on diplomacy has not moved entirely beyond the dominant themes of the past; the shadow of potential decline still lingers over much of the discussion of the nature and role of diplomacy. The 1997 Wilton Park conference was entitled, for example, Diplomacy: Profession in Peril? (Sussex, UK, 21-25 July; see also Smith 1996c). Echoes of Eayrs' critique of diplomatic practice also continue to preoccupy a distinctive strain in academia. If less robust in presenting the scenario that diplomacy will inevitably wither away, this critical voice is no less certain of the normative benefits of shifting the centre of attention away from the professional diplomat.[2]

The tendency continues, as well, to label any shift in diplomatic practice as "new." This way of framing trends is not in itself misleading. The problem is that it may confuse, as layer after layer of "new" diplomacy is added. New diplomacy, to Harold Nicolson and others of his generation, meant "open" as opposed to "closed" or secretive diplomacy (1939). Alternatively, new diplomacy to those who wrote the 1969 Duncan committee report meant more emphasis on multilateral relations (United Kingdom 1969). Finally, to Susan Strange and John Stopford in the 1990s, "new diplomacy" means an extension of state-firm and firm-firm modes of diplomacy (1991). Overused by succeeding generations, the term "new" risks not only substantive confusion but intellectual devaluation.

Thematic continuity notwithstanding, the contemporary literature tackles a number of puzzles at the heart of emergent diplomatic practice. The first puzzle of this type relates to the diffuse question of diplomacy being drawn away from its traditional mode of operation. To be sure, some academics continue to concentrate their attention almost exclusively on the traditional attributes of diplomacy with a fixed image of conventions and notion of a special diplomatic disposition. Other academics, however, have broadened their parameters to take into account diplomacy's adaptive machinery as well as its age-old institutional features. Out in front of this more nuanced wave of recent literature is Gil Winham's overview of the pattern of continuity and change in contemporary diplomatic practice (1993). Winham's work shows that the level of conceptual analysis (as opposed to just thick description) of contemporary diplomatic practice can be raised, while elaborating on how diplomacy actually works in practice. Winham appreciates the general interaction between system change and the evolution of diplomatic method, and he is aware of the way the traditionally separate functions of diplomacy and the policy process have been drawn closer together. Large United Nations conferences on technical as well as "political" topics, in addition to smaller ad hoc meetings of ministers have become a more pervasive form of conducting a multitude of "diplomatic" interactions. When we speak of "diplomats" therefore, we now mean officials of the foreign ministry at home and abroad, working in embassies, at multilateral conferences, and conducting bilateral negotiations. We also mean leaders and ministers, and officials of "domestic" departments. Extending his earlier path-breaking work (1977), Winham has shown how complexity, the new technical qualities, and bureaucratization in particular, contribute to this evolution.

The source of debate is, nonetheless, as much about prescription as description. Those academics who have openly questioned the value of turning the focus away from the diplomats' "traditional source of authority and raison d'etre" toward "the skills they possess and the jobs they do," (Sharp 1997, p. 609) tend to believe this alternative research agenda would ensure a loss of professional status. As Paul Sharp has written, this trend raises "the possibility that diplomacy's identity as a discrete practice may be subsumed under broader notions of conflict resolution and bargaining" (ibid.). For Winham, by way of contrast, integrating diplomats far more deeply and widely into the technical aspects of decision making has the opposite effect — rather than making diplomacy redundant, it allows diplomatic players and functions to take on a great deal of additional significance.

A second related puzzle — has the communications revolution reinforced the trend to integrate diplomacy into policy making? This question seems particularly relevant in terms of the competing scenarios laid out in the older literature, represented, for example, by Jim Eayrs and John Holmes, about the relationship between ambassadors and embassies with headquarters. For Eayrs, not surprisingly, the impact of technological changes in communications pointed to the downgrading, if not the eventual elimination, of the ambassadorial/embassy function. For Holmes, equally consistently, this prediction was just another example "of the superficial treatment of a subject scholars have too often disdained to take seriously." As he went on to say, "Communications work in both directions, and the part the ambassador can now play in the devising of his instructions has been greatly increased" (1973, p. 5). Notwithstanding a lack of forecasting ability about societal change opening up diplomatic representation (most clearly, in terms of gender), it appears that Holmes rather than Eayrs may have possessed the more accurate crystal ball on the future of diplomacy. Pessimistic assessments of externally-based diplomats marginalized by technological change have not played out; in contemporary affairs ambassadors are more "plugged in" because of the closer and faster connection between the various components in the diplomacy/policy-transmission belt.

A third connecting puzzle has to do with the speed with which diplomacy has been applied. If states have become more like firms in the onus they place on bargaining, states have also copied the practices of some firms in offering forms of "just in time" diplomatic practice. Indeed, the emphasis on speed is a frequent theme of the contemporary literature on diplomacy.

The academics who tackle this theme, nonetheless, bring very different orientations to the endeavour. Some attend to the changing structure of the international system. Strange has noted, for example, that "states today have to be alert, adaptable to external change, quick to note what other states are up to" (1992, p. 10). James Der Derian, from a post-modernist perspective, is even more emphatic on this point, suggesting that time has in many ways replaced space as the crucial factor in diplomatic communications, delivery and response (1987, p. 208). Still other academics see speeding up primarily as a specific form of response to an external stimuli (often in the form of a specific situational or institutional demand, but sometimes in the form of a cumulative learning process). Fen Hampson gives pride of place, for instance, to the triggering effect of a particular set of exogenous factors in launching Canadian issue-specific activity on pollution control and other environmental issues (1989/90; 1990). Finally, going back to Putnam, some consideration is given to how domestic imperatives affect diplomatic initiatives (1988). Against the ideological/policy background of the 1980s and 1990s, for example, international signalling has become a useful device in a state's campaign for economic and/or social reform.

Winham's work also acts as a guide in introducing a fourth overlapping puzzle. As varied forms of technical negotiations become more prominent, a greater salience is given in contemporary diplomacy to issue-specific expertise and administrative capacity. Yet this tendency does not appear to have reduced the possibilities of what may be termed initiative or mission-oriented diplomacy; a phenomenon described by Winham as diplomacy "when and where you needed it" (Winham 1993, p. 9). Indeed, some of the recent cases best described as illustrations of mission-oriented diplomacy (land mines, for instance) are also issues with a highly technical component. (See Cooper and Hayes, forthcoming.)

A fifth puzzle centres on the range of diplomacy. This puzzle emerges from the widening agenda of international politics. As long as the old Cold War order remained intact, the parameters of Canadian diplomacy were severely confined. Without these imposing structural limitations, the scope of diplomatic activities has broadened considerably. As opposed to the traditional fixed concerns (with primacy of place being given to territorial integrity) the state must not only try to "do something," but be seen "doing something," across a wider continuum of international issues. These issues arise, for example, from the non-military security agenda and from efforts to promote economic well-being and social welfare.

Still, if Canada has had considerable incentive to respond to the multiple and expanded pressures of being a good international citizen its ability to do so has been severely contested. Indeed, the gulf between will and capabilities serves as a key sub-text in the debate about Canadian diplomacy. A strong push-pull dynamic exists between intense (albeit uneven) demands and uncertain resources. The result has been a growing sense in public discourse that Canada must carefully choose areas of diplomatic activity (Potter 1996). This logic helps encourage a mode of niche diplomacy, that is to say, "concentrating resources in specific areas best able to generate returns worth having, rather than trying to cover the field" (Evans and Grant 1991, p. 323; see also Cooper 1995).

A sixth puzzle involves how contemporary diplomacy is applied. The prominence of "access" to both information and power points is an increasingly important theme. (For an early discussion see Haskel 1980). As a consequence, the "public" face of diplomacy is stressed either in direct lobbying or in relations with the media and society. The dissemination and the management of knowledge are essential ingredients in this public face of diplomacy. It can be expressed either in direct lobbying of decisionmakers (an "insider" strategy) or in relations with the media and society (an "outsider" strategy).

Mobilizing a sophisticated form of public diplomacy, as a number of case studies confirm, offers considerable rewards.[3] However, many of the same studies reveal that campaigns of this sort should not be oversold. Although often valuable and necessary, public diplomacy must be done right to ensure benefits. When executed without expertise or crudely, these campaigns can result in a public relations backlash. The practice of public diplomacy fascinates and perplexes because it is both an art and a science.

A seventh puzzle has to do with the increasingly intricate relationship between state and societal actors. The impression given by Eayrs' work, as with most of the older literature, is that this relationship has been riddled with ongoing and intractable tensions. A strong current in the contemporary literature, conversely, showcases at least the potential for "creative statecraft" between state and societal actors. Evans, Jacobson and Putnam, in an influential edited collection, refer to this constructive form of interaction as part of a shift toward "double-edged diplomacy" linking the domestic and the international (1993).

This theme is brought out more explicitly by Hocking's use of the term "catalytic" diplomacy to describe the development of some degree of symbiosis between the "official" and "unofficial" practices of state and non-state actors. Although tensions persist between the state and firms and between the state and non-governmental organizations, Hocking concludes that there is also some mutuality of interest between these actors on an issue-specific basis (1995). To be fully convincing as an operational concept, this argument needs to be buttressed by a greater variety of empirical work. There is a dearth of in-depth studies, especially of the state-firm relationship. While cases abound portraying the relationship between states and firms as either openly conflictual or as instances of cronyism, the more subtle forms of interaction between these two actors remain a puzzle.

An eighth and final puzzle relates to how diplomacy is "managed" bureaucratically. A number of writers have commented on the extensive administrative decentralization evident in contemporary diplomacy. To give just one illustration, in a keynote presentation to a recent conference on "Foreign Ministries: Change and Adaptation," [Lord] William Wallace, stated that, "Government-to-government relations have substantially replaced relations via foreign ministries and embassies, at least among developed countries. Direct and continuing contacts among ministers and officials make for cross-cutting coalitions; defence ministries support each other against finance ministries within NATO, central banks form an effective trans-national 'club'." (1997, p. 2)

Yet, as Karvonen and Sundelius (1987), among others, show, the changes are not all unidirectional. If there is a pronounced trend toward extended forms of diversification, there are also countervailing tendencies toward some forms of consolidation vis-à-vis the authority of professional diplomats. Following Canada's lead, a number of other foreign ministries have moved to consolidate bureaucratic responsibility for international trade relations in the foreign ministry. There are also abundant signs that foreign ministries can successfully assert (or reassert) control over some aspects of the international agenda. A case in point is the diplomatization of peacekeeping/peacemaking/peacebuilding activities. What is required is a fuller assessment about how, why, and where these differing results occur regarding fragmentation/consolidation of authority.

CONCLUSION

The purpose of this chapter has not been to tackle directly questions relating to the institutional structure or role of ambassadors and missions. Rather it has been to try to ground these specific players and functions in the larger body of literature about the nature and significance of diplomacy. The two tasks are interconnected. At least in Canada, apart from the work of a few ex-practitioners, the constellation of roles assigned to and delivered by diplomats abroad has never received the academic attention it deserves. As noted, the reasons for this neglect are both specific to Canada and universal. For many students of Canadian foreign policy, the activities of ambassadors and embassies simply held little interest. The exciting task was to try to settle questions about Canada's position in the world. For others, the activities of these figures and institutions were not only irrelevant, but doomed to the rubbish heap of history. The only agreement between these camps was the implicit idea that ambassadors and embassies existed on the margins; they might prove a useful source for anecdotes or historical insight, but otherwise were of little consequence.

Cast in the light of the larger set of debates about contemporary diplomacy, these narrow lens will no longer do. Although not without recognizable gaps, we can discern the attempts of an increasing number of academics to locate and try to understand better the varied puzzles of diplomacy at the end of the twentieth century. What stands out in this scholarship is an appreciation that not only does diplomacy matter more now, but that much about diplomacy is being transformed. While some are tempted to identify this diplomacy as new, the image of decline no longer reflects what has been occurring in practice. A volume such as this represents an opportunity to move to a different stage in this process of rethinking and adaptation. Reflecting the "ever thickening texture in international diplomacy" (Langhorne 1996, p. 12), it speaks to the need for refinement and segmented focus in research as well as in the operational agenda. To suggest that the study of diplomacy is about to become an academic growth industry for students of international relations may be an exaggeration. However, there clearly is sufficient richness — not only in country-specific and comparative case material, but conceptually — in the subject area to justify concerted activity. A key component of this ongoing exercise is the attempt to more fully and accurately appreciate the work of missions and ambassadors.

NOTES

1. The scholarly literature on the subject has risen sharply in recent years. While perhaps lacking some of the "Small World" flavour of the activities of their academic counterparts, serious journalists have also taken up the theme that diplomacy (and diplomats) are "back in." For this theme, set against the Canadian context, see Cohen 1994. For general surveys see Hamilton and Langhorne 1995, Berridge 1995, and Melissen 1998, aided and abetted by the interest that some publishing companies, notably Macmillan, have shown in diplomacy. The number of conferences with a central focus on diplomatic themes has also risen. In addition to the workshop that served as the genesis for this volume, the nature and features of contemporary diplomacy have been discussed in major meetings hosted by the United States Institute of Peace, the Mediterranean Academy of Diplomacy, as well as Wilton Park in the United Kingdom. The International Studies Association (ISA) added a Diplomatic Section in 1997 to follow in 1998 at Minneapolis and Vienna.

2. See, for example, Scholte 1993. In Canada this critical voice may be seen, most recently, in Healy and Neufeld 1997. "Teaching IR from a critical perspective," these academics suggest, "means that students who assume that IR can be understood as the preserve as diplomats and generals will be rattled. (On the other hand, those who are not interested in the distant goings-on of missile counters and diplomats will be reassured that their questions have a place in the classroom." p. 29.)

3. On the South Korean experience of lobbying in the United States see Moon 1988. On the Canadian case, see Cooper 1989.

PART I

DIPLOMATIC MISSIONS

3

Diplomacy at the Coal-Face: A Mission to Pakistan in the 1990s

Louis A. Delvoie

INTRODUCTION

Canada's high commissioner to Pakistan cannot rely on material power to influence affairs of state. Canada is a far-off country, locally significant mostly for being rich. Pakistan is, for Canada, a strange faraway place, a heavily populated Asian country of 120 million people, a country of regional, but not global importance. The two countries have nevertheless maintained close diplomatic relations for five decades. The challenges, demands, and obstacles I faced as Canadian high commissioner to Pakistan from 1991 to 1994 are not atypical of those faced by many Canadian heads of mission in comparable countries. This chapter, therefore, is an attempt to provide one of many possible answers to the question: What do heads of mission do and how do they do it? My approach is largely descriptive and analytical rather than prescriptive or normative. I outline the context in which my mission took place, set forth the mandate I was given by the Canadian government, and examine some of the main activities I undertook in pursuit of that mandate. My selection of material is intended to highlight both the functional and sectoral aspects of my role as a head of mission. I touch on representation, communication, advocacy, analysis, reporting and management, and I draw my examples from the realms of politics and security, aid and development, trade and investment, narcotics control and immigration, and human rights and good governance.

In the conclusion I argue, not surprisingly in this book, that the role of individuals "on the ground" remains indispensable to the development of relations between countries and governments. I must stress that this importance does not attach only to the head of mission. Most of what follows is written in the first person singular in order to avoid the charges of lèse-majesté attendant on the use of the first person plural or the even more damning charges of Gaullism or Dolism attendant on the use of the third person singular. This linguistic convention does not mean, however, that I am not profoundly conscious of the degree to which heads of mission are dependent on the support of their officers and staff in whatever they do and in whatever they may be fortunate enough to achieve. If I had been asked to discuss the role of the mission rather than that of the head of mission, this chapter would have been very different in tone and character.

BY WAY OF CONTEXT

Pakistan was one of the first developing countries in which Canada took a significant and enduring interest in the years immediately following the end of the Second World War.[1] Pakistan was one of the founding members of the modern multiracial Commonwealth, whose establishment was viewed in its time as a major Canadian foreign policy priority. Canadians saw Pakistan, like India, as the wave of the future in post-colonial Asia, one of a growing number of independent Asian countries with which Canada should seek to interact as it sought to affirm its international personality after decades of quasi-isolationism. As the Cold War took hold, Canada's interest in Pakistan intensified. On the one hand, the poverty, sectarianism, political instability and inter- and intrastate conflicts of the South Asian region were seen as providing ideal conditions for Soviet interference and the expansion of Soviet influence. On the other hand, Pakistan's generally pro-Western inclinations and orientations made it a bulwark in the effort to contain Soviet expansion in Asia where the United States built politico-military links, and eventual membership in regional alliances such as the Central Treaty Organization (CENTO) and the Southeast Asia Treaty Organization (SEATO).

Commonwealth links and the creation of the Colombo Plan in 1950 provided Canada with a framework for bilateral relations. Pakistan became one of the first and largest beneficiaries of Canada's developmental programs in the Third World. Over the ensuing four decades, Canada devoted nearly $2 billion in economic and technical assistance to Pakistan. The Pakistani landscape is dotted with the products of this effort: hydro dams, irrigation schemes, a nuclear power plant, schools and training centres, hospitals, and clinics. Hundreds of Canadian engineers, technicians, economists, and teachers worked in Pakistan while hundreds of young Pakistanis studied in Canadian schools and universities. Canada came to enjoy an excellent reputation as a generous and effective contributor to the country's socio-economic development, and especially as a country that did not attach political strings to its aid program.

A relationship generally described as "very good" or "close" was not devoid of bad patches. The Canadian government did not hesitate to express its dismay when the military seized power in Pakistan in 1958 and again in 1977, and on each occasion held onto it for approximately a dozen years. In 1971, Canada expressed criticism of the heavy-handed tactics used by the Pakistani army in repressing a separatist movement in East Bengal, soon to become the state of Bangladesh. Canada has also on various occasions expressed its disappointment that its very large investment in aid to Pakistan has not been parallelled by the development of a more substantive trading relationship. But in all these instances, the Pakistani government accepted Canadian criticism with relative good grace.

The only serious cooling in the relationship occurred in the mid-1970s over the question of bilateral nuclear cooperation (see Azmi 1982, pp. 95-116; Delvoie 1995, pp. 29-34). After the Indian nuclear explosion of May 1974, the Canadian government reviewed its nuclear export policies, and made them far more restrictive. Several months of difficult negotiations with the Pakistani government had revealed a willingness on the part of Pakistan to accept the most stringent of safeguards on the Canadian-supplied KANUPP reactor and on all nuclear materials provided by Canada, but an unwillingness either to sign the Nuclear Non-Proliferation Treaty (NPT) or to accept international safeguards on its entire nuclear program. Under the terms of its new policy, which applied to all non-nuclear weapons states, the Canadian government terminated all of its nuclear cooperation arrangements with Pakistan. The decision was viewed in Pakistan as a unilateral abrogation of three bilateral agreements that Pakistan had always honoured. It was portrayed as Canada punishing Pakistan for the sins of India, although Pakistan had always been far more forthcoming than India on all questions related to nuclear safeguards and had not, of course, violated its agreements with Canada by conducting a nuclear explosion. The bitterness engendered by this episode endured for several years in Canada-Pakistani relations.

Canada-Pakistan relations survived lengthy periods of military rule, Canadian criticism, and Pakistani displeasure with the abrogation of nuclear cooperation because the relationship had broader political and economic significance for both sides. In the late 1980s and early 1990s, however, a series of events external to the relationship had a direct impact. The Soviet withdrawal from Afghanistan, the end of the Cold War and the collapse of the Soviet Union all significantly decreased the geostrategic importance of Pakistan to the West. The conclusion of the major East-West arms control agreements (INF, CFE, START) reordered Western arms control priorities, and gave pride of place to the issue of nuclear weapons proliferation; Pakistan and India stood out on the Western arms control agenda as two large and mutually hostile countries with unconstrained nuclear weapons capabilities. The triumphal march of democracy from Managua to Moscow and from Prague to Phnom Penh inspired many Western governments to once again believe that the world was politically perfectible, and to attach a much higher priority than before to human rights and good governance in their foreign policies and relations. Pakistan's record in these domains was scrutinized and found wanting.

These harsh new realities were first communicated to Pakistan by the United States. In October 1990, the US announced that it would terminate its program of economic and security assistance because Pakistan had crossed a certain threshold in its nuclear weapons program that it was unwilling either to cap or reverse. This was a severe blow given that the value of the American aid program was US$500 million annually and represented roughly 25 percent of the assistance that Pakistan received from the Western donor community. Subsequently the United States and two of Pakistan's other major benefactors, Japan and Germany, insisted on Pakistan engaging them in sustained bilateral security dialogues to come to grips with the nuclear proliferation issue. Within the Western aid consortium for Pakistan, countries such as Germany, the Netherlands, and Canada increasingly insisted that Pakistan mend its ways on issues such as the rights of women and religious minorities, the imbalance between social and military spending in the state budget, institutional reform, and the reduction of political corruption. These and other modifications in the approach taken by Western countries toward Pakistan led less to actual change or reform and more to creating a deep sense of betrayal among Pakistani elites. The image of Pakistan, the loyal ally of the West in the struggle to contain Soviet expansionism, being discarded as soon as it no longer served vital Western interests became a commonplace of editorials, conferences, and government statements, and led to calls for Pakistan to reorient its foreign policy in the direction of the Islamic world. I did not arrive in Islamabad at the best of times for bilateral relations.

THE MANDATE

Like many newly appointed Canadian heads of mission, I was provided with a letter of instructions from the secretary of state for external affairs setting out the parameters and objectives of my mission as high commissioner to Pakistan. My letter, signed by Barbara McDougall, was dated 22 November 1991 and reached me by diplomatic bag nearly two weeks later, three months after my arrival in Pakistan. When well-crafted, these letters can be invaluable to new appointees. (For excerpts from recent letters see Appendix B.) Letters of instructions provide a set of considered official views on Canadian government priorities in the country of accreditation, outline a number of expectations, and leave the appointee enough leeway to take the initiative and to act in pursuit of government objectives in the absence of more specific instructions related to particular issues or events. I found my letter a highly useful and flexible document, since I was not overburdened with specific instructions from Ottawa during my three years in Pakistan.

After dealing generally with the responsibilities incumbent on all heads of mission, the letter from the minister set forth the general parameters of my mission in the following terms:

> Your challenge is to promote Canadian interests in a broad range of Canadian/Pakistani activities in the context of a country that has only recently returned to civilian, democratically-elected government and to the Commonwealth, and which confronts an innate conservatism in social and religious matters in addition to a difficult law and order situation.

The letter went on to outline four principal goals that I was to pursue: (i) to support Canada's interest in encouraging moderation in Pakistan's foreign and domestic policies; (ii) to encourage regional nuclear non-proliferation, reduced defence expenditures, and the signing of the NPT by Pakistan; (iii) to promote trade and investment opportunities for Canada in Pakistan; and (iv) to direct Canada's development assistance programs into those sectors in which Canadian International Development Agency (CIDA) had determined it could have the greatest positive influence.

The main body of the letter of instructions dwelt on the tasks and activities I was to undertake in pursuit of these and other goals. In summary, I was instructed:

- To monitor and assess political developments in Pakistan and Afghanistan, with particular reference to the threat of a military clash between Pakistan and India over Kashmir, tensions in the Punjab, growing lawlessness across Pakistan, and the prospects for a settlement to the civil war in Afghanistan.

- To be sensitive to the potential for a dialogue on nuclear non-proliferation and arms reduction, given the commitments by the new governments in both India and Pakistan to improving consultations on security matters.

- To report regularly on economic developments, especially those likely to have an impact on Canadian commercial activities and interests.

- To report regularly on patterns of government expenditure, especially military expenditures, as they relate to Canada's development assistance program.

- To manage the implementation of Canada's development assistance program for Pakistan, with annual allocations of approximately $45 million.

- To manage the immigration program with its family reunification, refugee and business immigration components, and to further efforts to contain immigration fraud and misrepresentation.

- To manage the consular program, with its concomitant workload increases due to the deteriorating law and order situation.

- To maintain an adequate level of communication with the media, in the absence of funding for any other public affairs activities.

- To supervise the programs and activities of the Department of National Defence (DND), Royal Canadian Mounted Police (RCMP) and Canadian Security Intelligence Service (CSIS) officers assigned to the mission.

- To ensure the effective and efficient use and management of mission resources, including a staff of 175 and an annual operating budget of $1.6 million.

The letter concluded with an injunction: "it is incumbent upon you to set an example of probity in your official and personal conduct that is beyond reproach" and to ensure that mission personnel understand that "their personal conduct must stand up to the same scrutiny as your own."

PRESENCE AND PROFILE

How to translate this mandate into reality? My first few weeks in Islamabad were spent, in part, in assessing my assets. What were the sources of the influence I was supposed to exercise, or to put it more crudely, what was my leverage? To carry on the day-to-day work, I had inherited from my predecessor a well-managed mission, staffed with competent and dedicated personnel. This was certainly a plus. So too were Pakistani perceptions of Canada: Canada continued to be viewed by Pakistani elites as a country that had been a prominent, generous, and disinterested partner in Pakistan's socio-economic development; many Pakistanis spoke warmly of contacts or friendships with individual Canadians. When I presented my credentials to the president of Pakistan, he spoke in the fondest terms of the Canadian engineers and technicians who had arrived in his home province to build the Warsak Dam in the 1950s. They were, he said, the first foreigners he had ever met and they had made an indelible impression on him. But what became readily apparent was that so many of these sentiments were expressed in the past tense. They referred largely to a 30-year period, running roughly from the early 1950s to the early 1980s, when Canada had indeed been a major source of development assistance to Pakistan, had been clearly identified with big projects that had attracted national attention, and when Canada had ranked among Pakistan's most important foreign partners, almost immediately after the United States, China, the Soviet Union, and Great Britain.

But the reality that confronted me in the early 1990s was quite different. In both absolute and relative terms, the value to Pakistan of Canada's bilateral development assistance program had declined sharply, nor had this growing gap been filled by any upsurge in Canadian trade or investment. By 1992 the Canadian program represented less than 2 percent of the aid received by Pakistan from the Western consortium, and Canada had slipped from the major to the minor leagues within the Western-donor community, behind the Netherlands. Sharp decreases in bilateral development assistance were part of the federal government's efforts to reduce its budgetary deficit and to redirect funding to the countries of Central and Eastern Europe. In early 1991, the indicative planning figure for CIDA disbursements to Pakistan over the next five years was reduced from $300 million to $190 million. By 1993 it had been reduced still further to $140 million. Given that the bilateral aid program had for decades been the cornerstone of Canada-Pakistan relations, it was evident that a cut of nearly 55 percent in that program signalled a period of change and transition in the relationship in the early 1990s. On the political front, the Canadian government had displayed little direct interest in Pakistan; more than 20 years had elapsed since the last visit of a Canadian prime minister and more than five since the last visit of a Canadian secretary of state for external affairs. Canada had played no significant role in the major peace and security issues that had preoccupied or were preoccupying Pakistan, whether it was the war in Afghanistan or the insurgency in Kashmir, which was once again exacerbating relations with India. On the other hand, several other countries had begun to make their presence felt on the Pakistani scene in the 1980s, most notably Japan, Germany, France, and South Korea. Within a matter of a few years these countries had come to surpass Canada (and Britain) in importance as economic partners for Pakistan.

Without any indication that the Canadian government was prepared to devote more resources or give higher priority to the relationship with Pakistan, I concluded that the only way of countering the effects of Canada's declining position and retaining as much influence as possible in the pursuit of Canadian political, security, and commercial objectives, was to devote much of my time and energies to a *politique de presence* aimed at raising the Canadian profile among Pakistani elites. To try to convince those elites that Canada was still an interested player in Pakistani affairs my watchwords would have to be presence, visibility, and coverage. In pursuit of these goals, I would have to rely on my own efforts and on the support of my staff. With no high-profile Canadian visitors on the horizon and since the High Commission's budget for public affairs and public diplomacy had recently been cut to virtually nothing, there would be no visiting scholars, no film festivals, and no art exhibitions to showcase Canada.

The first part of the program involved securing enhanced media coverage for what Canada was doing in Pakistan. Every new agreement signed, every new project launched — no matter how minor — became the object of a High Commission press release. These press releases were hand carried by our Pakistani public affairs officer to known contacts in the newsrooms of a half-dozen major press and broadcast outlets. I also revived a quarterly, illustrated publication called *Pakistan-Canada Highlights*, issued by the High Commission and paid for out of the sole remaining public-affairs budget of $1,500 per year. This publication, which was widely distributed to the media, as well as to key actors in government and business, featured not only short stories on Canadian activities in Pakistan, but also profiles of major Canadian industrial and technological sectors, thereby serving as a trade promotion tool.

The second point of the program was to create news by embarking on an active public speaking program. I rarely, if ever, turned down an invitation to speak, and in fact engineered many. These invitations took me to chambers of commerce and industrial federations, Rotary Clubs and civic organizations, universities and think tanks in all of Pakistan's major cities. These appearances were always accompanied by press releases, and I usually had with me a one-page summary of my speech or statement to facilitate the work of the journalists in the audience, which paid off in the amount and accuracy of the media coverage. The CIDA program, and especially the Canada Fund for small projects, which was administered by the mission, provided other opportunities for making news. By officiating at the inauguration of numerous projects, cutting ribbons, participating in folkloric celebrations, meeting local dignitaries and making short speeches, I managed to bring home the reality of Canada to people in remote areas of Pakistan while at the same time providing stories and photo-opportunities for the regional media. The coverage underlined the presence of Canada and the diverse sectors in which it was involved: constructing causeways, dikes, and water pumping stations; establishing rural schools and clinics; funding vocational training centres and women's entrepreneurship programs; and supporting human rights monitoring organizations.

Since I discovered that establishing contacts with Pakistani political leaders, senior officials and businessmen was relatively easy and did not require the extensive use of the financial resources I had for representational entertaining, I decided to channel most of these resources into a few large, profile-raising receptions rather than into smaller luncheons and dinners destined to develop and exploit contacts. These receptions highlighted the Canadian presence and interest in Pakistan's two major commercial and financial centres, Karachi and Lahore, where unlike other G7 and Western countries, we had only a minimal official presence. Our honorary consul and one-man trade office in Karachi did great work for Canada, but could not compete with the full-blown diplomatic and consular establishments of most of our major competitors. Among the guests at these receptions were always a good number of journalists, who unfailingly attended in the knowledge that there would be free food and drink, that there would be photo-opportunities, and that they could rely on being able to conduct an interview with me either during or after the reception. The coverage achieved was usually well worth the effort.

In my efforts to sustain and raise the Canadian profile, I was greatly aided by my wife. Not long after our arrival in Pakistan she became president of one of the most active and best-known charitable organizations in Islamabad. At the head of a group of 500 women — half Pakistani, half expatriate — she mounted a long series of imaginative and highly successful fundraising activities, several of which were held on the grounds of the Canadian High Commission. These not only highlighted the caring side of the Canadian presence in Pakistan within Islamabad society, but also attracted considerable positive media attention. My wife was interviewed by the press not only about her charitable work, but was also asked to comment on the role of women in modern societies and was eventually featured on the cover of a national women's magazine. In short, she got for Canada the kind of coverage that money could not buy.

While it is impossible to measure with precision the effect of all of these activities, I am convinced my efforts to develop our presence, increase our visibility, and expand our coverage were helpful in giving additional weight to our interventions on issues in the realms of politics and security.

POLITICS AND SECURITY

The foreign policy questions of primary interest to Canada in Pakistan and in South Asia generally were directly interrelated: regional stability, the proliferation of nuclear weapons, the confrontational relationship between Pakistan and India, and the long-standing Kashmir dispute. On these and related issues, my officers and I reported regularly to Ottawa and made periodic demarches to the Foreign Ministry, whether on our own initiative or on instructions. The demarches on regional security counselled moderation, compromise, and the pursuit of peaceful, negotiated solutions; these were usually greeted with assurances of complete Pakistani agreement and statements of regret that the fault for whatever was going wrong in Indo-Pakistani relations lay squarely in New Delhi. Demarches on nuclear proliferation advocated the untrammelled joys of renouncing nuclear weapons and of signing the NPT; the response here, too, was eminently predictable — Pakistan would adhere to the NPT as soon as India did so, but could not renounce acquiring a nuclear weapons capability as long as India, with proven hostile intentions toward Pakistan, continued to possess one. Indeed, neither the demarches nor the response had varied much in 15 years. These demarches, taken in conjunction with those made by other Western countries may have served a useful moderating purpose in reminding the Pakistani authorities of our concerns, and that their actions, as well as those of India, were under constant outside scrutiny. They did not, however, seem to have any noticeable effect on the fundamentals of the situation.

The best hope of altering those fundamentals would have been a well-coordinated multilateral approach, bringing together the countries with the most interests and the most clout in South Asia (see Delvoie 1995, pp. 37-44). There was, however, no sign of that on the horizon. A second best would have been a series of well-coordinated bilateral approaches, aimed at engaging both Pakistan and India in sustained, in-depth dialogues on security issues. During my time in Pakistan, the United States, Japan, and Germany, as well as to a lesser extent France and Britain, initiated such dialogues with the Pakistani government; and I recommended that Canada should do the same. Ottawa, however, seemed reluctant to adopt this approach, which would have entailed a new policy effort and committing the time and energy of already hard-pressed senior officials and military officers to visiting Pakistan at fairly regular intervals. Under the circumstances, I undertook a series of informal conversations with Pakistani ministers on security issues. These were ministers whom I had got to know reasonably well, who often had no responsibilities for foreign policy, but who were politically influential and carried more weight in the government than did the foreign minister.

In these conversations with Pakistani ministers, I usually emphasized the significant mutual advantages that Pakistan and India could derive from a resolution of their differences, particularly the economic advantages of decreased military expenditures and a normal bilateral trading relationship between the two countries. I also outlined the merits of the building-block approach to conflict resolution featuring political dialogue, exchanges of people and ideas, confidence- and security-building measures, and conventional and nuclear arms control agreements which had helped to end the Cold War. I drew heavily on the lessons of the Middle East peace process, which had made remarkable progress and which had brought to the negotiating table countries such as Israel and Syria whose mutual antipathies were certainly no less strong than those between Pakistan and India.

In general, I found my interlocutors prepared to discuss these points pragmatically and dispassionately, and open to arguments and evidence drawn from outside the immediate confines of South Asia. But I almost invariably ran up against counter-arguments that had little to do with the foreign and security policy issues themselves and everything to do with domestic political realities. In their essentials they ran as follows: a coalition government dependent on the support of small parties for its majority in parliament could not afford to make concessions on either the Kashmir or the nuclear weapons questions, because public opinion would not tolerate it and the government would be immediately brought down; furthermore, the life of any political leader who was to do so would be in danger, especially with no evidence of Indian willingness to make similar or larger concessions. One Pakistani minister made this case to me in particularly stark terms. While Pakistanis disagreed among themselves about virtually everything, he said, there was an undeniable national consensus on one point: if India had nuclear weapons, Pakistan should also have them. In his words, even totally illiterate peasants who could not name five foreign countries subscribed wholeheartedly to this consensus. The leader who unilaterally gave up Pakistan's nuclear weapons option would be dead within a matter of days! In a country in which one president and two prime ministers had met violent ends in a 40-year period, this claim did not strike me as particularly exaggerated. My rejoinders, to the effect that there was indeed a need for courageous political leadership and that in every process of accommodation somebody had to take the first step, left them largely unmoved as they dwelt on their own and the country's immediate political future and fortunes.

HUMAN RIGHTS AND GOOD GOVERNANCE

As had so often been the case in the past, Pakistan's domestic politics were highly unstable in the early 1990s. The coalition government in power when I arrived in Islamabad was carrying out an ambitious program of economic reform, deregulation, and privatization, but it was politically handicapped by dependence on the support of Islamist parties for its majority in parliament and under constant attack from opposition forces, which questioned its legitimacy and did not hesitate to mount strikes and demonstrations to make their points. This government collapsed in 1993, a year in which the office of prime minister changed hands four times, with the ever-present risk that the army might once again feel the need to take power to avoid political disintegration. If these circumstances were not particularly propitious for advancing Canada's foreign and security policy agenda in Pakistan, they were even less favourable for promoting our objectives in the fields of human rights and good governance. The governments in power between 1991 and 1994 were not ones likely to take bold initiatives in these areas, and certainly not initiatives that might offend either the Islamist parties or the army. This did not, however, stop us from trying, with mixed results.

I personally focused on the so-called Hudood Ordinances. These were a series of decrees adopted in the mid-1980s by the late president and dictator, General Zia Ul Haq, to shore up his position with an appeal to Islamic legitimacy. These Ordinances not only prescribed harsh "Islamic" penalties (stoning to death, the severing of limbs) for a variety of offences but they discriminated against women in all cases involving rape, adultery, and pre-marital sex. Unlike so many other forms of discrimination against women that existed in Pakistan, these were not merely the result of custom or practice, they were enshrined in law — they resembled the apartheid laws in South Africa that had actually legislated racial discrimination.

In my conversations with selected Pakistani political leaders, I pointed to the discriminatory nature of the Ordinances and noted that their existence on the statute books had a highly detrimental effect on Pakistan's image abroad, particularly in the Western aid community. I especially brought up these points in conversations with Benazir Bhutto while she was still leader of the Opposition, reasonably confident that as a Western-educated woman she would not need much persuading and would agree that the revocation of the Ordinances would do much to repair Pakistan's image in Western circles. In that I was right, but when she became prime minister again in October 1993, she did not feel politically strong enough vis-à-vis the Islamists to address the issue directly. The most she attempted was the creation of a series of "women's police stations" in major cities to spare women the indignities and sexual abuse they regularly endured while detained in conventional police stations.

Another dimension of my activities in the field of human rights arose out of a decision of the government to issue new national identity cards to all Pakistanis. Under pressure from the Islamists, the Cabinet rather hastily and reluctantly agreed that these cards should be colour coded to indicate religious affiliation. This decision caused great consternation among Pakistan's main religious minorities — Christians, Hindus, and Parsis — who saw the decision itself as a form of discrimination, and who feared that such an obvious identification of their status would expose them to repeated acts of discrimination in their daily lives. At the instigation of the Papal Nuncio, representing the interests of the Christian minority, three or four other Western heads of mission and I mounted a very discrete but relentless campaign with senior Pakistani ministers to alter their decision. I pointed out that, beyond the merits of the issue itself, the Pakistani government should also be conscious of Pakistan's image in the West, where memories of Nazi Germany's use of yellow stars were still fresh. In the end, our efforts paid off. While reluctant to publicly rescind its decision, thus losing face and incurring the wrath of the Islamists, the Cabinet decided simply not to implement it, and to continue issuing identity cards in the normal way. A small victory for preventive diplomacy.

Given regional and domestic political realities, there was little that we or other outsiders could do to effectively address the central governance issue — the enormous imbalance in the budgets allocated to the defence sector and to the social sector. While ritually repeating Canadian concerns on this issue, I had little hope that they would lead to change, and unfortunately I was not proved wrong. I did, however, seize the opportunity presented by the general election of 1993 to take a few modest initiatives in the realm of good governance. On the advice of one of my CIDA officers, I allocated monies from our Canada Fund and our Women in Development Fund to a number of Pakistani non-governmental organizations (NGOs) that were endeavouring to educate women about their political rights, to explain the electoral system to them and to encourage them to vote. We also provided funding to one of Pakistan's major human rights organizations which was setting up monitoring teams to guard against electoral fraud on the day of the vote. On instructions from Ottawa, I lobbied leading figures in the two main political parties and in the state electoral commission to persuade them to accept a team of Commonwealth observers to monitor the election. Once the team reached Pakistan, my Australian colleague and I provided it with briefings and support, and I know that we breathed a collective sigh of relief when the Commonwealth observers submitted an official report declaring the elections to have been "free and fair."

Suggesting to the authorities of another country that they should accept international monitoring of their elections is a delicate matter, for it tacitly calls into question their competence or integrity or both. I can well recall the sense of wounded national pride evident when I first broached this topic with the then-chairman of Pakistan's electoral commission. When toward the end of our conversation he very reluctantly assured me that his commission would give its full cooperation to the Commonwealth observers, he asked me only half in jest whether Pakistanis would be invited to monitor Canada's next general election.

THE NARCOTICS TRADE AND ILLEGAL IMMIGRATION

In addition to broad Canadian concerns, with matters of regional security or domestic good governance, Canada had direct interests in Pakistan, notably in two law enforcement issues that came to the fore in Canada-Pakistan relations in the early 1990s: the steady rise in the volume of illegal narcotics traffic and a sudden surge in the number of illegal immigrants.

According to RCMP statistics, nearly one-third of the heroin imported into Canada in 1990 either originated in, or had transited through, Pakistan. The "Golden Crescent" of Pakistan, Afghanistan, and Iran was beginning to rival the "Golden Triangle" of Southeast Asia as a source of illegal narcotics on the market in Canada. In trying to combat this trade, we adopted two approaches with the Pakistani authorities. On the one hand, we progressively expanded cooperation between the RCMP and the Pakistan Narcotics Control Board (PNCB). This cooperation included not only the exchange of intelligence through liaison channels, but also joint operations that resulted in numerous arrests and the seizure of significant quantities of narcotics in Canada. On the other, we sought to exert gentle but constant pressure on the Pakistani authorities to reform their anti-narcotics legislation and to enforce it more widely and more effectively. Whether bilaterally, or together with other representatives of the so-called "Dublin Group" of Western countries, I met on numerous occasions with both ministers for narcotics control and the interior to drive home our concerns. These efforts had a modest payback in the form of new and improved legislation, but my colleagues and I had few illusions about the effectiveness of our lobbying in terms of actually stamping out the drugs trade. We had three reasons for our scepticism. First, the "drug lords" were often well connected to politicians and members of parliament. Second, the law enforcement agencies were ill-equipped to deal with the sophisticated operations and fire power of the traffickers. Third, much of the production and processing of narcotics took place in mountainous tribal regions along the Pakistan-Afghanistan border, regions that the Pakistani authorities, like the British and Russians before them, were unable to subdue or control.

My work on the narcotics issue in Pakistan gave rise to one of the more curious episodes in my diplomatic career. One fine morning early in 1992, the Islamabad newspapers were full of stories about an operation mounted in Baluchistan by the PNCB and a force of border troops that had resulted in the seizure of 23 tons of hashish and 3 tons of heroin, a truly remarkable coup. (For purposes of comparison, the RCMP had seized a total of seven pounds of heroin in all of Canada during 1990.) At the instigation of our police liaison officers, both the British high commissioner and I sent letters to the minister of narcotics control congratulating him on this highly successful operation and suggesting that he might consider the public destruction of these drugs as a way to impress both domestic and international public opinion that his government was indeed serious about combating the drug trade. Our unspoken concern was that these drugs might otherwise filter out the back doors of ramshackle government warehouses, guarded by underpaid and vulnerable police officers. About two weeks later, I received a most unusual invitation that read: "The Federal Minister for Narcotics Control requests the pleasure of the company of H.E. Mr. Louis Delvoie to witness the destruction of one of the World's biggest seizure of narcotic Drugs taking place at Turbat, Baluchistan."

On the appointed day I was one of six Western heads of mission to board a small charter aircraft for a remote location in the stony desert of Baluchistan. On arrival, we were seated under a marquee tent set up on a hillock, about 100 feet away from the largest bonfire I had ever seen. Policemen were dousing it with kerosene to ensure a spectacular show for the dignitaries and the Pakistani, American, British, French, and Canadian media in attendance. When the minister with all due solemnity put the first torch to the bonfire, the show was sufficiently spectacular to make us all think for a moment about our life insurance coverage. But this concern was largely overshadowed by a sense of satisfaction that at least these drugs would not make their way onto the streets of Europe and North America, and we had given the minister a politically attractive idea to which he resorted several times in the ensuing months with lesser drug seizures.

Although perhaps less serious in its effects than the narcotics trade, immigration fraud was also an ongoing problem for Canada in Pakistan. It was generally estimated that 40 percent of the immigration application files in the High Commission contained forged or otherwise falsified documents, and that on average between 1,000 and 1,100 people from Pakistan made their way illegally into Canada each year. This problem required our immigration officers to be ever vigilant and thorough in their investigations of prospective immigrants and visitors. The question took on alarming proportions in 1992 when reports from the immigration authorities in Ottawa indicated a surge in the number of Pakistanis entering Canada with forged documents or simply without any documents at all. By the end of the year it became apparent that the number of identified Pakistani illegals had risen to over 4,500 and that they exceeded the number of those who had immigrated legally.

It did not take us long to identify the source of the problem. It turned out that members of the Pakistani government, as a form of political patronage, had secured jobs for particularly venal individuals at the middle management level of both the Federal Investigation Agency (FIA) and Pakistan International Airways (PIA). In exchange for certain considerations, these officials were prepared to turn a blind eye to the forged documents or lack of documents of passengers boarding PIA flights to North America. Our response to this situation was two pronged. First, we obtained from Ottawa the services of a resident Immigration Control Officer who made random checks of passengers boarding flights for North America both in Lahore and Karachi, and who worked in tandem with counterparts at the American embassy to secure the maximum coverage possible. Secondly in representations to Pakistani ministers and senior officials I made it clear that, if remedial action were not taken, it would be open to the Canadian government either to oblige PIA to post a multi-million dollar performance bond or to cancel PIA's landing rights in Canada altogether. I also stressed the further damage that would be done to Pakistan's reputation in Western countries if this problem attracted any more public attention, particularly at a time when Pakistan was seeking to fend off American threats to label it a country sponsoring state-terrorism. My Pakistani interlocutors seemed susceptible to the merits of these arguments, and in 1993 the number of Pakistani illegals entering Canada dropped by more than 75 percent, back to the more normal figure of about 1,000.

AID AND TRADE

The CIDA aid program represented the single most important managerial challenge I faced during my time in Pakistan. Although dwindling in budgetary terms, the program's nature and orientation were changing. Whereas before it had focused on a half-dozen large infrastructure projects at a time, it was now dispersed over two dozen smaller projects related to capacity building and human resources development. I spent much of my time overseeing this transition from a hardware to a software approach to ensure that it took place in a manner consistent with Canadian foreign and aid policy priorities, and at the same time met genuine Pakistani needs. While the CIDA staff of the High Commission handled the day-to-day management of existing projects, I was often heavily involved in the identification, selection, and launching of new projects. I was also often required to intervene at senior levels in the Pakistani government when projects ran into bureaucratic roadblocks.

While I am convinced that most of our CIDA projects directly benefited Pakistan, they also occasionally produced unexpected spin-off dividends for Canada. For example, CIDA was the first foreign aid agency to offer assistance to the Pakistani government as it slowly came to grips with issues of environmental degradation and protection in the mid- to late 1980s. Over a period of five years, CIDA provided financial and technical support in the development and elaboration of Pakistan's national conservation plan, which was launched with great fanfare not long after my arrival in Islamabad. As a result of this program, the High Commission enjoyed very close and cordial relations with both the minister and the Ministry of the Environment.

When the time came for me to lobby the Pakistani government in support of objectives that the Canadian government would be pursuing at the 1992 Rio summit on the environment, I already had an important friend at court in the person of the minister of the environment. This was doubly important because not only would he be the effective head of the Pakistani delegation at Rio, he would also be chairing the caucuses of the G77 group of countries, of which Pakistan held the presidency that year. I sought the minister's support for two Canadian initiatives in particular, one dealing with the protection of forests and one designed to promote the role of coastal states in the protection of fisheries and oceans. On the first, the minister was quite frank in telling me that we could not expect much support, since Pakistan had few forests, and within the G77 would be following the lead of countries such as Malaysia which had far more at stake in the issue. On the other hand, he did promise his complete support on the fisheries and oceans question, and when the time came, he delivered.

Some of the new directions in which we were taking the CIDA program also produced genuine partnerships between Pakistani and Canadian institutions, from which both benefited greatly, such as the links established between the Lahore University of Management Sciences and the Faculty of Business Administration of McGill University, or between the Aga Khan University of Karachi and the Faculty of Health Sciences of McMaster University. These ventures frequently involved relatively novel ideas, and precisely for this reason often ran into obstacles in both the Canadian and Pakistani bureaucracies. I was frequently required to intervene personally to help overcome these obstacles and to bring these projects to fruition.

If there was some considerable personal and professional satisfaction to be derived from the direction of the aid program, the same could not be said of the trade program. Despite my best efforts and those of the officers in the Commercial Section of the High Commission, the value of Canadian exports to Pakistan stagnated at or below the $100 million mark annually throughout my time in Pakistan. I certainly did not discover any magic formula that had escaped my predecessors in trying to jump-start our export performance. It seemed to me there were two root causes of the problems. First, the Pakistani business community did not see Canada as a source of imported industrial goods or technology, as it did countries such as the United States, Japan, Germany, France, and Britain. Rather, Canada was perceived primarily as an aid giver and as a source of raw materials and agricultural products. Second, most Canadian companies willing to venture beyond North America and Europe were content to go no farther than the rich markets of the Far East and the Middle East; the predominant image of the South Asian market was one of poverty, political instability, and stultifying government regulation of the economy. An ancillary problem was that we did not have the resources to match the trade promotion efforts of most of our major competitors in Pakistan's two largest commercial centres, Karachi and Lahore.

In trying to address and overcome some of these problems, the High Commission not only carried out all of the normal trade promotion functions on the ground, but also systematically reported back to Canada on changes occurring in the Pakistani marketplace as a result of the government's program of economic deregulation and privatization. I seized every opportunity to give speeches to business audiences emphasizing Canada's industrial and technological capabilities in areas of particular interest to Pakistan, especially telecommunications, oil and gas exploration and processing, and thermal- and hydro-power generation. I called frequently on the heads of government agencies and on the presidents of private sector corporations to explore possibilities for joint ventures or to promote bids submitted by Canadian companies for the supply of goods and services. When commercial projects seemed to need some political impetus, I did not hesitate to call on the relevant minister or deputy minister with the executives of the Canadian firm concerned.

Our efforts in the commercial field did achieve a few encouraging results. The High Commission was instrumental in securing the first ever commercial sale of Canadian wheat to Pakistan, a contract worth $20 million. By dint of hard work and high level interventions, my officers and I were able to salvage for Canada a $10 million per year contract for the sale of coal to the Pakistan Steel Corporation after the Canadian company that had originally obtained the contract became paralyzed by strikes and lock-outs, and eventually declared bankruptcy. Similarly we assisted Canadian companies in concluding initial contracts with the soon to be privatized natural gas and telecommunications authorities, contracts that held out the promise of additional business in years to come. That said, however, we certainly did not achieve any major breakthrough in significantly increasing the volume and value of Canadian exports to Pakistan.

AFGHANISTAN

One of the more unusual aspects of my mission to Pakistan was my responsibility for covering Afghan affairs. This was not a normal non-resident accreditation to a second country, since Canada had suspended diplomatic relations with Afghanistan at the time of the Soviet invasion of 1979. Not only did I have no official status in Afghanistan, I was not even allowed to visit the country or have any contact with the representatives of what passed for an Afghan government. Although three of my officers were allowed to make very brief visits to Afghanistan under UN auspices, we were largely dependent on sources in Pakistan for our analyses and assessments of what was taking place. These sources included the representations of international agencies working in Afghanistan, the diplomatic representatives of countries that had reestablished relations with Afghanistan, and above all the leaders of Afghan political groups and guerilla movements who still maintained headquarters in the northern Pakistani city of Peshawar. All of these sources were highly useful and helpful, and permitted us to report to Ottawa on the unfolding of the Afghan civil war and on the various initiatives taken to bring it to an end, but they were no substitute for first-hand knowledge. Keyhole diplomacy has its limits, and more than its fair share of frustrations, as one tries to reconcile diametrically opposed second-hand accounts of events.

The Afghan civil war varied in intensity during my three years in Pakistan, and parts of the country enjoyed periods of relative peace, but the destruction and loss of life were never-ending. After the Soviet military withdrawal in 1989, Afghanistan's ranking on the list of priorities of the international community fell dramatically. The UN and the regional powers (Pakistan, Iran, and Saudi Arabia) tried without success to devise solutions to Afghanistan's internal conflicts. For a country like Canada, which had never been more than a marginal player in Afghan affairs, the best we could hope to do was help attenuate the suffering by providing humanitarian and reconstruction assistance, and we concentrated our efforts on that goal.

Between 1991 and 1994, CIDA allocated from $20 million to $24 million each year for aid to Afghanistan and to the Afghan refugees in Pakistan. This allocation did not, however, represent a normal or stable program commitment, due to the ever changing situation within the country and in the refugee camps. Each year the High Commission in Islamabad had to formulate policy recommendations to CIDA headquarters on the level and allocation of budgets, which in turn meant assessing not only the changing needs of the Afghans, but also the effectiveness and relevance of the actions being undertaken by the various international agencies through which most of the Canadian funds would be channelled. For me personally, this responsibility involved maintaining contacts with the heads of the offices of numerous international governmental and non-governmental organizations (e.g., UNHCR, UNICEF, ICRC, OSGAP, UNOCHA, MSF, etc.), each of whom was expert at pleading the special merits of his or her program. It sometimes also proved difficult to prod CIDA to accept the merits of non-traditional forms of aid. Thus, it took time and effort on my part and on the part of the Canadian Forces attaché to get CIDA to overcome its ingrained reluctance to be involved in anything having a military flavour and to provide funds to the UN organization carrying out mine clearing operations and training in Afghanistan.[2]

In addition to the CIDA funds channelled through international agencies, we also had a Canada Fund of $1 million per year for Afghanistan which was administered by the mission under my direction. This fund permitted us to intervene directly and assist many of those whose lives had been shattered by more than a decade of war in Afghanistan. We supported programs to provide literacy and vocational training to war widows and to orphaned young women, and to provide rehabilitation services and trades training to war amputees. These programs and others were particularly welcome to the proud Afghans, men and women, who resented their status as helpless refugees dependent on international charity and wanted to be able once again to earn their own living. Toward the end of my stay in Pakistan, we were able to begin to funnel funds to reconstruction projects in the pacified areas of Afghanistan. I derived particular satisfaction from the assistance Canada provided to the Afghans and from my involvement in it. In the midst of all of the triumphalist rhetoric about how the West had won the Cold War, it behoved us to remember the heavy price paid by many Third World peoples in the course of that struggle, not least the Afghans.

CONCLUDING THOUGHTS

I have dwelt primarily on the external manifestations of my task in Pakistan rather than on my responsibilities as the manager of the High Commission, because those responsibilities are largely generic, not peculiar to any particular country or set of circumstances. On the one hand, all heads of mission must coordinate the programs and operations of the mission to ensure that they meet government objectives and are, to the greatest extent possible, mutually supportive. For example, the economic analysis and reporting function must not only serve the needs of the politico-economic community in Ottawa, but must also be supportive of the trade and aid programs. On the other hand, all heads of mission must manage to best effect, and in conformity with law, the human, financial, technological, and physical resources of the mission. Always something of a challenge in Third World countries, this responsibility poses particular difficulties in a time of budgetary austerity and cutbacks. For example, reducing the staff of the High Commission in Islamabad from 175 to 125 between 1991 and 1994 involved some gut-wrenching decisions to lay off Pakistani employees with 20 or more years of service to the Canadian government.[3] And, of course, after a certain point, the much touted nostrum about "doing more with less" must give way to the professionally disquieting reality that one can only do less with less, or at the very least, do it less well.

While some personnel and financial cutbacks can be compensated for through technological innovation and change, they are in my experience the exception rather than the rule. In a country like Pakistan, it is only people on the ground who can properly assess local conditions and identify the "pressure points" where influence can most usefully be brought to bear in pursuit of national interests. It is only people interacting with people who stand any prospect of exercising that influence to maximum effect. And finally, among diplomats, it is only ambassadors and high commissioners with their special status, and their often vainglorious titles, who can play a significant role in stamping their sending country's imprint on the political map of the host country and in gaining access to the real holders of political, financial, and commercial decision-making power.

NOTES

1. The literature dealing with Canada's relations with Pakistan is not abundant. See Morrison (1976, pp. 1-59), and W.M. Dobell (1989, pp. 349-73). For a Pakistani perspective, see Azmi (1982).
2. This is the only reference to military affairs in this paper, largely out of deference to the level of security classification at which most military information is pegged. The same holds true of information dealing with security intelligence and terrorism.
3. Some readers may be surprised by the large size of the High Commission staff. In Pakistan, as in many developing countries, the staff includes many low-paid employees whose services would be secured on a contract basis in industrialized countries, for example, guards, gardeners, cleaners, repair, and maintenance workers.

4

Small Missions in Hard Times: Lagos, 1996-1997

Janet L. Graham

Canada's High Commission in Lagos, Nigeria, like any Canadian mission, is both a symbol of the two countries' mutual recognition as legitimate members of the international community and an office of the Canadian government with many functions to perform. From 1993 to 1997 the simultaneous deterioration in Canada's relations with Nigeria and in conditions in Lagos ended when both roles became impossible. I was acting high commissioner in Lagos from August 1996 until Canada temporarily suspended operation of the mission, largely for security reasons, on 13 March 1997. My challenge was to run a small mission with very limited resources at a time when there was considerable interest in Canada-Nigeria relations in Ottawa and a great deal of hostility toward Canada from the Nigerian government.

"Small missions" are posts with fewer than ten program officers (both Canada-based and locally-engaged). These missions, normally run by a head of mission, handle more than one program, are likely self-sufficient administratively, and are staffed by a Canada-based administrative officer. Lagos, originally with 6 Canada-based and about 18 locally engaged staff, was categorized as a small mission.[1] Our programs included aid, trade, immigration, general relations, and consular affairs — all backed by an administrative section.

I begin by providing some background to the difficulties in our bilateral relations with Nigeria before describing the consequences for the work of the head of mission. I conclude with a summary of the special management issues faced by small missions everywhere, with specific reference to Lagos. During my six months in Nigeria the hostility increased to the point where Canada decided to suspend mission operations in Lagos. This difficult relationship certainly affected my role as head of mission, particularly when it came to access to senior government officials, but the small size of the mission also made my work more difficult.

CANADA'S RELATIONS WITH NIGERIA

Canada's relationship with Nigeria is long-standing, diverse, and relatively important in the context of our involvement in Africa. Canada opened a high commission in Lagos in October 1960, the first month of Nigeria's independence from Britain. Our bilateral relationship with Nigeria, the most populous country in Africa (100 million plus), a fellow member of the Commonwealth, and an important and influential regional and Third World leader, has historically been one of the most important in Africa. Nigeria has also been an important multilateral partner, notably within the Commonwealth on issues such as ending apartheid in South Africa.

Nigeria has been one of our major trading partners in Africa, largely due to their significant production of oil. In some years, Canada has transferred up to $600 million in payment for oil, while the value of our exports has ranged between $20 million and $60 million yearly. These exports, high by African standards, are generated largely by commercial not developmental activities. If the value of our trade in services to Nigeria could be captured the figure would no doubt be higher, given the number of Canadian engineering, communications, and oil service companies doing business there. Canadian firms with local Nigerian offices include Lavalin, Hydro Québec, Spar, Reed Crowther, and Pulsonic.

Canadian non-governmental organizations (NGOs) have historically played a significant partnership role in Nigeria. One of CUSO's largest programs in Africa was based there, and many prominent Nigerians received their early education from CUSO teachers. Its work in civil society, however, made CUSO highly unpopular with the current Nigerian military regime, which refused to renew the CUSO Memorandum of Understanding in 1996. The few remaining CUSO volunteers were expelled from Nigeria just before Christmas of that year. One of the only assistance programs Canada now finances in Nigeria is the Democratic Development Fund, implemented by a coalition of Canadian NGOs.

Approximately 800 Canadians are registered at the High Commission; many of them are dual nationals, children born in Canada while their parents were studying here. As well, a significant number of Canadians work for the multinational oil companies.

In sum, if general relations were normal, Canada's commercial, development, and consular interests in Nigeria would certainly justify a small diplomatic presence. But relations are not normal, and they may not be for some time. Although potentially one of the richest countries in Africa with considerable regional importance, Nigeria is also a poor and turbulent country whose leaders in their suspected corruption and evident contempt for democracy have frequently offended Western governments. It is fair to say that the country has squandered its opportunities.

BACKGROUND TO THE PRESENT POLITICAL SITUATION

Since independence Nigeria has been plagued by political instability and its people have suffered numerous coups and military governments. In June 1993 the Babangida military regime held elections deemed free and fair by international observers. Unfortunately, these elections were annulled, and an interim civilian government was overthrown by General Sani Abacha in November of 1993. Abacha dissolved existing democratic structures and reversed many of the economic reforms initiated under a structural adjustment program. He also jailed prominent opposition leaders, including Moshood Abiola, the presumed winner of the 1993 elections, as well as journalists, labour leaders, and human rights activists. Many prominent Nigerians critical of the regime were killed or they mysteriously disappeared.

In response to the annulment of the election and the coup, Canada adopted a number of limited measures against Nigeria, including suspending military and police training and imposing an arms embargo. The high commissioner who left in the summer of 1994 was replaced by the political officer who was given the title of acting high commissioner — a clear signal of displeasure with the regime. Many other Western countries temporarily withdrew their heads of mission and imposed limited sanctions. Canada took a prominent role in multilateral actions to condemn Nigeria. In July of 1995, Flora MacDonald, a former secretary of state for external affairs, led a delegation of the NGO Commonwealth Human Rights Initiative to Nigeria which subsequently issued a report critical of the Abacha regime. Christine Stewart, then a junior minister in the Department of Foreign Affairs and International Trade (DFAIT), joined with other Western and Commonwealth leaders in calling for clemency for the alleged coup plotters, including former President Obasanjo, who were given harsh sentences. She also met with leaders of the Nigerian National Democratic Coalition.

During the Commonwealth Heads of Government meeting (CHOGM) in Auckland in November 1995, the Nigerian regime, following a trial and conviction by a military tribunal, executed Ken Saro Wiwa and eight other Ogoni activists. Heads of government responded by suspending Nigeria from the Commonwealth pending its return to democratic civilian rule and establishing the Commonwealth Ministerial Action Group (CMAG) whose mandate was to recommend collective Commonwealth action in response to serious and persistent violations of the Harare

Declaration.[2] CMAG was to study and make recommendations vis-à-vis the situations in Nigeria, the Gambia, and Sierra Leone. Canada, along with Zimbabwe, Ghana, the United Kingdom, Malaysia, New Zealand, Jamaica, and South Africa became a member of this Action Group. At the CHOGM, Prime Minister Jean Chrétien, in concert with President Nelson Mandela of South Africa, took a leading role in condemning Nigeria and calling for measures to restore democracy.

Most Western and many Commonwealth countries again recalled their heads of mission. Both the European Union and the United States strengthened their sanctions against Nigeria, and the United Nations Third Committee issued a resolution against the regime. Nigeria became a pariah in many Western countries, but its power and influence in Africa left it far from isolated. The Nigerian military drew most of its members from the Muslim north, and the regime began looking to other Muslim states for alliances. Nigeria became a founding member of the Democratic Eight, a Muslim grouping of Third World countries. In addition Nigeria looked to Asia, particularly China, for investment in oil and infrastructure in order to reduce its reliance on the West.

At the various CMAG meetings, Canada took the lead, but was by no means alone, in calling for concrete action against Nigeria. The composition of the CMAG is broadly representative of the regional distribution of the Commonwealth. Within CMAG there was, and probably still is, a divergence of views, with Canada on one extreme and Ghana on the other. These differences relate more to strategy than to views on the human rights record in Nigeria or the importance of a return to democracy.[3] All members shared a concern that instability in Nigeria could spread to the region with devastating effects. Nevertheless, at the June 1996 CMAG meeting, a face-to-face discussion with the Nigerians in London, Minister of Foreign Affairs Lloyd Axworthy announced that Canada would unilaterally impose sanctions against Nigeria, although some CMAG members were not yet prepared to recommend this step to the Commonwealth.[4]

In Nigeria, our mission and the acting high commissioner were actively and publically supporting human rights groups. The Canada Fund, which makes funds available for aid projects, was increased and a significant portion of the monies available set aside for human rights projects. Other Western countries were also providing assistance in this area, some directly and some through NGOs. The position of the Canadian government in CMAG, and the various public statements of our ministers critical of Nigeria were widely reported in the local press. It was also repeatedly and erroneously reported that Canada was actively assisting political opposition groups, and the Nigerian government eventually accused Canada of trying to destabilize Nigeria by funding opposition groups through our Democratic Development Fund. In the view of the Nigerian regime, Canada, along with South Africa and the United States, was one of its greatest critics, and we were regularly attacked in public statements by ministers and in the government-controlled press. Bilateral relations when I arrived in August of 1996 were obviously poor.

ACTING HIGH COMMISSIONER

Canada sent me to Lagos as an acting high commissioner, the second head of mission so styled. Although I was fully responsible for the operations of the mission, Canada wished to signal continued displeasure with the political regime in Nigeria. A few weeks after my arrival, I was called to Abuja, the site of Nigeria's new capital, to meet with Foreign Minister Tom Ikimi. Prior to this summons, I had had a number of meetings with officials in the Ministry of Foreign Affairs (MFA) as well as with chairmen of various transition committees.[5] It seemed my "acting" status and the state of Canada-Nigeria relations were not to affect my access to senior officials. My initial successes, however, were short-lived.

Foreign Minister Ikimi met with me to deliver a diatribe against Canada and my predecessor. At the end of the lecture he handed me a note advising that the Nigerian High Commission in Ottawa was closing for economic reasons. As I left the meeting, I tried to seek clarification from the MFA officials in attendance, but they scattered quickly in embarrassment. This meeting was the last time I was allowed to meet with an MFA official in Abuja until a week before my departure, six months later.

After my meeting with Foreign Minister Ikimi I was essentially placed in diplomatic Coventry and was unable to make any appointments through normal channels. The Nigerian government required that diplomats make all appointments with representatives of government ministries, state administrations, or even political parties through the MFA. Some missions complied, most did not. All missions had great difficulty communicating with the MFA and getting appointments with MFA officials in Abuja. The distance involved was not the only factor.[6] Some colleagues in friendly missions, representing both First and Third World countries, told me they had spoken to officials at senior levels of government on Canada's behalf to try to reopen channels of communication. All to no avail. I was, however, able to make contact with some advisors in the president's office, and this was one of the few direct channels of communication I was able to maintain.

While the obstacles to continuing a dialogue with the Nigerian government about their transition program were a major problem, there were other more immediate problems to consider. For example, with the Nigerian mission in Ottawa closed we needed to know where Canadians should apply for visas and how Canadian officials were to obtain them. We never did get answers to these questions and Canadians had great difficulty getting travel documents.

My status as acting high commissioner did not, however, have any noticeable effect on my relations with diplomatic colleagues. I was able to work at all levels, perhaps more easily than might otherwise have been possible. I attended working lunches and substantive meetings of heads of mission as well as get-togethers of economic counsellors, "number twos" of like-minded missions, and donor meetings to discuss human rights projects. As the only political, economic, and aid officer in the mission, I attended these sessions regardless of the level of participation in order to obtain as much information as I could, particularly from colleagues of larger embassies.

Our strategy in dealing with the Nigerians became controversial, particularly among members of the Canadian business community with offices in Nigeria. One of my roles was to ensure that officials in Ottawa were aware of their concerns; another was to help the business community understand the reasons behind the Canadian government position, and to clarify some of their misperceptions. (The Canadian business community has since developed a Global Code of Best Business Practices, initially in response to the Nigerian situation.) I also played a similar reporting/explanatory/advocacy role with the NGO community, both Canadian and Nigerian.

The problems of running a small mission in a dangerous city — Lagos is a sprawling, chaotic, violent, and unhealthy city — when political relations are deteriorating all came together for us in January 1997 when the mission security manager left for medical reasons. We nominated a successor, but the Nigerian authorities refused to issue a visa. Two other staff members were scheduled to leave and it was evident their replacements would have the same problem. We had clearly reached the stage where we could not carry on, even as a virtual mission, particularly given the security concerns.[7] At this point Canadian Foreign Minister Axworthy spoke with Nigerian Foreign Minister Ikimi by telephone in an attempt to resolve these issues. This demarche was followed up with a letter, but the Nigerians failed to respond. The Canadian High Commission was closed in March 1997.

A British scholar says that "the first duty of an embassy ... is to promote its country's policy — and this may actually require a diplomat to behave in an unfriendly manner.... However, if the ambassador can achieve the respect of the local decision makers and get along well with them ... the interests of his state will indeed be well served" (Berridge 1995, pp. 35-6). In retrospect, therefore, I wonder if Canadian interests would not have been better served if a full high commissioner had been appointed in Lagos. It would have made it easier for the Nigerians to respond more appropriately to our concerns, and it would have allowed them to save face, given that titles are sometimes more respected than function in many African countries. One of our objectives was to try to pursue a dialogue with the Nigerian regime. To a certain extent we hobbled ourselves diplomatically by downgrading the level of representation. Certainly all other major Commonwealth and Western countries, with the exception of Japan, eventually returned their resident heads of mission after the Saro-Wiwa execution.

SMALL MISSIONS

The difficulties caused by strained relations with the host government were compounded by management problems. The Canadian High Commission in Lagos in August 1996 was a small — and soon to be smaller — mission. The phenomenon of small or virtual missions is growing. Missions of less than full size are grouped in two categories. A "micro-mission," also referred to as a "satellite office," is normally staffed by one or possibly two Canada-based staff and a few locally engaged employees. These missions often perform niche functions; our aid missions in Africa at Kigali and Maputo are examples. Many micro-missions are run by "officers in charge" who report to non-resident ambassadors. Some micro-missions, however, such as Zagreb and Bamako, are headed by officers with ambassadorial rank and perform a wider range of functions. Consulates, like those in Saint Petersburg, San Diego, and Nagoya, in countries with resident ambassadors are the more traditional micro-missions. Of Canada's 157 missions and offices abroad (see Appendix A), about 50 are categorized as micro-missions or satellite offices and 25 as small missions — almost one-half of all our missions abroad now fall into these two categories. Most of the small missions are in Africa and the Middle East; micro-missions are more evenly distributed geographically.

The growth in the number of small missions does not appear to have been prompted by a deliberate strategy, rather the small mission has evolved as a practical response to the implicit political decision that Canada ought to be represented in as many countries as possible. As a result of this ad hoc growth, management procedures for these missions have been emerging "from the bottom up," although the Resource Planning Bureau and the Office of the Inspector General have now done a good deal of work developing management guidelines for small missions.

Clearly the major challenge for small missions like Lagos is the gap between client expectations and the services the mission can provide with its limited resources.[8] The role of the head of mission, especially as perceived by clients, is virtually the same at a small mission as it is at a large one. An ambassador is always an ambassador. Small and emergent states naturally think that the act of recognition implicit in having resident foreign missions is significant, and they tend to treat even satellite offices as full-blown missions. Diplomatic colleagues are likely to react in the same way. The responsibilities of advocacy, representation, and public diplomacy are no different in a small mission. What is different is that the head of mission is required to deliver the programs. Even micro-missions perform consular work beyond their niche function because our clients — Canadian travelers and business people, the host country governments, and the local public — expect all programs to be available whenever the Canadian flag goes up. Small missions have limited resources, and staff — including the head of mission — must be flexible, able to work as a team, polyvalent, and trained in administration, finance, communications, consular affairs and trade promotion. Knowing how to use and even fix minor technical problems with communications equipment is sometimes critical.

Technology is helping to close the gap between expectations and available resources. Our new communication systems, SIGNET and MITNET, described in the chapter by Richard Kohler in this volume, have dramatically improved our ability to provide reliable service at small missions. It is now a practical option to rely directly on administrative and financial support from Ottawa or a large regional mission.

Staff in the Audit and Area Management and Resource Management Bureau developed, with post-administrative officers, the "hub and spoke" concept to manage small and micro-missions. Spoke missions rely on the hub mission for a range of administrative and financial support, depending on their own level of resources, as well as for support in other programs such as general relations, trade, and immigration. Administrative officers at hub missions work directly with spoke heads of mission or officers in charge. This sometimes gives rise to accountability problems and loss of autonomy, but by and large it has proved to be a cost-effective mechanism. Temporary duty from the hub mission should be undertaken regularly so that hub staff are familiar with spoke operations. Regular telephone contact with headquarters and the hub are also important because a lone officer at a small post can feel very isolated.

In Lagos, we were the spoke to Abidjan's hub on financial management and to Accra for immigration and communications technical support. This generally worked well, although the financial link was complicated by communication difficulties between our English-speaking local staff in Lagos and his French-speaking counterpart in Abidjan. We also relied on Accra and Abidjan for unofficial advice on administrative issues and for back-up staff when Lagos-based staff were absent. Small missions have no back-up, making this support from a larger mission critical. For Lagos, this was particularly important during the initial staff evacuation and closing of the mission. Accra staff, with multi-entry visas were able to support those left in Lagos while the post was closing down.

It appears likely that a micro-mission staffed by only one Canadian is not a viable operation, particularly in countries designated as "hardship" postings for

Canadian staff. The administrative burden and thus the cost of maintaining one Canada-based employee may be greater than the output of the post. A critical mass of at least two Canada-based staff may be required. Even with two Canadians, the best way to maximize our investment in small operations is by hiring more skilled local staff, including expatriate Canadians. This move would, however, require changes in departmental classification levels and pay scales for locally-engaged staff. In Lagos for example, the demands on our immigration program required the use of expatriate staff in the visa section, a practice DFAIT discourages. As we reduce the number of Canada-based staff we risk control problems, particularly in the administration of the visa and passport programs. My experience in Lagos was certainly not typical of the challenges faced by Canadian heads of mission, but it does illustrate some of the novel problems we face in small missions.

CONCLUSION

The work of the Lagos mission could not continue after March 1997. Had it been a larger mission with a full high commissioner, would there be an office of the Canadian government in Lagos today? Our downgraded level of representation was essentially a rebuke and Nigeria responded by refusing to extend normal diplomatic courtesies. We will never know whether a full high commissioner would have been treated differently, but the Nigerians would have had one less excuse for not engaging in a dialogue. It is possible that small missions may not be effective in hard times, but the exception should not undermine the general principle. If our relations with Nigeria had not been so difficult, the small size of the mission would not have been a constraint — indeed it would have been an appropriate and effective level of representation given our interests in Nigeria.

If we continue to believe that Canada's public purposes are best served by having diplomatic missions in as many countries as possible, then the realities of budget ceilings will lead to more not fewer small missions. If the telecommunications links are in place and the missions are staffed by the right people (and these are the two most critical factors), I believe that small missions can be very effective mechanisms for delivering Canadian foreign policy objectives.

NOTES

1.   Prior to the withdrawal of the high commissioner in 1994, Canada-based staff included the head of mission, a political officer, an immigration officer, a secretary, an administration officer, and a military security manager.

2. Through the Harare Declaration issued at the Commonwealth Heads of Government meeting held in Harare in 1991, member governments agreed to work together to promote democracy, good governance, and fundamental human values throughout the Commonwealth.

3. There was certainly unanimity among CMAG members evaluating the situation in Nigeria during a CMAG visit to Lagos and Abuja in November 1997.

4. The United Kingdom as a member of the European Union already had imposed similar sanctions as had the United States.

5. In 1995 Abacha had announced a three-year transition program to democracy. This program was being monitored by CMAG as progress here would indicate whether the regime's democratic objectives were sincerely held.

6. A Latin American colleague told me he always sent his Nigerian driver to deliver demarches because the driver did not mind flying on Nigerian Airways and could get into the MFA without an appointment. In any event, the ambassador knew he would not get an answer even if he made the trip himself.

7. One of the services offered by our mission was a response to conditions in Lagos. The chaos and crime common during airport arrival and departures made our offer of an airport clearance and pickup service in an armed vehicle for Canadian business and NGO visitors popular. The service, which was offered on a cost-recoverable basis, is an unusual example of how special services to Canadians can be sustainable at small missions with limited resources.

8. This discussion is based both on my own experience and the comments of other foreign service officers in small missions.

5

Fish, Forests, Fur and Canada's Fortunes in Bonn

Paul Heinbecker

Definitions of diplomacy abound. My experience leads me to believe that an ambassador is one part pundit, one part saloon-keeper, one part salon-keeper, one part bean-counter, one part advocate, one part impresario, one part psychiatrist, and one part flag pole. In Germany I was Canada's eyes, ears, and mouth and, all too often, stomach.

The stakes were high. Germany has become a pillar of democracy, an engine of stability, on occasion an effective voice on Canada's behalf in Europe, and a world leader. Germany is also an economic giant, the world's third largest economy, third largest spender on research and development, and fourth largest foreign investor. The dominant country in the European Union, it is a champion of free trade, and the industrial powerhouse of all Europe, east as well as west. For Canada, Germany is a rich market, an outstanding technology partner, and an important source of foreign direct investment. It is also a strong steady ally at the heart of Europe, a vital member of the North Atlantic Treaty Organization (NATO) and the leader in the effort to expand the Euro-Atlantic zone of peace and prosperity to the countries of Central and Eastern Europe and the former Soviet Union.

Canadian and German governments have had good relations for a long time. The prime minister and the chancellor meet yearly at least at the G7 summits, and the ministers of foreign affairs, international trade, finance, and defence meet even more frequently at multilateral meetings of the G7, Organisation for Economic Co-operation and Development (OECD), International Monetary Fund (IMF), and NATO. With so many high-level contacts, and an exceptionally strong team in the Bonn embassy to keep Ottawa up-to-date on significant and relevant developments in Germany, and to advocate Canadian positions to their German foreign ministry counterparts, traditional foreign policy was not my highest personal priority in pursuing Canada's interests in Bonn, although the tragedies in the former Yugoslavia, especially Bosnia, did demand my attention, as did staying abreast of the issues that were likely to engage heads of government at G7/8 summits.

Before describing my work as ambassador in Germany, I want to pause to stress that my current role as an assistant deputy minister in Ottawa, or previously as a senior official in the Privy Council Office, is completely different. In Ottawa I advise the government on foreign policy goals and how they can be achieved. We are developing a value-added foreign policy. Shrinking resources and Canada's evolving place in the world community require us to develop niches. What Canada thinks about NATO enlargement is significant, but it is unlikely to determine the outcome of that particular debate. What Canada can do to bring about a land-mines ban can be decisive, however, as we saw during 1997.

The land-mines ban is an interesting example of "the new diplomacy." Canada is engaged in changing a significant international norm, akin in importance to the one against the use of poison gas. We have had to work against the objections of some of our major allies and back up our more familiar approaches to consensus-building and multilateral diplomacy with contemporary foreign policy techniques such as forming partnerships with non-governmental organizations and using both our electronic and personal communications savvy. We do not ignore our larger and more traditional interests. We do protect them. But we also seize opportunities to make a difference in the rapidly evolving global agenda.

The communiqué from the June 1997 Denver summit of the eight, where some of the "classical" arms-control issues were covered, is a good example of the change. The environment, terrorism, crime, drugs, human rights, peace-building, land mines, and disease all had a prominent place. In one sense, the communiqué reflects the dark side of globalization, which is as much on the agenda of most leaders these days as peace and security. To be sure, NATO enlargement and UN reform are important, but what we have to deal with on a day-to-day basis goes well beyond institutions and national security to affect the well-being of Canadians of all walks of life.

As a senior official in Ottawa, the information on which I draw to give advice comes first of all from our posts abroad, from delegations and embassies with whom the department is in communication, written or otherwise, every day. But the media, the good newspapers, Canadian and foreign, are also read and analyzed. *Newsworld* and *CNN* have become indispensable for breaking news, a clear change in the way foreign policy is conducted. When the Japanese embassy in Lima was attacked, for example, we knew what was going on in real time. We were watching it on television and also getting reports from the Internet and from the wire services. The Internet is becoming essential, particularly in authoritarian countries, because it is so hard for governments to control. Through the Internet we kept fully apprised of what was happening on the streets of Belgrade. Canada now has perhaps one of the best electronic communications systems of all the foreign services. Of course, gathering and evaluating information in order to give policy advice involves more than "surfing" the Internet, reading telegrams, and watching television. We try to stay abreast of academic thought through the learned journals. We have an in-house foreign policy institute linking us to work going on in universities and elsewhere. We also have direct contact with our counterparts in other governments — in my case, I have frequent formal consultations with my G7 counterparts, with my Russian counterpart, with the EU presidency and Commission, with the Japanese, and with the Nordics. We see the Americans periodically, the Chinese, members of ASEAN, and many others. Canada is also a member of dozens of international organizations where information is exchanged and judgements formed. Seen from Ottawa, our ambassadors are important diplomatic assets, privileged contributors to foreign policy development, often essential advocates of positions developed in Ottawa, but their role has evolved dramatically.

So what did I do in Bonn? My number one priority was investment advocacy. Canada had fallen off the radar of German business (if it had ever been on their radar) at a time when German industry was suffering from the structural constraints of rigid labour markets, and an overvalued Deutsche Mark. Many business leaders in Germany were looking actively, all over the world, for places to invest. They also felt strongly the need to be present physically in their major markets. Unfortunately, Canada was not a "top-of-the-mind" place for them to invest. In fact, they did not think of us at all. To Germans, Canada is a large nature park. They see Canadians as park wardens too inclined, for their taste, to fell trees. To most Germans Canada is a *traumland* and you do not build factories in paradise; you put factories in large, urbanized markets, such as the United States or possibly Mexico.

I reported back to Ottawa on Canada's invisibility in Europe, trying to make the case that it was in our national interest to raise our profile there. In Europe, generally, and in Germany, particularly, there are pools of technology and of capital from which we were, and are, not benefiting to the extent we could have and still should. Attracting investors to Canada is difficult but beneficial. For example, over a period of about 25 years, Siemens increased its staff in Canada from about 20 to 4,000 and their sales from about $80 million a year to nearly a billion dollars. Of that billion dollars, a large amount is exports, and a substantial amount of that is back to Germany. So attracting investment can pay off big and for a long time. That was the message that I was sending to Ottawa.

In Germany, promoting investment was retail work, best pursued one company at a time. We worked very hard at trying to get Canada on agendas throughout the vast German enterprise sector. We also devoted a great deal of effort to creating a framework to attract investment to Canada. There was no transatlantic Canada-Germany business organization at all, in contrast to the highly developed Canada-Japan Council. Trade with Japan is greater, but there is far more German than Japanese investment in Canada. With the help of some German contacts, I helped to establish the Canada-Germany Business Forum, a blue-chip organization comprised, on the German side, of very senior officials, often CEOs, of VIAG, Daimler-Benz, Deutsche Aerospace, Bayer, Deutsche Bank, Gerling, Volkswagen, BMW, Preussag and so on — literally a who's who of German industry. (Although far from being a household name here, VIAG was actually one of the biggest foreign investors in Canada, with a huge aluminum operation in Quebec.) After we got the Germans interested, I enlisted Canadian business people, primarily through the Business Council on National Issues. The Canadians needed a lot of persuading but, in due course, they started participating.

My second priority as ambassador was to put Canada on the German *political* radar screen and vice versa — Canadians can also be myopic. Germans have a high regard for us, largely as a consequence of the NATO connection. They take us seriously, probably more seriously than any of the other Europeans do. But their interest appeared at times to be unrequited. There were many more German visits to Canada than there were Canadian visits to Germany. Indeed, more Canadian ministerial visits took place to London or Paris in almost any month, and even in quite a few weeks, than took place to Bonn in almost any year. Part of the explanation is that access to Bonn from Canada is not ideal; Bonn remains a small town in Germany. Part of it might be the legacy of the war, although Tokyo seems to get its share of Canadian visitors. Part of it might be the difficult German language, although, again, the Japanese language does not deter visitors. Successive prime ministers did visit, but not many other ministers did. Whatever the reason, I believed that improving Canada's fortunes in Germany required raising the profile of the relationship between the two countries.

A third and transcendent priority for me was public relations. Here it was mainly the three Fs — fish, forests, and fur. My task was to explain the Canadian position, which I did with enthusiasm, especially after Greenpeace scaled our fence to protest forest practices in Clayoquot Sound. Countering misinformation required going to editorial boards around the country to present our side of the story. We also held conferences, sponsored symposia, imported experts, and organized visits of German foresters and media to Canada for a first-hand look at what was happening in Canadian forests. We worked actively with the European representative of the Canadian Pulp and Paper Association.

Our opponents tried to characterize the protagonists as Goliath and David, but I think they misidentified the players. Greenpeace Germany had a budget seven times ours. Nevertheless, we marshalled our resources to get all the facts out and to prevent a boycott of Canadian forest-product exports to Germany. It was an uphill battle partly because of misconceptions and romantic ideas among the German media and public about clear-cutting, old-growth forest, plantation planting, and many other things. The totally different scale of forests and forestry in Canada and Germany also impeded understanding. German forests are to Canadian forests what backyard gardens in Ontario are to wheat farms in Saskatchewan. We ultimately succeeded in neutralizing often ill-informed and inaccurate criticism of Canada in the German media.

The "Turbot War" was another public affairs challenge, and we responded with what I would call modern diplomacy. At the outset we had no support and few friends in the German government on the issue. If we had wanted their help, I was told, we should have brought this problem to them sooner; we were just greedy; the Spanish were a good European Union partner; we were contravening international law — that was the most fundamental charge — and we were bullies. Not a very promising starting point.

In response, we conceived and implemented a public relations campaign to persuade the Green movement in Germany to support us. We convinced them that, though Canadians were not blameless in the depletion of the fish stocks, the issue had become essentially one of conservation. Once we were able to convince the Greens, the media were our next target, followed by sympathetic members of the Bundestag with whom we had previously established contact. The ineptness of the European Community and the showmanship of Brian Tobin, then minister of fisheries and oceans helped. Tobin's hoisting of an illegal fish net outside the United Nations headquarters gave us wonderful pictures of the pathetic size of the fish being caught in gigantic nets. We made sure that every television station had good graphics comparing adult-sized turbot with what some fishermen were actually catching. In short, through an aggressive public relations effort, we turned the issue around. The German government, which had begun by seeing us simply as violators of international law, proceeded to convey Canadian perspectives in Brussels and to help bring about a solution.

The third public affairs issue, fur exports, began during my time as ambassador and continued many months after I left Bonn. Our objective was to apprise the Germans, especially the media, but also members of the national parliament and of the European Parliament, that the livelihood and culture of Aboriginal communities were at stake. Acquiescing in the objectives of the International Federation of Animal Welfare would have real consequences for real people. We used many of the same techniques we had used on fish and forestry, staging conferences and helping organize visits of Canadian First Nations' representatives to inform German decisionmakers.

I recently read excerpts from Charles Ritchie's memoirs, paying particular attention to those pages devoted to his posting in Bonn in the 1950s. Times have evidently changed a great deal. He seemed to have had ample time for picnics and fancy-dress balls, and I was surprised to learn how much of his effort seemed to involve the British Embassy, despite the proximity to the war years. Things are dramatically different today: the ambassador is run off his feet and it is definitely more important to relate to Germans than to other foreigners. I made it my business to see virtually every corner of Germany. I learned what was going on in the former East Germany, in Bavaria, along the Baltic, in Berlin and Frankfurt. This was not idle curiosity — knowing Germany and the Germans was essential to advocate our interests effectively and to report to Canada accurate and relevant political and economic information.

I spent much of my time with German senior officials and politicians, with business people, with the media and with academics — probably in that order. I had access to some ministers, when I had something concrete to tell them, but not to the chancellor and not to the foreign minister. Judging by embassy invitation lists in Ottawa, Canadian ministers appear to be much more available to foreign ambassadors. For ambassadors everywhere, official hospitality remains extremely important. Ambassadors, and all diplomats, have only a limited amount of time at a post and have to meet and cultivate people to do their job. It is not like public service in Ottawa. Foreign service officers abroad do not have a lifetime to build connections. Hospitality funds allow them to telescope a process that would otherwise take years. Monies allotted to social functions are not there for entertaining friends and neighbours at taxpayer expense. And diplomats do not just entertain other Canadians, except of course on Canada Day. Nor do they entertain just other diplomats, beyond those few who can help with access to local decisionmakers. Ambassadors do build a circle of contacts and try to consolidate it. Their targets are business people, officials, politicians, media people, representatives of non-governmental organizations, everybody they need to know to do their job effectively. This hospitality work is integral to effectiveness, and it makes for very long days.

Diplomats are usually also managers, and in that capacity I was accountable for the expenditure of an $8 million, plus, budget. I imparted strategic direction to the work of my collaborators, dealt with difficult personnel problems, from harassment cases to family crises, and generally did what you have to do to keep the auditor general satisfied. One administrative objective was to find a new embassy in Berlin and to keep "helpful" land developers at arm's length in the process.

Embassies have been getting smaller, particularly as globalization advances. It is counter-intuitive given the stakes involved in Bonn, but our embassy there is substantially smaller than it once was. I reduced the staff and budget by about a third while I was there. By the time my successor leaves, the post will likely have been reduced further. This reduction comes at a time when the tasks assigned to embassies have multiplied. When Canada's finances had to be restored to good order, the Department of Foreign Affairs and International Trade had no diplomatic immunity from cost-cutting.

In an age of "soft power," we still have to have a military and it still has to be combat-ready. Hard power underwrites soft power. Modern communications have, nevertheless, changed the ways of influencing the world. Image is a crucial issue. If there is one very significant dimension of diplomacy in which we are not succeeding, I think it is in projecting our image. The German foreign ministry budget for what I would call "image work," though they call it their cultural budget, is a little over a billion Canadian dollars a year, compared to our global budget of, I believe, $18 million. The result of all our cutbacks is that fewer people are working harder, with some help from technology, but overall they are, collectively, probably producing less. In particular, a good part of our capacity for reflection and assessment has had to be sacrificed to transactional imperatives.

What makes a good ambassador in the 1990s? The same thing that made a good ambassador at any time in history: leadership, integrity, perspicacity, communication skills, and management skills. One of the participants at the workshop that gave rise to this volume was one of my distinguished predecessors in Bonn, the late John Halstead, ambassador to Bonn two decades after Ritchie, and two decades before me. During the discussion, Halstead said:

> I think the blurring of the distinction between domestic affairs and foreign affairs is one of the most striking characteristics of the changing international environment, and it has implications for heads of mission abroad. Most so-called domestic departments now have foreign agendas they pursue through direct contact with corresponding departments or agencies in other countries. For the head of mission, the question is how to conduct the orchestra in the foreign environment without trying to play all the instruments. It requires the explicit mandate to coordinate the activities of all the departments represented in their mission, and it requires information. International relations are no longer a matter of relations among nations, among governments, they involve the totality of the interchanges and contacts among nations. They involve more non-governmental actors, and they involve a wider variety of subject matter. The head of mission must be able to deal with a range of topics that goes far beyond the traditional subject matter of diplomacy. The head of mission must also deal with people far beyond official circles. I have in the past had occasion to describe diplomacy as a contact sport. The last place you should be is in

your office. If you are not in contact with the range of people that are dealing with the range of subjects that international relations now encompasses then you are not doing your job.

I think Halstead was right and I am pleased that this distinguished public servant's judgement and mine coincide. Being an ambassador is still a wonderful job. Today's issues may be more prosaic than dramatic, but they are the stuff of people's lives. I am honoured to have been given the duty of resolving some of them.

6

Post-Cold War Diplomacy: Prague and Washington in the 1990s

Paul Frazer

At the height of the Cold War, it was possible to think that diplomacy had been reduced to the confrontation between the superpowers. Indeed, nobody who was in Prague in August of 1968 could have overlooked that central reality. Nevertheless, in 1992, when I arrived as ambassador to Czechoslovakia, soon to become ambassador to the new Czech Republic with non-resident accreditation to Slovakia, the people and government were finding their way in a world where the Cold War no longer provided guidance. I now work closely with our ambassador in Washington, where claims of "national security" were once used as the Cold War trump card in policy disputes. In both cities, one the capital of a small country on the periphery of western Europe and the other the capital of what is still the mightiest power the world has ever known, diplomacy is vital; but post-Cold War diplomacy does not mean dealing mainly with the foreign ministry. In both cities diplomacy is more public than ever.

The rules of the game for diplomacy once provided for a civil, correct means of doing business even under the most difficult circumstances. Diplomats knew when to make a formal demarche and when to call on an official in the foreign ministry with an aide mémoire. Having met with senior officials in the foreign ministry, an ambassador could reliably report to headquarters on the views of the host government. In turn, the foreign ministry official could be relied upon to convey the views of the ambassador's government to the foreign minister and other senior government officials. Traditional diplomacy provided order when the environment was chaotic. It brought a degree of certainty to channels of communication, with procedures to deal with an issue from beginning to end. Being largely invisible, it allowed a diplomat to exit discreetly or to save face. Not only were ambassadors expected to deal through specific channels, they were also never to be seen to be interfering in the domestic affairs of the host country.

The formal rules are the same, but the practice is considerably altered because public diplomacy has gained prominence. The reasons public diplomacy has become so important are complex, but since the end of the Cold War came about as part of the same set of forces, it becomes a useful symbol. The short "explanation" is that public diplomacy matters because of democratization and participation. In Prague as in Washington, more people are active participants in public life. The issues that confront diplomats have not changed much, nor have some of the major diplomatic functions. What has changed is that we work much more in public.

PRAGUE AFTER THE WALL CAME DOWN

The formal priorities of the old diplomacy characterized diplomatic life in the countries of the former Soviet sphere until 1989. When the Berlin Wall fell diplomatic practice began to change.[1] Diplomats did not adjust to the new order easily or quickly, as the following anecdote illustrates.

When I arrived in Prague three years after the Wall came down, I gradually realized that my ambassadorial colleagues frequently called on the senior foreign ministry official responsible for their area. They were anxious to understand the nuances of Czech and Slovak relations with their neighbours, Prague's hopes for reintegration into European institutions, and to consider the forces that might lead (and did lead) to a division of the country into two new republics on 1 January 1993. My officers and I called on offices of the MFA when a specific issue required it, either on instructions from Ottawa or on our own initiative. We had excellent contacts throughout the ministry and I was confident that I could see anyone, including the foreign minister, as the situation warranted. Rather than focusing on the foreign ministry, I travelled outside Prague to raise Canada's profile in the key cities of the then Czechoslovakia and later the new Czech Republic. I also travelled frequently to the Slovak region and, after independence, to Bratislava to meet and get to know the president, prime minister, and other senior officials of the new Slovak Republic. Indeed, because economics, trade, and technical assistance are key elements of our bilateral relations, I invested time developing relations with Cabinet ministers and senior officials in various government departments. The needs of the new diplomacy, I thought, did not require me to live at the foreign ministry.

Nonetheless, as a first-time head of mission, I thought I might be missing opportunities that my more experienced European colleagues were pursuing at the foreign ministry. My sense of unease prompted me to call upon a senior MFA official. I informed him that my failure to darken his door regularly did not mean I wasn't interested in discussing key issues. I was confident that the bilateral relationship was in excellent shape, that we had a first-class working relationship with the ministry, and that if he needed me for anything he would call. I added that, given the papers piled high on his desk, I assumed he was busy enough.

My host responded with a weary sigh, thanked me, and commented that he wished other ambassadors thought as I did. As I rose to leave he asked me for my views on a particular matter. Some ambassadors had been insisting that he explain the foreign policy model the Czech Republic would adopt and when it would be in place. In the first months of the new republic he had not thought it necessary to be so specific. What would I do in his shoes? Aware that an injudicious response could be misinterpreted I replied on a personal basis; I did not wish my remarks to be construed as reflecting the views of the Government of Canada. Later that day my interlocutor informed me that he had briefed the foreign minister on our discussion and that the minister wished to see me. Our lengthy tête-à-tête the next day was an invaluable opportunity to review our bilateral relations, to seek the minister's views on the future of the relationship, to discuss a variety of other international questions, and to review Canada's experience in developing its postwar international role. I was later told that my initiative had demonstrated that Canada was sincerely ready to talk frankly, not hidebound but open to new ideas, and prepared to do business in a serious substantive manner. These events convinced me that the old diplomacy had not completely disappeared. An ambassador's ability to represent his country at the highest levels of the receiving state is still important.

Nevertheless, it was also clear that the rapid return of democracy to central Europe, new countries with new people in new jobs, and liberal contact with any diplomat (really with anyone) meant that new ways were supplementing and superseding old ones with amazing speed and far-reaching consequences. Understanding the new context and determining the most appropriate strategy for Canada proved to be a three-part challenge.

Learning how to make Canada's presence felt in an effective way in federal Czechoslovakia and subsequently in the Czech Republic and Slovakia was the first part of the challenge. The old regime had been brought down by the massive public opposition so well described by Rob McRae (1997) in his account of his assignment to our embassy between 1988 and 1991. Public diplomacy was essential, because the new country was being created by its citizens. We developed a variety of community activities, used the emerging free and open print and electronic media; and we allied ourselves publicly with leading Canadian companies seeking business (in competition with the United States and Europeans). We highlighted Canada's technical assistance program as a means of creating a greater awareness of Canada's role and activities in supporting the development of democratic institutions and a market economy. I hosted and/or spoke at the opening of Canadian corporate offices, provided public support for community-related activities, and sponsored the launch of Canadian cultural products. I spoke about the bilateral relationship, and the embassy's role in the community to business councils, foreign policy groups, universities, business schools, and the media.

The second aspect of the challenge was to engage officials in Ottawa in the effort to develop a substantive relationship between my countries of accreditation and Canada. As it turned out, events made this task very difficult. It was unnecessary to await Ottawa's instructions to act initially: in a country about to divide, it was obviously essential to travel extensively and speak with opinionmakers in order to report events and their implications for Canada's interests. However, in late 1992 neither Prague nor Ottawa were in a position to engage in detailed efforts to enhance significantly this new, open bilateral relationship. Czechoslovakia was facing disintegration; then, the republics were newly formed countries understandably self-absorbed. Domestic developments preoccupied Canadians: this was the time of the Charlottetown Accord and the subsequent referendum; Prime Minister Brian Mulroney retired; and the Tories elected a new leader and the country a new government. Officials in the Department of Foreign Affairs and International Trade working on Central and Eastern European affairs were forced to concentrate their attention on developments in Russia and the former Yugoslavia. In such circumstances embassies get on with the job without waiting for guidance.

The third part of the challenge was essentially administrative: how to adjust the size and nature of our operation to a changed political and operational context in Prague and fiscal change in Ottawa. In the early 1990s, no post was immune from pressures to reduce the costs of the federal government. The embassy budget was reduced and a number of positions eliminated at significant cost savings. Advances in technology allowed us to redefine some jobs and to reduce the labour component of some tasks. Under the old regime the embassy had needed a large staff in order to be as independent and self-reliant as possible. We no longer had to do everything ourselves, but could purchase goods and services at competitive prices and only when they were needed. In fact, in the quickly transforming market economy of the Czech Republic and Slovakia, we were able to buy many services locally. Contracting-out saved us time, made our operations more efficient, and allowed us to focus on the new bilateral priorities and opportunities.

Some tasks are common to the "old" and the "new" diplomacy: diplomats continue to seek the generic access to officials that all ambassadors should establish. As we might have done during the days of more formal diplomatic practice, we began a monthly luncheon series for ambassadors of G7 summit countries with the Czech prime minister as the first speaker. This initiative highlighted Canada's international role and allowed us to compete with the private EU monthly discussions, which as non-members we did not attend. Such functions complimented the many other more public contacts initiated to make Canada's presence felt. All of our public activities, my speeches for example, supported the message we tried to convey to the government. It was important to demonstrate that Canada was a significant player in Prague and Bratislava, that we were seriously interested in supporting efforts to develop a free-market economy and democratic institutions, and that we were committed to working with the Czechs and Slovaks over the long term, which included supporting their early membership in such organizations as the OECD and most recently NATO. To do this we presented our case in many settings, as publicly as possible, in ways that would have been impossible before the end of the Cold War.

NEW WORLD ORDER DIPLOMACY IN WASHINGTON

The challenges of diplomacy in the 1990s are similar in Washington to those in Prague, but there Canada has more resources and the ambassador works in a much more complicated environment. As it has elsewhere, the invisible, quiet world of the old diplomacy long ago ceased to exist in Canada's dealings with the United States. In his memoirs, Arnold Heeney, a distinguished former Canadian ambassador to the US (1953-57 and 1959 to 1962) wrote that in 1965 he called on a senator about an important regional issue. It was his only call on a member of Congress during his years in Washington. "Quiet diplomacy" was preferred, if at all possible, as Heeney and Livingston Merchant, a former American ambassador in Ottawa, argued in their eponymous report on managing the bilateral relationship.[2] By comparison Ambassador Raymond Chrétien had over 50 meetings with *individual* senators and congressmen in the last year.

Diplomatic practice between the United States and the rest of the world has also changed. A study published by the bipartisan US Advisory Commission on Public Diplomacy (1996) argued that US policies will only succeed with the support of publics at home and abroad; and powerful information technologies give the United States new ways to understand and influence governments and publics. Surprisingly, this group's main conclusion is that even the United States needs a "new diplomacy and a new diplomat." The new diplomat, they explain, understands that a meeting with an environmental action group could have more long-term value than a meeting with the local minister of the environment.

Readers who suggest that there is nothing new here are partially correct. It has always been important to understand the local context. For example, the diplomat has always needed to have a good relationship with the environment minister, as well as contacts with environment NGOs, and environment writers for the mainstream and specialized press. But the balance between official and non-official sources of influence has shifted, and there are many more issues and players in the policy arena. Ambassadors accredited to the Government of the United States learn quickly that they must deal with an immense, contradictory, and constantly changing collection of power centres.[3]

Television correspondents often report from Washington with the majesty of the Capitol or the White House behind them, as if power there has a focal point. It does not. Formal power rests with the president, the Cabinet secretaries and senior officials in the public service, the Supreme Court, and the 535 members of Congress. Now try to imagine the action generated by almost 20,000 congressional staffers, the thousands of lawyers and lobbyists who try to influence the politicians, the trade associations members, the estimated 5,000 reporters and correspondents (600 accredited to the State Department), and the hundreds of think-tank employees and political action committees. All of these people flourish because of the fragmentation inherent in the American political system with its division of powers. One consequence is the lack of party discipline in Congress. Some 10,000 pieces of legislation are introduced each year. Of course, most never see the light of day and many are combined with others, but all represent a vast array of interplaying interests. The daily round of public departmental briefings, press conferences, committee hearings, talk shows, conferences, think-tank seminars and political debates generates announcements, policy decisions, research findings, and partisan political statements thrown into the daily mix where pundits and journalists and sometimes diplomats find grist for their daily mill.

A country with as much at stake as Canada ignores this vast open-air policy bazaar at its peril. The variety of forces, people, and interests creates a new political context every day. This constant realignment on issues brings us friends one day who can be our opponents the next. Allan Gotlieb (1991) recalled that he spent his time in Washington (1981-89) working on the issues that cause the greatest conflict between the two governments. These issues tended not to be strictly within the foreign policy domain of the State Department, nor did they become problems to be solved because someone in the United States had set out to pick a fight with Canada. Conflicts usually arose over the consequences for Canada of American domestic policy. When an American special interest group lobbies a congressman for a new regulation, the administration does not normally consider its possible impact on Canada. It is up to the staff at the Canadian embassy to know how the regulation will affect Canada, who wants it, who their allies are, and what approach might be used to solve any potential problems.

Ambassador Chrétien argues that "Elements of the U.S. debate can affect Canadian interests and require appropriate Canadian responses. American initiatives to reduce [domestic] expenditures can have a direct impact [on Canada].

For example, deregulation and budget cutting may undermine transboundary cooperation if the U.S. is unable to meet its international obligations. If development-minded legislators were to limit the reauthorization and funding for the Environmental Protection Agency and for statutes such as the Clean Water, Clean Air and Endangered Species Acts there would be profound implications for Canada" (1996, p. 143). Hence his many one-on-one meetings with senators and members of Congress in the course of a year and the dozens of mailings (110) and telephone calls to targeted congressmen on a wide variety of issues such as Helms-Burton legislation, cross-border documentation, softwood lumber, Pacific salmon, and wheat. The ambassador talks to Americans about such foreign policy issues as land mines, human rights, hemispheric relations, United Nations reform, and new trading relations with Latin America, the Asia-Pacific region, and Europe. But given our relations with the United States, the talks also include clean air and water, Porcupine Caribou herds, protection of cultural industries, and what we call national unity. Canada must constantly try to win friends on the issues that are important to us.

The Canadian ambassador in Washington travels extensively in the United States. At each stop the program invariably includes a policy speech to a leading organization, such as the board of trade or the World Affairs Council; an on-the-record meeting with a newspaper editorial board; and separate newspaper, radio, and television interviews. The ambassador calls on leading corporate executives to discuss bilateral economic-trade relations and to outline why Canada should be the company's next major investment destination. In each state capital he meets with the governor and other political leaders. The ambassador also calls on the major university in the area to discuss their Canadian and international studies programs, often speaking to graduate and undergraduate students about Canadian foreign policy. This public diplomacy allows the ambassador to use a concentrated one- or two-day visit to meet those leaders and opinionmakers of importance to Canada in all regions of the United States. It is an opportunity to address a full range of bilateral issues and to focus on relevant local issues.

On some issues, it is strategically more effective to influence the American public first. For example, although half of Canada's acid rain problem was created in the United States, our initial efforts to persuade American government officials of the urgency of the problem were unsuccessful. We, therefore, made Americans aware of their own acid-rain problem and its impact on their environment, hoping they would bring effective pressure for change on state and federal governments. We encouraged a wide variety of environmental groups, researchers, journalists, local governments, state governments, farmers, the tourism industry, hunters and fishermen and others to create an influential *American* critical mass on this issue. Lobbying from their own interest, they played a significant role.[4]

When the task is to change how an issue is perceived, advocacy may be essential, but some issues are not susceptible to the new diplomacy. No ambassador received more attention for the role of the diplomat as public advocate than Allan Gotlieb (Cooper 1989). Gotlieb was well known for his public profile, because "working" the Congress is not private but public diplomacy, with its attendant risks and opportunities. In Washington, Gotlieb learned, "If the Administration is strongly opposed to the position of the foreign government, the potential is high for a foreign lobbyist both to increase resistance and breed resentment in the Administration's midst and to contribute to a backlash on the Hill." Fighting acid rain, for example, was different from most issues, because the administration opposed the Canadian position, so "lobbying" on the Hill was "lobbying" against the US government (Gotlieb 1991, p. 66). In a traditional intergovernmental conflict, lobbying and public relations were less acceptable, and other factors affected the outcome.

In the era of public diplomacy an issue raised by a regional lobby group or politician can almost instantly become part of the politics of the day in Ottawa. Someone in Montana calls a senator in the morning about Canadian wheat. Later that morning the senator is on the phone to someone in the White House and by noon calls are coming in to the embassy from the executive branch. In half a day we can easily have a new trade irritant rooted in local politics, trade-offs on the congressional floor, the interests of a key governor or a combination of the three. Invariably, one of the parties concerned will contact the media, and Canadian journalists in Washington will ensure that the topic receives high priority on Canadian front pages and on television news broadcasts. If the House of Commons is sitting, the topic is raised in Question Period, and journalists may question the prime minister or a Cabinet minister in a scrum outside the Commons. As in Prague, so in Washington and elsewhere, bilateral issues are now seldom managed quietly and rarely by "quiet diplomacy" alone.

CONCLUSION

The trend to a more public diplomacy has been building since the post-First World War era of "open diplomacy," the reaction to the supposed secret deals of classical European diplomacy that were thought to have pulled the world down the slippery slope to war. Making the fact of diplomacy and its results public proved not to be the same as negotiating in public, however — something every negotiator knows is impossible. Being economical with the facts about one's ultimate intentions, bluffing, in other words, is still a daily diplomatic reality, but it has been harder to do since the 1960s because of the mounting public interest in open government. Openness was not prized in the former Soviet empire, of course, and it was not prized in Washington at the height of what Daniel Patrick Moynihan calls the national security state. An insistence on openness increased in Washington after Vietnam and Watergate: in domestic and foreign affairs, the public demanded to be informed, and Congress refused to defer to the president.

Now in the 1990s, a desire for increased transparency affects public life in the new democracies as much as the old. Canada's challenge is to seize the positive development to advantage — working in capitals to promote and defend not only more narrow bilateral interests but also working to assist governments in taking on the ideals and principles to which we subscribe and the practices of national comportment which we hold to be basic to effective and productive nation states domestically and internationally. Representatives of the Canadian business community, non-governmental organizations, the media and the travelling public come through our embassy doors daily. They all have a role in Canadian foreign policy, as do their counterparts, the vastly increased range of people and organizations to whom the ambassador is accredited in the practice of the new diplomacy.

NOTES

1. For a Canadian diplomat's reflections on the momentous events immediately before and after the transformation, see McRae 1997. McRae reports, for example, that his monitoring of some of the early anti-regime demonstrations in 1988 was both unusual for senior diplomats, and discouraged by the authorities. In contrast, when Havel, as president, presided over his first National Day celebrations he was mobbed by ambassadors who would not have been seen with him one year earlier.
2. Portions of the text of the Heeney-Merchant Report of 1965 can be found in Granatstein 1986. For the views of a principal, see Heeney 1972.
3. For an interesting commentary on the interplay of Washington political forces and the structure of the political system see Chrétien 1996, p. 137.
4. For an account of how the Mexican government learned to play this game in order to build public and then congressional support for giving the administration "fast-track" negotiating authority for NAFTA, see Bertrab 1997.

PART II

DIPLOMATIC FUNCTIONS

7

Great Expectations, or What We Demand from the Head of Mission Today

Lucie Edwards

In my reflections on the role of the ambassador, I came across a wonderful article by John Kenneth Galbraith, a Canadian who I like to think we loaned to the Americans. He wrote, "some 30 odd years ago, while serving as Ambassador in India, I discovered that if I did no work that my staff could do as well or better, I could finish everything in not over three hours a day. The occasional crisis, excepted. So, with a reasonably good conscience, I spent the time writing instead. Two or three books emerged ... The role of an ambassador is one of happily available leisure. Let there be no doubt, to have poets staffing the diplomatic corps is a wonderful idea." This comment initially distressed me, as I had not found the time to write a single book during my own time as the head of a mission or post, but it did cause me to reflect. What are the characteristics of a head of post that are unique to this function, as opposed to the general responsibilities of any foreign service officer at Canadian missions abroad? We expect all of our foreign representatives, including the ambassador, to be responsible for interpreting the nature of their host country's society and relaying it to the Canadian government. Conversely, they are responsible for explaining what Canada is all about to their contacts in the host country. That is the job of an embassy. But what is the unique quality, the special value-added of the ambassador alone? I think that is what Galbraith was alluding to when he called for ambassadors who were poets.

Canadian ambassadors have one of the best jobs in the modern public service. I stress the word modern for this old role is as demanding as any that today's managers must perform. My current managerial functions in the department are far removed from the poetic. Without indulging myself by repeating all the gloomy details, in a presentation to outgoing heads of mission it was my responsibility to cover: financial management in a time of cuts; the extraordinary challenges of managing our worldwide information technology systems; the extreme importance of managing people well; the necessity for stewardship of public assets, including our extensive property portfolio; the need to constantly reengineer mission operations to cut red tape and find the resources for new initiatives; the need to provide services in both official languages; the importance of the ambassador setting the mission's standards by becoming personally involved in the consular program; and the need for ambassadors to "think like taxpayers" about ambassadorial perks such as the official residence, representational funds, and the official car. I concluded this presentation with the prayer, "and deliver me from temptation," which was intended to make the point about the difficulty of managing conflict of interest issues. But the more I spoke the more I found myself tempted to go out on a posting, so the person who needed to be delivered from temptation was myself! For all the difficult management issues associated with being an ambassador, it really is a wonderful job.

In this chapter, however, I want to discuss a headquarters' perspective on the management challenges associated with being an ambassador in these times. We have lofty expectations of the ambassador, a role I have entitled "the very model of the modern major-general." We do seem to expect a renaissance person who can be proficient in a dozen different crafts, including, I suppose, poetry, and who can do it in an office abroad that has been shrinking — today's heads of mission must make do with fewer staff and a smaller budget than their predecessors.

When I speak to new heads of mission, I begin by talking about the honour and burden of command. Few functions in government — I would identify two, the head of mission and the head of a peacekeeping operation — have a great responsibility that is also personalized. The individual who is the head of mission is delegated an extraordinary level of duty and undertakes this task thousands of miles from headquarters. If you look at positions of equal responsibility within the domestic public service, such as assistant deputy ministers and directors general, the striking thing about these senior managers is that they work in teams, inside their own departments and horizontally across the government. They are constantly in touch with their deputy ministers and ministers. Decisions are made collegially, and it is rare for them to be made alone, in isolation from others and under great time pressures. But heads of mission regularly find themselves in that situation. When something happens, and there is no time to consult, heads of mission must take the decision and live with the consequences. During the evacuation of the Canadians from Rwanda, staff had to be ordered to leave and I determined what route they should take to safety. If we had got it wrong, they would have been ambushed and could have been killed. The burden of command is an exceptional responsibility, and a lonely one, but it is also a very great privilege.

In addition to command, a number of other functions fit Galbraith's criteria of work that the head of mission cannot delegate to others. A critical one, in my mind, is leadership, and the developing of a common vision for the operations of the mission. Again, it is a duty that is to a great extent personalized around the head of mission. I think, for example, of the role our ambassador in Beijing played in June 1997, a critical time in Canada's relations with China and Hong Kong as the two were rejoined. He must ensure that every member of staff understands precisely what the mission is there for, and that they are motivated to act in the same direction.

Leadership in a post abroad demands that ambassadors set an example by their own behaviour. One domain where such leadership is vital to our country is bilingualism, where we require all foreign service executives to be proficient in both official languages, which helps set the tone for the operation of the mission as a whole. Leadership also requires extensive team-building. Our missions are teams made up of Canadians along with locally-engaged staff. The local staff, now the larger part of our employees abroad, may be Canadians in some cases, but generally they are proud citizens of the host country. We have to turn a multicultural, multinational group into a single team working to a common purpose. Well-run missions have an extraordinary level of esprit de corps and solidarity; and display intense pride in the fact that they are working for Canada. The ability to create that feeling is a central function of the ambassador.

Another function, and one that has been the subject of a great deal of general discussion in public administration, is the concept of the "single window" for all government services. Canada's most senior public servant, Jocelyne Bourgon, says that citizens expect that the benefits of new technology will offer them more responsive service, with work organized to suit people not departments. They expect to get what they need in one place, without knowing whose job it is. In the single window model, government departments work together (horizontal integration) as do different levels of government (vertical integration) (Bourgon 1997, p. 13). A great deal of work is underway to make it possible for Canadian citizens, wherever they may be, either to pick up the phone or to go to a kiosk for the answer to any question they might have about their government, to have a public service that is truly responsive to their needs. Anyone who has been caught up in an endless series of voice-mail messages knows how far we are from achieving this ideal, but one prototype of an effective single window already exists within the federal government — the embassy abroad. It is the one place where you can go to the receptionist's desk and be referred to somebody who can either answer your questions or know how to find the answer. The ability to provide this seamless web of services to the individual takes an extraordinary amount of knowledge and gymnastic flair. It takes team building within the mission where staff with diverse skills may come from and/or report to many government departments, and it takes training. The results are worth the effort. I am always struck by the number of business people I meet who tell me that if they have a question about trade or tax or travel conditions abroad they do not call Ottawa; instead, they call the post, because staff at the post will knock themselves out to try to help.

In the traditional model, our missions abroad tend to be a kind of box where people can go to get whatever services they need, a box hedged in by security marooned in the capital city. Our most entrepreneurial missions are breaking out of that box. They are developing brilliant Web sites, like the consulate general in New York; setting up a network of mini-offices in tourist centres throughout the country, such as the mission to Mexico; or taking their services on the road by organizing Canada Weeks in provincial capitals, as in Brazil. They are turning the chanceries into people places, like the cultural centre in Paris, where visiting Canadians feel comfortable dropping in. The ambassador has to lead the way in turning that august and intimidating institution, the embassy, into a people place.

The head of mission is also the voice of the country. This is the person who gets to field questions from the local media about what is going on in Canada, about the bilateral relationship, and often, about what Canadians think is going on in the host country. To serve as advocate for our country and for its aspirations is one of the most important challenges facing our ambassadors. One of our senior managers was complaining good-naturedly the other day that if he had known he would be a television performer, he would have trained differently 30 years ago. We not only have to field difficult questions, but often do it in foreign languages. Few of us have had the requisite training, and it has become an enormous challenge for our heads of mission to become master communicators in another, and very different, society.

The ambassador remains one of the government's most important policy advisors, able to see all parts of the Canadian team interested in their domain, whether they are located on post, in a domestic department or in the Pearson Building in Ottawa. Forty-five years ago, Harold Nicolson argued that "An ambassador in a foreign capital must always be the main source of information, above all the interpreter, regarding political conditions, trends and opinions in the country in which he resides ... It must always be on his reports that the Government base their decisions upon what policy is at the moment practicable and what is not" (Nicolson 1962, p. 111). At our workshop, a former Canadian ambassador argued in similar terms that the ambassador remains the ultimate interpreter of the state to which he or she is accredited. I think that centrality is gone, for the ambassador is just one signal against a sky-full of information noise. The ambassador and staff cannot monopolize the information or advice flowing to Ottawa, but leadership, advocacy, and managerial skills still allow them to be at the heart of all affairs. They work on instructions, but their advice often has a major influence on those instructions, though not as much as they might like. Senior ambassadors are appointed because they have the confidence of the prime minister, and yet they must act on instructions written by junior desk officers in Ottawa. And so they should — the desk officer can be the broker of a process that involves provinces and many other government departments. Technology allows ambassadors to participate in the policy process, but decisions are taken in Ottawa. Of course, instructions can be quite general, leaving the person on the spot to determine how best to carry them out. It is one thing to tell our ambassador in Washington to influence official perceptions of over-fishing for salmon, it is another for Raymond Chrétien to decide to go to Alaska to do it.

The ambassador as advocate also has a role in Canada. There is a famous story about an ambassador some years ago who visited the Pearson Building in Ottawa while on vacation. The under-secretary of state for external affairs frowned on seeing him and said, "What are you doing here? You should be at your post." If you were to tell that story to Lloyd Axworthy, the present foreign minister, he would fall over himself with laughter — he sees a critical part of the function as communication to Canadians, to ensure that they understand what is going on in the bilateral relationship. It would be helpful if we could clone some of our ambassadors in major posts — Washington, Tokyo and Havana, for example — because we could have one on post and the other on the road trying to explain our relations with that country to Canadians.

Finally, the ambassador has to be a people person. If there is one quality we ask from our ambassadors, it is the recognition that bilateral relations have to be built one person at a time. This includes the ability to empathize and work with people to generate the necessary loyalty, energy, and enthusiasm within the mission, and to have the ability to recruit the kind of people needed from the local community to make the attainment of Canadian objectives possible. To put it simply, to make friends for Canada.

Here in Canada, these qualities of communication and networking are traditionally more required of politicians than of bureaucrats, which may explain why so many politicians have become highly effective ambassadors. Our best ambassadors are getting out of the office, meeting people, maintaining a constant dialogue with opinionmakers and decisionmakers, inside and outside government and outside the capital city. They maintain excellent ties back home, with colleagues in government, with the provinces and with business people. These ties are nurtured so that when a crisis flares, the head of mission already knows who to call — in Canada and in the host country — to defuse the problem. All members of the mission network all the time, of course, but the head of mission has an ace in the hole: almost anybody, anywhere in the world, is prepared to meet a Canadian ambassador — you can literally see almost anyone, including Nobel Prize winners who are very busy people. It is an "open sesame" in a society if you are curious, since a lot of the most remarkable people you will see are not politicians. In my case it was very often people in remote areas doing development projects and working 18-hour days who somehow found the time to see me. An effective head of mission knows how to exploit the precious asset of access that comes with the prestige of the rank of ambassador.

One last point. A lot of work has been done in the past year, under the heading of "La Releve," about public service renewal. We are trying to develop the leaders the public service will need in the future. The model is a renaissance person with some 15 daunting attributes, including communications skills in both of Canada's official languages, leadership qualities, wisdom, strong ethical values, a deep commitment to client service, and stamina — a much under-valued asset. I think we ask our ambassadors to demonstrate all these things. The individuals who are trying to work up to this extraordinary standard of performance are doing it not just for this department but for the country as a whole. They represent a broad vision of public service. The demands we place on them, to be a people person, to offer service with a smile, to be the voice of the country, to serve as leader, team-builder and commander, are immense. Some of our heads of mission fail, some falter, others break their health under the yoke of their responsibilities. The remarkable thing is how many do the job so well.

8

Recruiting Tomorrow's Ambassadors: Examination and Selection for the Foreign Service of Canada, 1925-1997

Hector Mackenzie

For more than 70 years, the Department of External Affairs (DEA) and its successor, the Department of Foreign Affairs and International Trade (DFAIT), have principally relied for recruitment of Canada's foreign service on broad criteria for eligibility, careful scrutiny of the experience and academic qualifications of applicants as well as a distinct and often elaborate ritual of written and oral examination. This brief study may suggest some persistent preoccupations and problems which confronted those who yesterday recruited today's ambassadors. Continuity and change in perceptions of Canada's interests and values, and of how best to advance Canada's objectives, have had a considerable bearing on the origins and development of the foreign service, as well as on contemporary assessments of its performance and worth. From the beginning, the story of how Canada's diplomats were chosen was inseparable from the evolution of the foreign service itself.

PRELUDE TO A FOREIGN SERVICE

When Canada's first diplomat presented his credentials in 1927, it represented a deliberate break with the past. The *British North America Act* of 1867, which created the Dominion of Canada, made few references to international affairs and none to foreign policy. The latter omission acknowledged the diplomatic unity of the British empire, which prevailed despite the dominion's autonomy in internal affairs. The British Foreign Office, with its network of ambassadors, ministers, and officials, remained formally responsible for imperial relations with foreign countries, though it might enlist help or seek views from dominions or colonies. Canada's first representative abroad was an emigration agent named William Dixon, who had been working in the United Kingdom before Confederation on behalf of the Province of Canada. The Dominion Agency for Emigration in London was established within two years of Confederation, with Dixon as its first chief. As with other Canadian emigration agents in Britain and Europe in the nineteenth century, Dixon was appointed politically, without competition and without specified qualifications (Skilling 1945, p. 3; Mackenzie 1995, p. 17).

The search for new markets for Canadian goods prompted the appointment of part-time commercial agents in 1892. Two years later, what became the trade commissioner service (TCS) began when John Larke was sent to Australia as Canada's first full-time commercial agent (Knowles and Mackenzie 1994, pp. 15-17; Hill 1977, pp. 45-51). Within 17 years, there were 21 trade commissioners in 16 countries, with five additional part-time commercial agents.

How did one join the TCS? Before the First World War, the TCS was invariably staffed by political patronage — Larke was no exception — often with disappointing results. After George Foster became minister of trade and commerce (DTC), one disgruntled trade commissioner depicted the TCS as a refuge for "political and other derelicts" who were "entirely unfitted by character or attainments for their position." Even that informant did not demand exceptional standards for the TCS. "No specially great ability is required in a Trade Commissioner but he should be possessed of average common sense, of enough energy, industry and enthusiasm, to prevent his lapsing into lazy habits" (see Hill 1977, p. 121). Foster, who flirted with dangerous and heretical notions such as recruitment by merit and professional performance, made a first step to reform in 1914, when he asked the principal of McGill University and the president of the University of Toronto to nominate individuals trained in economics who might join the TCS. The nominees had to submit essays on a set topic to the minister. Thereafter, political patronage would no longer govern the selection of trade commissioners.

Politics, however, was critical in determining suitability for the most prestigious and vital quasi-diplomatic post, that of high commissioner in the United Kingdom. Successive holders of this office were distinguished not only by political influence and social prestige, but usually also by personal wealth. The first and second high commissioners — Sir Alexander Galt and Sir Charles Tupper — were both Fathers of Confederation and the third, Lord Strathcona, had earlier been head of the Canadian Pacific Railway and the Hudson's Bay Company. Strathcona's conspicuous success for 18 years under both Conservative and Liberal governments lent a non-partisan gloss to the office, but his replacement by a minister without portfolio in the government of Robert Borden clearly demonstrated that the political justification for the position had not been forgotten during his long tenure. No indigents or political neophytes need apply.

Initially at least, the approach taken to representation in France was more casual and the results less impressive. In 1882, the Government of Quebec appointed Hector Fabré to represent its interests in France. While there he was paid by the federal Department of Finance "to report directly to the Secretary of State." Cabinet records describe him as "Agent of the Canadian Government in France" and he was eventually identified as the Commissaire générale du Canada in France. He does not appear to have been a faithful correspondent and when his failure to keep Canada informed was brought to his attention, Fabré apparently ceased writing altogether. Fabré's qualifications were similar to those of his more diligent successor, Philippe Roy. Both were journalists, Liberals, and members of the Senate before their appointment. Fabré served for 28 years in Paris and Roy represented Canada for 27.

Though the focus of this chapter is on representation of Canada abroad, the changes that had the greatest impact on development of the foreign service took place in Ottawa and the most influential officials never served overseas, except temporarily as advisers to Canadian delegations. Sir Joseph Pope, the undersecretary of state, took advantage of his appearance in 1907 before a royal commission investigating the civil service to advance his proposal for a department of external affairs to deal efficiently with international questions affecting Canada. What he had in mind, as John Hilliker has demonstrated, was more than a "post office" but less than a foreign office — though the gloriously brief and vague legislation eventually presented by the government of Sir Wilfrid Laurier and approved by Parliament in 1909 provided sufficient "legislative authority" for the latter development and for eventually creating a foreign service (Hilliker 1990, pp. 30-42; Eayrs 1960a, pp. 14-32). When the legislation was amended in 1912 to designate the prime minister as secretary of state for external affairs, the enactment of Pope's recommendations was complete. Pope believed firmly in the diplomatic unity of the empire and he did not advocate a distinct Canadian policy in international affairs nor the elaboration of a separate diplomatic network (Hilliker 1990, pp. 32-33).

Without consulting Pope, Prime Minister Robert Borden hired Loring Christie in 1913 as legal adviser in the Department of External Affairs after a personal interview. Though Christie was certainly qualified, there was no formal competition (Bothwell 1988, pp. 18-20; Granatstein 1982; Hilliker 1990, pp. 64-66). Borden had interviewed others but had made no formal appointment. Whatever his nominal title, Christie became Borden's principal adviser on imperial and international relations in a period of questioning and reassessment in both spheres. That prompted consideration of a distinct Canadian foreign policy, with its logical corollary, separate diplomatic representation for Canada. During the First World War, the British government accepted in principle that the dominions could be represented by diplomats who would report to dominion governments and in May 1920 the Borden government announced its intention to appoint a Canadian minister in Washington, who would serve in the British embassy. Partly as a result of resistance from Borden's successor, Arthur Meighen, that appointment was not made and the Canadian war mission in Washington, which had stayed open as a bridge to a more permanent arrangement, was closed.[1] Though Borden "hoped in due course to see established a Canadian Foreign Service," nothing had been done before William Lyon Mackenzie King became prime minister and secretary of state for external affairs in 1921.[2]

KING'S REPRESENTATIVES

King was certainly a more convinced autonomist than Borden or Meighen, though his initial steps were characteristically cautious. In 1922, King replaced the high commissioner in London, Sir George Perley, but his choice for the "the highest [office] within the gift of Government" was consistent with the nineteenth-century precedents — Peter Larkin, the president of the Salada Tea Company, a close friend of King and a financial backer of the Liberal Party, was sufficiently wealthy that he considered it "undignified to draw a salary" (Hilliker 1990, p. 105; [Gelber] 1980, p. 31). Dissatisfied with the form earlier favoured by Borden, King left unresolved the question of how Canadian interests and policies should be represented in Washington. That enabled him to await more propitious political and constitutional circumstances, as well as to search for a suitable candidate for the patronage appointment which would inevitably follow. Meanwhile, he relied for information on relevant American affairs on confidential "despatches" from a Canadian journalist, Tom King, who wrote directly to the prime minister, rather than the more formal Canadian "agent" in Washington, Merchant Mahoney, whose office was located in the British embassy (Eayrs 1961, pp. 133-34). Though Canada's ambiguous international status had been advanced by membership in the League of Nations, the government saw no need for permanent representation in Geneva until December 1924, when it appointed as "Dominion of Canada Advisory Officer" Walter Riddell, who was already there working for the International Labour Organization (Riddell 1947, p. 19; Veatch 1975, p. 22).[3]

Unquestionably more important for the future of the Department of External Affairs and the development of the foreign service was Mackenzie King's source of advice on Canadian foreign policy. Without expectations of Pope or his long-time assistant W.H. Walker, and mistrusting Christie, King sought the informal counsel of political contacts before developing confidence in the ability, dedication, and judgement of a distinguished scholar, Dr. O.D. Skelton, then dean of arts at Queen's University. Skelton's suitability was not diminished by his Liberal sympathies nor by his laudatory biography of King's mentor, Laurier. But what convinced King was an address Skelton made to the Canadian Club in January 1922 on Canadian foreign policy. Over the next few years, King increasingly relied on Skelton, as a delegate, as a special adviser for imperial conferences, as a counsellor and finally, on 1 April 1925, as Pope's successor. Skelton's performance had confirmed King's assessment, so that no alternative for deputy minister was considered. Skelton firmly believed in Canadian autonomy in international affairs and he was convinced that a stronger Department of External Affairs, a professional foreign service, and separate diplomatic representation were essential instruments for that purpose (Hilliker 1990, pp. 93-94; Dawson 1958, p. 454).

By then, reform of the civil service had transformed the process for recruitment for both the immigration service and the trade commissioner service. In 1919, the Civil Service Commission (CSC) supervised the first competitive examinations for entrance into the TCS and three years later promotion by merit was introduced. Lest anyone forget who was in charge, however, the minister fired four recent recruits in 1924, apparently to save money. More serious concerns were raised about what qualifications were appropriate for the TCS. Under the new regime, applicants were expected to have a university education "preferably with the degree of Bachelor of Commerce or with specialization in political economy," though critics contended that practical experience of business was more worthwhile. Prospective trade commissioners had to undergo a written examination "on Canadian resources, products and industries, and on the principles of export trade, including placing and selling goods, trade terms, foreign exchange and financing," an oral examination and optional tests of language proficiency. Once recruited and trained, their choice of career usually meant "a life-time spent abroad," as there was little rotation between headquarters and posts (Skilling 1945, pp. 63-64). Between the wars, expansion of the TCS slackened, then halted, with the last entrants in 1934 (see Hill 1977, chapters 14 and 23).

With immigration curtailed during the First World War, reduced from its prewar heights thereafter and restricted during the Depression, the context for reform of the immigration service (IS) was even less favourable. The first competitive examinations, written and oral, for emigration agents took place in 1924. The qualifications for candidates, not surprisingly, reflected the expectations about prospective immigrants to Canada. Thus, the academic standard was lower than for the TCS, with "education equivalent to high school graduation, preferably with graduation from an agricultural college," but there was a requirement for "four years' practical experience in farming in Canada and a knowledge of farming conditions throughout Canada" (Skilling 1945, p. 29). For the first time, agents were required to be British subjects who had lived in Canada for at least three years (ibid.). When Skelton set out to recruit for the foreign service, therefore, there were precedents for qualifying standards and entrance procedures.

But the process Skelton devised, and the way it was implemented, demonstrated a different approach to recruitment. For the first opening, the position of counsellor, Skelton was determined to apply the merit principle, with competitive entrance. But he set a high qualifying standard for eligible men (women were not allowed to apply): "a law degree or membership in a provincial bar association, two years of post-graduate studies in international affairs, practical experience in legal work, and a good knowledge of both English and French" (Hilliker 1990, p. 102). As a result, the only qualified candidate, Jean Désy, professor of international and constitutional law and political history at the University of Montreal, joined DEA in July 1925 (ibid.).

Undaunted, Skelton devised a specialized examination for foreign service officers in time for a second competition in 1927. To be eligible, candidates had to have graduated with a university degree or its equivalent, preferably with graduate work in political science, political economy, or international law. The questions Skelton posed in the four parts of the written examination clearly indicated that he wanted what are now called "generalists" rather than "specialists." Apparently, he was also looking for autonomists: "The first essay, which was usually on nationalism and internationalism, was designed to elicit the candidate's attitude toward Canada's role in the empire and enabled the department to determine whether he accepted the government's position as enunciated at recent imperial conferences." Another essay tested knowledge of Canadian and international affairs, while a third involved a choice from a list of topics drawn from the qualifying disciplines. Another component of the examination, which could last for two days or more, was a précis. Leaving nothing to chance, Skelton graded the papers, assigned a value to the examinee's curriculum vitae, usually chaired the interview panel, and often introduced the prospective foreign service officers to the prime minister, who as secretary of state for external affairs was politically responsible for the department and the service (Hilliker 1990, pp. 101-7, 118-20; Lalande 1969, pp. 32-33).

Though there is understandably greater evidence of the written examinations, the interviews with the superior candidates were essential parts of the process. One veteran Canadian diplomat implicitly justified that emphasis. "Much international business is transacted orally," Benjamin Rogers wrote. "A tremendous amount of paper is used within governments, but very little passes between governments" (1976, chap. 4, p. 1). In addition to the academic standards, candidates for first-secretary were expected to possess "undoubted integrity, tact, astuteness, keen perception, good judgment, and good address."[4] The oral examination may also have ensured qualifications that could not be tested on paper, as John English has suggested. "Skelton sought out Canadians who would be neither rustic nor colonial, who should know that one sipped cognac but downed aquavit; that one used 'one' in certain company ... Proper, to be sure, but stuffy never, for Skelton's strongly democratic instincts meant that the department rejected the formal trappings that traditionally accompanied diplomacy" (1989, p. 147-48).[5] In effect, Skelton was "constructing" the Canadian foreign service "in his own image" (p. 139).

For Skelton, the results of the competition in 1927 were disappointing. There were few applicants and only two successful candidates: E. D'Arcy McGreer and J. Scott Macdonald. To his other roles in the process, Skelton then added that of recruiting officer. Relying on an elaborate and effective political and academic network, Skelton personally encouraged likely prospects to apply, with impressive consequences, as there were more than 60 applicants.[6] Examinations held in 1927 for first-secretary and third-secretary eventually resulted in the hiring of six individuals, five of whom had taught in university: Lester Pearson, Kenneth Kirkwood, Hugh Keenleyside, Norman Robertson, Paul-Émile Renaud, and Keith Crowther. From this group would emerge not only ambassadors but three deputy ministers, one of whom would later serve as secretary of state for external affairs and later still as prime minister. Skelton had recruited his successors.

"There were no gimmicks or gadgets in 1928 to test one's IQ or one's skill at not putting square pegs in round holes," Pearson recalled in his memoirs (1972, p. 59). Nor was there an evaluation of competence in French. Pearson wrote his optional paper on "The Rise of Fascism," along with compulsory ones on international affairs, modern history, and international law. With the précis, this trial took place over four days in late June. The interview must have followed soon after, as Pearson received a telegram offering him the position of first-secretary on 10 August 1928 (ibid., pp. 58-60; English 1989, pp. 137-45). Other applicants, then and since, did not receive their offers so promptly. Keenleyside, who applied for both positions and wrote two sets of examinations recalled the oral examination as "a very pleasant experience," with "most of the questions" about "my prospective book on Canada-United States relations" (1981, pp. 211-15). After an informal meeting with Skelton at the Rideau Club, Keenleyside was then summoned to dinner with King, who according to Skelton "had been taking a great personal interest in the recruitment of staff for the department" (ibid.). Robertson very nearly wrote no papers, as he was unable to write the examination in Washington or Montreal, eventually performing the task in Ottawa. When the first positions were filled by Pearson, Keenleyside, and Kirkwood, Robertson was placed on an eligibility list — an impressive achievement for one so young. Not until late May 1929 did Robertson report for work (Granatstein 1981, pp. 25-30).

What Skelton achieved in these early examinations and in others to follow was an impressive beginning for the professional foreign service, particularly when one considers the qualifications and expectations in relation to contemporary

Canadian society. In other respects as well, those who would represent Canada were not representative of its population, but they did exemplify the qualities and abilities which Skelton believed were important to define an autonomous diplomatic presence internationally for Canada. Moreover, these aims and the process Skelton devised to realize them, would profoundly influence later recruitment for Canada's foreign service. The procedure today for recruiting tomorrow's ambassadors owes a great deal to Skelton's legacy. But the appointment of heads of post in 1927 and 1928 was certainly not his responsibility. Nor were all of the lower ranks filled by Skelton's method, even then. As prime minister and secretary of state for external affairs, King was determined to exercise his prerogative to choose Canada's first diplomats (Skilling 1945, pp. 212-18).[7] His choices demonstrated similar criteria as for Larkin's earlier appointment, with an even more pronounced partisan aspect.

As minister in Washington when Canada opened its own legation in 1927, King eventually selected Vincent Massey, a patrician aesthete who "combined an academic background with some experience in public affairs" as well as "an adequate private income" to meet the representational expenses of the new office (Neatby 1963, pp. 192-93). Massey had served briefly in King's Cabinet as a minister without portfolio before being defeated at the polls in 1925. He presented his credentials on 18 February 1927. Massey personally hired the staff for the legation, including Laurent Beaudry, Tommy Stone, and Hume Wrong, who thereby entered DEA and the foreign service by selection, not competition. Though all were able, there were considerable tensions within the small mission, which prompted King to take a greater interest in recruitment (Bissell 1981, pp. 224-26; Hilliker 1990, p. 118).

When King elevated the office in Paris to a legation and appointed a minister to Tokyo, he redesignated as minister Philippe Roy, who had been Commissaire générale du Canada in France, and chose Herbert Marler, whose qualifications for the post closely resembled Massey's, to represent Canada in Japan. Like Massey, Marler had been a minister without portfolio in King's government before suffering electoral defeat, though his parliamentary career had been longer and more distinguished. Marler was also independently wealthy. Marler interviewed prospective staff for the legation, rejecting Robertson and approving Keenleyside.

Of some concern to Skelton, as well as to the new diplomats, was political opposition to these developments. As Conservative leader, R.B. Bennett had mocked Marler as "a glorified trade commissioner seeking publicity," while his colleague T.L. Church had denounced the legations as "sink holes" for tax dollars. Neither had welcomed the break with imperial diplomatic unity (Skilling 1945, p. 258; Marler 1987, p. 118). Moreover, DEA and the foreign service had been created by a Liberal regime, with which Skelton was closely identified. Yet, as prime minister and secretary of state for external affairs from 1930 to 1935, Bennett was more cautious than his partisan rhetoric had presaged. Massey, who had resigned as minister to Washington before his nomination to succeed Larkin as high commissioner in London, was the sole diplomatic casualty of the change of government. With some justification, Bennett argued that the high commissioner, unlike other representatives, required the political confidence of the government, which Massey, as a former Liberal minister, would not enjoy. Thus Massey's diplomatic career was interrupted by his resignation from the Washington post and his unsuitability for London. For Washington, Bennett chose his confidant and future brother-in-law, William D. Herridge; for London, he selected the premier of Ontario, Howard Ferguson, who was certainly not a diplomat. Marler and Roy both kept low profiles and their jobs, as did the foreign service officers in their missions. Meanwhile, back in Ottawa, after an uneasy transition, Skelton proved as indispensable to Bennett as he had been to King.[8]

The Bennett interregnum was as important for continuity as it was for change. Though Bennett's diplomatic appointments were no less partisan than King's, the fact that Marler remained in Tokyo, and later replaced Herridge in Washington, suggested a limit to the sway of patronage. Recruitment for the foreign service continued, with examinations in 1930 and 1932-33 adding six officers, while two senior advisers — Lt. Col. Georges Vanier and Loring Christie — were appointed without competition. With the death of W.H. Walker and the departure of three members of the foreign service, the net expansion was modest, but in the context of the depression, any increase was important (Speaight 1970, pp. 150, 169-70).[9] As a successful candidate, Charles Ritchie (1978), recalled, Bennett continued his predecessor's interest, personally interviewing the group of new recruits. Though Skelton was relieved when King returned to office, DEA and the foreign service had not suffered unduly in his absence.

Neither Ferguson nor Herridge waited for King to decide his fate. Bennett had cleared Marler's transfer to Washington with King, so that left openings in London and Tokyo. King reconfirmed his earlier judgement that the right choice as high commissioner was Massey, who had since performed more good deeds for the Liberal Party. For Japan, King chose as minister a former lieutenant-governor of British Columbia, Randolph Bruce, who had been defeated as a Liberal candidate in the recent federal election. Bruce was prominent and wealthy, but he was 73 when he accepted the appointment and he had lost his eyesight. Meanwhile, Roy, who was 68 and hard of hearing, continued as minister to France. The three ministers prompted Hume Wrong's cruel observation that "Canada was represented abroad by the deaf, blind and dumb" (Keenleyside 1981, p. 291; Granatstein 1982, p. 120). Yet Wrong was not convinced that more dynamic diplomats would make a difference, as Canada did not possess a discernible foreign policy for the heads of mission to articulate. "Dining alone this evening," he wrote privately to Massey, "I developed a plan for the perfect representation of Canada at Conferences. Our delegate would have a name, even a photograph; a distinguished record, even an actual secretary — but he would have no corporeal existence and no one would ever notice that he was not there" (quoted in Massey 1963, pp. 234-35).

Undoubtedly the "low dishonest decade" was frustrating for the members of the foreign service, particularly given the qualities that Skelton had deliberately recruited, but their ranks and their opportunities were expanding. Wrong himself replaced Riddell in what was by then a diplomatic post in Geneva, while Vanier succeeded Roy in Paris in 1938. Désy became the first of Skelton's recruits to head a mission when he was named minister to Belgium and the Netherlands in January 1939. Later that year, Marler was replaced by Christie, though ill-health limited the latter's effectiveness. With McGreer acting as chargé d'affaires in Tokyo, Canada's representation abroad had been transformed on the eve of the Second World War. Over the previous three years, competitions had added six recruits, including James Gibson and J.W. Pickersgill, who soon found that they worked for King more as prime minister than as secretary of state for external affairs. Two others joined the foreign service without competition: Escott Reid, former national secretary of the Canadian Institute of International Affairs, who was personally recruited by Skelton; and Herbert Norman, whose expertise on Japan prompted his appointment as a "language officer" in 1939 before his posting to Tokyo — an exceptional specialist (Eayrs 1960b, pp. 59-80).[10] As yet, Canada had no ambassadors, but inter-war recruitment for the foreign service, principally through the process devised by Skelton, had produced heads of mission — and future ambassadors.

THE SECOND WORLD WAR AND POSTWAR EXPANSION

The Second World War and Canada's part in that conflict altered not only the international context but also the national expectations for a distinct Canadian foreign policy and for independent representation of Canada abroad. Though Canada's legations in Paris and Brussels were swept away by German advances in Europe and the one in Tokyo closed when Japan attacked in Asia, these closures were more than offset by the exchange of high commissions with other dominions and by the opening of new missions, particularly in allied countries, China and the Soviet Union, as well as in the neutral nations of South America.

At a special press conference on 11 November 1943, it was announced that Canada's minister in Washington would be elevated to an ambassador; a month later, the same treatment was extended to the Soviet Union, China, and Brazil. Three of the four new high commissioners and three of the initial four ambassadors were selected by King from outside the foreign service, though one ambassador — Dana Wilgress in the Soviet Union — had been a member of the TCS. The first foreign service officer appointed as an ambassador was Jean Désy, who achieved that distinction in Brazil. When King's choice for Washington, Leighton McCarthy, proved a disappointment, Lester Pearson was appointed as Canada's ambassador to the United States.

Though King still favoured friends and political associates for heads of posts, the wartime demands for quantity and quality in Canada's representation abroad provided unprecedented opportunities for Skelton's early recruits.[11] When Skelton died in late January 1941, he left the foreign service and DEA well placed to meet the challenges ahead and it was appropriately one of his recruits, Norman Robertson, who succeeded him as under-secretary of state for external affairs.

With the expansion of its diplomatic network and the lengthening agenda for Canada in international relations, including both wartime cooperation and post-war planning, DEA's responsibilities and personnel requirements grew extraordinarily. In 1940-41, 15 foreign service officers were added by competitive examination, among them 2 future deputy ministers (Jules Léger and Marcel Cadieux), one future Cabinet secretary (Gordon Robertson), and others who would distinguish themselves as ambassadors and senior officials after the war. For its other needs at headquarters, DEA hired a dozen university-educated women who were examined and employed as officers but were designated as clerks. In addition, there were 26 "temporary wartime appointments" without competition from the universities. Some would return to academe after the war, while others would play important parts in elaborating a constructive internationalist foreign policy for a "middle power" in the Cold War. In the spring of 1944, it was decided to recruit particularly from those who had served in the armed forces, with the result that 64 officers were added by 1946. For veterans, it was considered inappropriate and "unfair" to impose "a fairly severe examination of academic standards," so that a "simple examination" involving one three-hour essay was substituted, which was written by 1,000 applicants. As before, the essay shortened the list for interviews to a manageable number (Eayrs 1961, pp. 47-48; Granatstein 1981, p. 194; Freifeld 1990, p. 22). The special recruitment of women, academics, and veterans reduced the proportion of francophones in DEA, and women were still excluded from the ranks of the foreign service, though a clerk who had been with DEA since 1909 — Agnes McCloskey — was posted to New York as vice-consul.[12]

Under a special examination in 1947 five women clerks were promoted to FSO 2, and women were made eligible for the foreign service competitions, though bias and discrimination against women persisted. Marion MacPherson became the first woman to enter DEA as an officer in 1947. (Not until 22 years later would the first woman join the TCS). That year also marked the final competition under the wartime procedures. For the next competition, the applicant had "to hold a degree from a recognized university" which would qualify him or her to undergo a written examination which was designed to be "as difficult as possible, to ensure that only the best candidates were successful" (Hilliker and Barry 1995, pp. 17-18). DEA expected prospective recruits to write three essays, each lasting three hours: a general topic combined with a précis; one on Canadian and international affairs; one "to be chosen from the fields of economics, international law, history, or the political and social sciences" (ibid.). The purpose was to determine "the candidate's ability to read and interpret instructions, to write clearly, economically and precisely, to arrange ideas and facts logically, and to do all this under pressure and in the manner in which he will be required to work almost immediately after joining the department" (ibid.). By now under-secretary, Pearson stoutly resisted the efforts of the CSC to introduce "modern principles of objective examinations" such as multiple-choice questions, though those tests were later employed (ibid.). In fact, subjective assessment of the suitability of the applicant for the foreign service was a critical element in the process.

Though it was satisfied with the examination, DEA was dissatisfied with the results. After a review, Cadieux advised the head of personnel, T.W.L. MacDermot, that "the solution lay not in more rigorous examinations but in attracting better candidates" through publicity, promotional visits to campuses and adjustments to the questions to take account of the "distinctive educational and cultural background" of francophone candidates (Hilliker and Barry 1995, pp. 17-18, 58; Weiers 1995, p. 89). As part of DEA's efforts to publicize the foreign service and to attract better applicants, Cadieux wrote a book and MacDermot wrote an article. Both help us to understand what DEA was looking for in the period of sustained expansion after the war.

MacDermot attempted to specify the "qualities and qualifications" which were sought as "integrity, devotion to a job, reliability, adaptability, resourcefulness, love of hard work, 'personality,' or the impact of one individuality on another, humour, good judgment, and the capacity to assume responsibility." He linked these attributes to the advanced skills for analytical reading and writing and facility of oral expression that were fostered in university and applied in diplomacy. "A glance at any current issue of our external policy," MacDermot wrote, "will show it to contain at least three factors — economic, political and historical. A good honours degree, therefore, in any of these or related fields, such as political science, geography, law, which provides a basic equipment of thought and expression, will be entirely adequate." In fact, the advertisement for the next competition reiterated the preference for those who had done postgraduate work. While the written examination would more precisely assess the applicant's skills in these subjects, their "professional quality" would be evaluated in the interview and in the probationary first year of employment (MacDermot 1948/49, pp. 24-32.).[13]

One former head of personnel division at DEA described the critical requirements as "lucidity, knowledge of Canada and its role in world affairs, common sense and personal adaptability" — all "vague words" which "seemed to be meaningful" to him (Farrell 1969, pp. 84-89). An outline of the competition for 1953 defined "personal suitability" as comprising "such traits as intellectual capacity, moral and personal integrity, sense of responsibility, initiative, adaptability, effectiveness of speech, and appearance and manner," which were all assessed by the oral board in an interview "which normally requires about one hour." In other words, the subjective element, to which the CSC took exception, was present in the written examination but deliberately magnified in the critical oral examination. This despite the acknowledged fact that "it is extremely difficult to predict the adaptability of a candidate in a short interview" (ibid.; "Foreign Service" 1953, p. 219). Even from the perspective of a successful applicant, the arbitrary aspect of the "oral board" could be intimidating, though one later supposed that he had benefited from "some rapport" with one of the examiners and the fact that the members of the panel "seemed to have had a stimulating lunch" (Stoner 1998; Reece 1993, pp. 33-34). Others later attributed their success in that final phase to indifference to the outcome or, conversely, to devotion to the foreign service as a career.[14] No doubt unsuccessful applicants found the process equally mystifying. Yet "the department's notion of the ideal candidate remained much as it had been in Skelton's day: a well-educated generalist, male, and from the mainstream white population" (Hilliker and Barry 1995, pp. 58-59).

By 1958, candidates were expected to write, in two and a half hours, 2 essays from a list of 12 topics, in addition to the multiple-choice examination the CSC used "to test all university graduates who are seeking employment in any part of the public service." As recently as 1953, the challenge had been to write, in six and half hours, one major essay and three shorter essays and a précis and analysis of a sight passage (which was extracted from Arnold Toynbee's *A Study of History*). Though the trial had been shortened, it was still sufficiently demanding that DEA could observe that "the majority of successful candidates in the past have taken at least one year of graduate studies," though that was not formally required.[15]

Generally speaking, the educational qualifications of the recruits had improved, and more had studied abroad, but there were still complaints about the quality of entrants. More attractive and quicker employment offers from the private sector were seen as negative factors, but no changes were made. One experiment anticipated a later development. For reasons of economy, and with a presumption about common needs, the CSC insisted on joint competition for DEA and DTC in 1953, but that innovation was dropped the next year and the overall process of recruitment remained much as it had before. From 1949 to 1957, 137 foreign service officers joined DEA, only 6 of whom were women and 36 francophones. From time to time, specific needs for DEA were met by transfers and secondments from other departments or agencies. Another four "specialists" were recruited in a special competition in 1955, though some gaps remained unfilled. "On the whole," a DEA official commented after that experience, "we find it best to recruit at the bottom — at grade one level — and to promote people as their ability develops and as they acquire experience" (Hilliker and Barry 1995, pp. 96-97; Eayrs 1961, pp. 53-54). Thus, in a period of rapid expansion, entry into the foreign service was determined much as it had been when Skelton devised the foreign service examination.

That growth was prompted not only by the "more active role in world affairs" played by the Canadian government after the war, particularly with Louis St. Laurent as prime minister and Pearson as minister, but also because of the increase in Canadian representation abroad and the demands imposed by "the extension of the practice of diplomacy by conference" ("Foreign Service" 1953, p. 218).[16] Thirty years after Massey presented his credentials in Washington, Canada maintained more than 60 diplomatic, consular and other offices abroad, including 33 embassies and 8 high commissions ("Foreign Service" 1958, p. 225). By then, most heads of mission were career officers, usually among Skelton's recruits, who were at or near the peak of their careers. Others, including Arnold Heeney — who first joined DEA as under-secretary of state for external affairs, then embarked on a series of ambassadorial appointments — and several military officers, originated in other government departments or agencies. And there remained a few, including some left over from the King era, whose diplomatic careers had political roots.

When John Diefenbaker led the Progressive Conservatives to power in June 1957 after nearly 22 years in opposition, some readjustment was perhaps inevitable. Diefenbaker was suspicious of the "Pearsonalities" in DEA, whose policies and loyalties were seen as too closely identified with the Liberals. One of his early diplomatic appointments was a reminder of prime ministerial prerogatives — taking a leaf from Bennett's book, Diefenbaker appointed a former premier of Ontario, and his predecessor as party leader, George Drew, as high commissioner to the United Kingdom. Jean Bruchési, who had failed the examination in June 1928 but who had subsequently distinguished himself in Quebec's political and cultural life, was named ambassador to Spain. However, Diefenbaker made only three other political appointments to diplomatic posts, even as decolonization and differing regional priorities led to the expansion of Canadian representation abroad (Hilliker and Barry 1995, pp. 157-58; Bruchési 1976, pp. 12-14; Eayrs 1961, pp. 45-46).

From 1957 to 1962, DEA grew by nearly 14 percent and 89 new entrants joined the foreign service, but those statistics mask important changes that had an impact on senior management of the department as well as on the recruitment — and retention of the recruits — for the foreign service. Within a year, the deputy under-secretary and two of four assistant under-secretaries left DEA, while another assistant under-secretary died. Though the new under-secretary was a familiar figure, Norman Robertson, he confronted unfamiliar problems: poor morale, inability to compete with expanding universities (and public utilities such as Hydro Québec) for talented graduates, the diminishing prestige of DEA within Ottawa, the debilitating impact of a purge of presumed security risks which particularly targeted suspected homosexuals, and the greater likelihood that assignments overseas would be "to politically and climatically uncomfortable environments" (Eayrs 1961, pp. 55-56; Granatstein 1981, pp. 328-29; Eayrs 1982, p. 107; Lyon 1963, pp. 30-31). Not only were junior and senior officers leaving the foreign service, but more candidates turned down offers of employment in the early 1960s, a tendency that was especially pronounced among French Canadians. While half of successful English-Canadian applicants declined offers, two-thirds of French-Canadian candidates looked elsewhere for employment. This trend occurred despite reforms to the examination process to make it more attractive to French-Canadian applicants (including changes in the written and oral examinations to reflect French-Canadian education and communication). Meanwhile, the burden of evaluating the written examinations increased as more candidates applied.[17]

Yet DEA was reluctant to change a procedure which had worked so well in the past, particularly as those responsible had themselves been recruited in that manner. "The competitive examination for admission to the Department of External Affairs is reputed to be difficult, and justly so," Cadieux wrote in 1962. That standard was justified by the attractions of the work and by emphasis on the "moral qualities" and "wide scholarship" which were deemed to be essential prerequisites for success in diplomacy. Though Cadieux waxed poetic about the elements of character and skills which were manifest in the "careers of our ablest diplomats," he denied that its methods of selection were "capriciously subjective" (pp. 69-78) Others were not so confident that the examination achieved its purpose. In 1963, a study by Maxwell Cohen for the Royal Commission on Government Organization cited evidence that "the average level of persons entering the Department in recent years, while still high, is no longer able to sustain a diplomatic service with the intellectual standards that once characterized the Department" (Canada. Royal Commission on Government Organization 1963, pp. 113-17). Fewer students with graduate training were entering the foreign service and DEA resisted both specialist recruitment and transfers or secondments from other government departments. Neither francophones nor women were effectively encouraged and employed.[18]

With the opening of more overseas posts, staffing requirements and levels of recruitment soared to new heights from 1963 to 1968, with 193 new entrants to the foreign service, so that DEA became even more "bottom-heavy with new recruits" (Hilliker and Barry 1995, pp. 347, 349). One consequence of this growth and the associated increase in the volume of applications for employment was that it was taking too long to grade the papers; as a result, the "tendency had developed to use the essay examination only as an aid for the oral examination teams" (Farrell 1969, p. 89). In 1965, candidates for entry as foreign service officers in either DTC or DEA were expected to answer one question from a list of ten, with one and a half hours allowed for that part of the examination. In addition, there was the CSC's multiple-choice "objective" test for prospective public servants and a test of proficiency in the candidate's "second Canadian language," first introduced in 1963.

With the essays unread and the language test not a grounds for disqualification, the "objective" test had effectively become the instrument to short-list candidates for interviews. As fundamental attitudes toward this form of evaluation had apparently not changed in DEA, the examiners obviously now relied "very heavily on the oral examination" and on assessment of the short-listed applicant's curriculum vitae to rank candidates. Thus, when DEA eliminated the essay examination in 1968, it was simply formalizing its existing practice. Still, that shift was criticized for exaggerating the importance of "oral abilities while ignoring the fact that one of the chief skills requested of a Foreign Service Officer is his ability to write messages and reports" (Farrell 1969, p. 89).[19] At this time, personnel policy generally came under critical scrutiny, with questions raised about the virtually exclusive reliance on recruitment at the junior levels for the foreign service, particularly as "many first-class students are not participating in the foreign service officer competition," rather than encouragement of transfers, secondments or specialized recruitment at more senior levels. One way to focus recruitment, which was consistent with past hiring practices, would be to set a higher qualifying standard to sit the exam, including a graduate degree (Canada. Department of Supply and Services 1969, pp. 53-54, 60-61). That recommendation would eventually be accepted, 26 years later.

Though he defended the selection of heads of mission from outside the foreign service in his memoirs, Pearson as prime minister made only five political appointments, including Lionel Chevrier as high commissioner in London (1972, p. 64; Hilliker and Barry 1995, p. 360). But there were other, more serious, challenges to DEA and the foreign service in the 1960s. A study for the Royal

Commission on Bilingualism and Biculturalism, by a former foreign service officer, was highly critical of departmental procedures, including recruitment, for their impact on francophone personnel, though some of its findings were out of date by the time it was published (Lalande 1969; Hilliker and Barry 1995, pp. 348-51). Canadian academics and commentators became increasingly critical of Canadian foreign policy and of the attitude of DEA to scholarship (Hilliker and Barry 1995, pp. 403-7; Thordarson 1972, pp. 28-33, 111-13). But the questioning of its role that would have the greatest impact on the foreign service came from Pearson's successor as prime minister, Pierre Trudeau.

CONSOLIDATION AND CHALLENGE

Trudeau expressed disdain for Canada's avowedly internationalist policies in the postwar period, as well as for "quiet diplomacy" and the diplomats who had practised it. Trudeau mocked "the whole concept of diplomacy today" as "outmoded" in an interview telecast on New Year's Day, 1969. "I believe it all goes back to the early days of the telegraph when you needed a dispatch to know what was happening in country A," Trudeau posited, "whereas now most of the time you can read it in a good newspaper."[20] That this was not simply a glib remark may be adduced from the approach taken by Trudeau to international affairs, from cuts at DEA and abroad, and from the fact that similar sentiments inspired a royal commission ten years later. On the latter occasion (Canada. Royal Commission on Conditions of Foreign Service 1981), Trudeau said the image and self-image of the foreign service "are based on a concept of diplomatic practice grounded in an age which has disappeared and which, in any case, predates Canadian experience. Traditional concepts of foreign service have diminished relevance in an era of instantaneous, world-wide communications, in which there is increasing reliance on personal contacts between senior members of governments, and in which international relations are concerned with progressively more complex and technical questions." In requesting the investigation, Trudeau stated that he was "not convinced that our approach to foreign service adequately reflects this new era" (Canada. Royal Commission on Conditions of Foreign Service 1981, pp. vii-ix).[21]

Though the Trudeau government did not then adopt a recommendation in 1970 for a unified foreign service, it did take other steps to integrate Canada's approach to international relations, including supervision by DEA of "all government programs operating abroad" and leadership of an interdepartmental committee which was supposed "to guide foreign policy planning in Ottawa and policy implementation abroad" (Story 1993, p. 1; Nossal 1993, pp. 39-40). That latter responsibility was translated into the quest for a role for DEA as a "central agency," a search particularly identified with Allan Gotlieb, who was under-secretary of state for external affairs from 1977 to 1981 (1979, *passim*).[22] This assertion of a leading role for DEA could not offset the perceived decline of its influence and authority in the 1970s, which prompted many senior officers to seek opportunities in other government departments (Dobell 1972, pp. 20-21). Nor could that elusive prospect overcome the decline in morale in the foreign service as well as the perception that the department lacked "expertise," which was particularly important as the international agenda became more complex and varied (Tucker 1980, pp. 62-64).[23]

No longer was the generalist venerated as before, though recruiting for the foreign service in the early 1970s still aimed for the type of officer that Skelton and Cadieux had favoured. In May 1973, the secretary of state for external affairs, Mitchell Sharp, had depicted the ideal foreign service officer as "the highly intelligent officer who can turn his hand to any question and deal satisfactorily with it, something like the renaissance man" (ibid. p. 64). By November 1978, a successor, Don Jamieson, conceded the need "to beef ourselves up on the economic side," though he still valued the "broad way" that generalists perceived issues (1979). A study of recruitment and work in DEA in the 1970s questioned the familiar dichotomy between generalists and specialists. Whatever the intent, "at least partial specialization" had been fostered by the traditional preferences in recruitment (Keenleyside 1979, pp. 51-71; Freifeld 1990, pp. 187-92; Eayrs 1982, pp. 100-101).

Idealism seemed also to have been a casualty of changes in DEA and the foreign service in the 1970s. Whether or not that quality was as dominant in earlier years as recollections suggested, its absence was discernible in commentaries and surveys of new entrants. More inward-looking and wary as a result of rising unemployment and inflation as well as faltering national unity, Canadians generally were less disposed to take bold initiatives in external affairs. Moreover, the extraordinary expansion of DEA and government generally had fostered both bureaucratic attitudes and the introduction of collective bargaining to the relationship between the foreign service and its departmental employers. More than their predecessors, recruits worried about working conditions and career prospects, so that missionary zeal was less likely (Keenleyside 1980/81, pp. 75-84; Canada. Royal Commission on Conditions of Foreign Service 1981, pp. 399-401.). That shift toward practical priorities was reflected as well in the eventual consolidation of the foreign service.

In March 1980, the senior ranks of the foreign service were integrated and members of the foreign service from Employment and Immigration and the Canadian International Development Agency were merged with DEA. On 12 January 1982, Trudeau announced a reorganization of government departments dealing with economic development, which linked regional and national economic policies to international trade. Included in the package of measures was the re-structuring of the Department of External Affairs. With the addition of the trade commissioner service and other elements of the former Department of Industry, Trade and Commerce, there was effectively a new department whose "primary purpose was to pursue aggressively international export markets and to give greater priority to economic matters in the development of foreign policy." For the under-secretary of state for external affairs, the precise aim was "to ensure a greater measure of coherence in the management of Canada's international relations by making economic and trade considerations a more integral part of its overall for-eign policy." The integration at posts had now been followed by consolidation in Ottawa (Osbaldeston 1982, pp. 453-66).

By then, the examination for the foreign service had undergone yet another change, which brought it back from the abyss of exclusive reliance on "objective" tests. A series of multiple choice questions assessed the candidate's knowledge of Canadian and international affairs, while another group evaluated "their powers of judgement." From as many as 4,000 who sat the examination, the department(s) involved would interview "between the top 5 to 15 per cent," from whom "an annual average of about twenty foreign service officers have been chosen" (Eayrs 1982, pp. 110-11). Those selected, according to the promotional literature from the government, "must be of the highest calibre." The under-representation of francophones was overcome in recruitment during the 1970s, "but not that of Canadians who are of other than Anglo-Saxon origin, who come from families whose breadwinner is not in the professions, or who happen to be women" (ibid.). For example, when Lucie Edwards was one of five women who joined DEA in 1976, no other women were recruited "in the two years immediately before or after." The requirement that women resign from the foreign service after marriage had been dropped only five years before and there was still "no advertising that the foreign service could be a career for women" (Weiers 1995, pp. 121-3, 157, 237).

Trudeau may have disdained some habits of diplomacy, but he upheld his right to make diplomatic appointments. When the Canadian government established an embassy to the Holy See, Trudeau reached outside the foreign service to appoint John Robbins. Most of his other selections involved former political associates representing Canada in European posts: France (Léo Cadieux, 1970-75; Gérard Pelletier, 1975-81); the United Kingdom (Paul Martin, 1974-79; Don Jamieson, 1982-85); Belgium (Lucien Lamoureux, 1974-80); Portugal (Lucien Lamoureux, 1980-84); and Ireland (Edgar Benson, 1982-85). Pelletier later served as Canada's ambassador and permanent representative to the United Nations. According to the Professional Association of Foreign Service Officers (PAFSO), the net tally of patronage appointments from Trudeau's period in office was 17 in 16 years.

When Brian Mulroney became prime minister he affirmed, in response to a letter from PAFSO's president, that "the standard of professionalism so characteristic of our foreign service will be maintained by my Government and reflected in the diplomatic appointments we will be making." Apparently acting on that pledge, on 11 October 1984, the Mulroney government announced that it had rescinded the most conspicuous favours to the faithful: Bryce Mackasey as ambassador to Portugal, Eugene Whelan as ambassador and permanent representative to the Food and Agricultural Organization in Rome, and Maurice Dupras as consul-general in Bordeaux, France. In the latter two cases, the offices were eliminated. For Portugal, another Liberal — though one not as dear to Trudeau — Lloyd Francis, the former speaker of the House of Commons, was chosen instead (Leyton-Brown 1987, pp. 142-43; Robertson 1987, pp. 46-49; Andrew 1993, pp. 152-53, 161-62).

Soon it became evident that the attitude of the Mulroney government, with Clark as foreign minister, was less straightforward and less favourable to PAFSO's interests than snatching away the political plums had suggested. After the appointments of Stephen Lewis, a New Democrat, as permanent representative to the United Nations and Douglas Roche, a Progressive Conservative, as ambassador for disarmament, John Kirton discerned "a desire to retain a professional foreign service establishment at home, but to politicize it further, if on a multipartisan basis, abroad" (1985, pp. 25-26). If that pattern was maintained, the purpose of the foreign service examination would be to recruit tomorrow's desk officers rather than tomorrow's ambassadors.

With a total of 19 appointments in his first three years in office, including his friend Lucien Bouchard as ambassador to France, Mulroney soon eclipsed the record of his predecessors, so much so that his use of diplomatic "rewards" for political purposes became controversial. In January 1986, PAFSO wrote one of a series of letters to Clark on this subject, followed by a press release. Clark's reply contended that "important Canadian communities are inadequately reflected now in Canada's public appointments — most notably women, organized labour, and Canadians other than English and French." In other words, one purpose of patronage was to compensate for the inability of DEA to reflect "national priorities" in recruitment and selection. Tension rose again when Jean Drapeau was appointed as representative to UNESCO, prompting former minister Allan MacEachen to defend "professionalism in the foreign service" in a predictably partisan exchange in the Senate and to ask whether the government "has abandoned the notion of a Canadian professional foreign service."

What was especially galling to PAFSO was that this activity was taking place against the backdrop of budget cuts and post closures. When six posts were closed in February 1987, the only head to be reassigned at a comparable level was a political appointee, Pierrette Lucas, formerly an aide to Clark and a defeated Progressive Conservative candidate. The war of words between Clark and PAFSO culminated in a nasty exchange in July 1987, which received extensive coverage in the national media. Though he claimed in April 1988 that he had received a "bum rap" on patronage, Mulroney promptly replaced two political appointees — Roy McMurtry, high commissioner in London, and Lewis — with two more, Donald Macdonald and Yves Fortier.[24] PAFSO might balk, but both were highly qualified individuals who successfully advanced Canadian interests as heads of mission. Moreover, as Clark contended, the vast majority of diplomatic appointments still went to career officers.

The potential impact of this trend on recruitment for the foreign service was aptly caricatured by John Kirton. "Professors across Canada," Kirton wrote, "have difficulty in countering with evidence the theory of their most intellectually promising and politically sensitive students that the surest way to become an ambassador and exert influence on Canadian foreign policy is to turn down External's job offer, go into law or business, make a fortune in the private sector first, and then get a classmate-turned-politician to provide a fast track to the top" (1985, pp. 27-30). Kirton argued that the promotion of Canadian values and interests around the world necessitated "an expanded and strengthened diplomatic corps" to cope with the complexity of international relations in a changing world. What he perceived instead was "the decline in the status of Canada's professional diplomatic corps" from its earlier exalted position as "a high calling for the best and brightest young Canadians of the day" (ibid.). The Mulroney government had devoted considerable attention to redefining Canadian foreign policy, but not enough to the ways and means to implement it.

Political appointments attracted the most notice, but other factors influenced the foreign service and especially recruitment. To improve its policy-making capacity and its relationship with other government departments, DEA had encouraged lateral entries, often at ranks and salaries above those of the generalists recruited earlier (Copeland 1997; Gotlieb 1979, pp. 18-20). In a brief to the joint parliamentary committee on Canada's foreign policy, PAFSO noted the negative impact of lack of promotions, loss of positions and programs at headquarters and abroad, and a freeze on recruitment to the foreign service imposed for fiscal reasons ("Foreign Policy Review" 1986, pp. 32-34). When recruiting resumed, it responded to additional demands. The context had been unfortunate, but Clark's earlier observation about the composition of the foreign service was not without foundation. Recruitment was one way to address that concern about how well it mirrored Canadian society. In September 1988, Clark appealed to "Canadians of all backgrounds" to sit the exam. "The foreign service is Canada's voice and face abroad," Clark commented. "I want to ensure that the richness of our ethnic diversity and the vitality of our multicultural society is fully reflected — for the whole world to see — in the women and men who make up the Canadian foreign service" (Canada. Department of External Affairs 1988). Yet, to pare costs, recruitment had become intermittent and consequently even more unpredictable, thereby discouraging potential applicants.

Seen in that light, the decision of senior management of the department to restore annual recruiting even in the face of financial cuts was a vital step toward renewal of the foreign service. But one move, inspired by the mutual desire of the Public Service Commission (PSC) and the Department of Foreign Affairs and International Trade to save the time and expense of sifting through thousands of examinations, provoked criticism.[25] In August 1994, the PSC informed university employment officers that "the department is only considering applications from students graduating in economics, law, business administration or commerce," or others with "an acceptable level of language proficiency in Mandarin, Arabic, Japanese, Russian or Korean." To underline that qualification, the PSC stated that other candidates "even if they decide to write the tests" and "attain the highest scores in the country" would not be considered.[26] Stung by protests, particularly from political scientists, DFAIT depicted the restricted scope as an alternative to "no recruitment" and as an exceptional way to meet acute needs.[27]

Privately, the incoming deputy minister distanced himself from this exclusive approach.[28] Afterward, the president of the Canadian Political Science Association concluded that "some good may yet flow from the Department's otherwise parochial action," which reinforced the impression "that government departments are out of touch with the social and economic reality of the 1990s" (Smith 1994). Revised eligibility criteria suggested that the complaints had had an impact. Urdu, Punjabi, and Hindi were added to the list of qualifying languages, but the emphasis on business and economics was dropped, with law, international affairs and international development substituted as acceptable undergraduate specialties. As well, someone with a graduate degree in any discipline could apply.

Thus qualified, a candidate wrote three tests on 28 October 1995: a General Competency Test Level 2 (GCT2), a Written Communication Test (WCT); and a Foreign Service Knowledge Test (FSKT). The GCT2 was 90 multiple-choice questions divided into five types (vocabulary, figural relations, number and letter series, numerical problems, and analytical reasoning), for which the examinee was allowed two hours. The WCT was a précis (from 2,000 down to 450 words) which would be evaluated "on the basis of grammar, spelling, punctuation, style and content coverage," for which 90 minutes was allocated. The shortest test (45 minutes for 60 multiple-choice questions) was the FSKT, which included "knowledge of subjects related to each of the three career streams in the Foreign Service," though some likened it to a trivia contest (Hantel-Fraser 1993, p. 82).

According to the PSC, the way to prepare for the FSKT was "by becoming well-informed about Canada and international affairs through relevant sources (e.g., daily newspapers)," which would presumably help one to avoid a misapprehension that Bob White was the "chief Canadian negotiator for the Canada-US free trade negotiations" [1995]. As for the oral examination, it comprised not only an individual interview but also a "group simulation exercise" and, for those select few, "a written forty-five minute essay on a political, economic, immigration, or international development subject" (Hantel-Fraser 1993, p. 83).

For 1996, Urdu, Hindi, and Punjabi were dropped from the qualifications. Another variation on the educational theme was offered by the stress on a "graduate degree in any field," a law degree or other bachelor's degrees "only if combined with significant experience in international commerce or with an acceptable level of proficiency in Mandarin, Japanese, Arabic, Russian or Korean." Applicants were also informed that "foreign language knowledge, especially German or Spanish, is an asset and is recognized in the selection process."[29] Even with these stipulations, there were 3,600 candidates across Canada and overseas for the foreign service in 1996. For 1997, the educational requirements for 60 positions in the foreign service (50 at DFAIT) again emphasized graduate training, law, and language skill.[30]

After 70 years, DFAIT has decided to abandon the last unique written element of the foreign service examination — the FSKT — and to rely instead on other PSC tests to screen applications from qualified candidates and on interviews and assessments of experience and education to select entrants to the foreign service. That revised procedure undoubtedly reflects not only the limitations of the FSKT as an evaluation, but also significant changes in the role of the department and in the demands on foreign service officers. "We live in a CNN world," a personnel director commented a few years ago, "we don't have time to produce scholarly, thoughtful papers on what's happening in Yugoslavia" (Weiers 1995, pp. 241-43). But, as Andrew Cooper has argued, the "constricted fiscal climate," the diversification of the international agenda and the preoccupation of other departments with national rather than international priorities may contribute to the "reinvigoration of the 'professional' foreign service" (1997, p. 63). In other words, diplomatic skills developed from the personal qualities and experiences sought by Skelton and his successors may have an enhanced rather than a diminished role in the articulation and advancement of Canada's values and interests in international affairs.

For today's — and even more likely for tomorrow's — ambassadors, the qualifications and expectations have been transformed by national and international circumstances, with the result that an elaborate ritual devised for the formative years of Canada's foreign service no longer meets the requirements of DFAIT or the Government of Canada. Today's selection system, however, still resembles the one devised in 1925. Senior officers of the department still use a mixture of educational requirements, exam results, and personal assessment at interview to make an informal guess about which young Canadians will mature in foreign service into future ambassadors. Their judgement is shaped by the policy needs and budget restrictions the department faces, but the results are also shaped by the motivations and attributes of those who apply to join the foreign service.

NOTES

1. The Canadian War Mission, which had opened only four days before the armistice, closed on 31 March 1921. Its secretary, Merchant M. Mahoney, was appointed on 27 May 1921 as the "agent" of DEA in Washington, with an office in the British embassy. When the Canadian legation was opened in February 1927, Mahoney became commercial secretary there. See Thibault and Moreau 1991, p. 200; Hilliker 1990, pp. 84-86; Skilling 1945, pp. 196-200.

2. The quotation is from Ritchie 1974, paraphrasing a letter he received from Borden, a close friend of his father, in 1921. Apparently, Borden's letter was prompted by a comment from Ritchie's mother about the interest expressed by her son (age 15) in international affairs. "Thus was planted," Ritchie comments in his foreword, "the germ of an ambition" (p. 9).

3. At the time of his appointment, Riddell did not have diplomatic status.

4. Quoted in Granatstein 1981, p. 25. "Only a saint," Granatstein comments, "could have fulfilled all those conditions."

5. "They [Skelton's recruits], too, reflected the man: like Skelton, they were academically-minded, frequently with postgraduate training, accustomed to critical thought and abstraction; pragmatists who were flexible, versatile, and adaptable; widely-read and articulate generalists with a concern for culture and history, and a talent for written communication; liberal idealists, sometimes given to political moralizing; anti-imperialists, suspicious of the worst excesses of both British and American power; resolute Canadians with a commitment to a wider world" (Hillmer 1992, p. 14). Vincent Massey (1963, p. 135) was more reluctant to give Skelton credit for the creation of the "diplomatic service."

6. The estimated number of candidates comes from Hilliker 1990, p. 120, though Keenleyside (1981, p. 213) states in his memoirs that he was informed "that the total number of applicants for the two posts was 256."

7. Even so, the appointment of the minister to Washington and the others that followed were controversial, with R.B. Bennett especially critical of "the end of our connection with the empire" (Neatby 1963, pp. 192-93).

8. On the transition, see Hilliker 1990, pp. 135-42 and Skilling 1945, pp. 244-47.

9. In the competition for 1932, there were more than 500 applicants (Hilliker 1990, p. 120). The alternative of unemployment, and the attractions of the career, inspired applicants to the TCS as well (Manion 1960, p. 18). Manion joined the TCS in 1931. By 1939, there were 60 members of the TCS in 32 offices in 26 countries.

10. On recruitment and personnel moves in the late 1930s, see Hilliker 1990, pp. 190-98; Gibson 1987, pp. 12-14; Rogers 1989, pp. 20-22.

11. On the wartime developments, see especially Skilling 1945, pp. 285-326, and Hilliker 1990, pp. 217-321.
12. On the circumstances of McCloskey's posting, which was designed principally to remove her from headquarters, see Freifeld 1990, pp. 66-67; Weiers 1995, p. 33; Granatstein 1981, p. 191.
13. The educational standard was stated as follows: "A degree from a university of recognized standing is a further qualification for applicants, and knowledge of a foreign language is advantageous. Preference is given to those who have done post-graduate work in one or more of the following subjects: political science, history, geography, economics, and law; but those who have a good training in other subjects, and who are interested in a career in Canada's Foreign Service, should also submit their applications to the Civil Service Commission" ("Foreign Service Officer Examinations," 1949). See also Cadieux 1949. By the time Cadieux's volume appeared he had succeeded MacDermot as head of the personnel division. Most francophone recruits in the 1950s had read Cadieux's book.
14. See especially Dorothy Armstrong's account of her written examination and oral board in Weiers 1995, pp. 99-100.
15. See "Foreign Service," 1958. The examination paper for 1957 (without the objective test) was reproduced as an appendix to that article. The questions for 1952 were reprinted in "Foreign Service Officer Competition," 1953.
16. The prime ministerial and foreign affairs responsibilities had been separated in 1946, when St. Laurent became secretary of state for external affairs. Two years later, St. Laurent succeeded King as leader of the Liberal Party and then as prime minister, with Pearson moving from deputy minister to minister. St. Laurent linked Canada's postwar internationalism with the growth of the foreign service in his major statement of Canadian foreign policy, the Gray Lecture of January 1947. For the text, see MacKay 1970, pp. 388-99.
17. See Caldwell 1965, especially pp. 73-78. For information about the number of candidates see Table 8, p. 59.
18. A comparison of entrants in 1947-49 with those from 1967 suggested that the latter group "on the whole tended to be younger, better educated (in terms of degrees obtained) and to have had relatively less pre-departmental working experience than their colleagues who joined twenty years earlier" (Caldwell 1965, p. 4). That suggests either that admission standards improved during the 1960s or that Cohen's criticism was overstated. The former group still included nearly 90 percent with military service (ibid., Figure 1).
19. See also "Recruitment of University Graduates," 1966. The essay component of the examination for 1965 is appended to the article.
20. See Thordarson 1972; Andrew 1970, chap. 6; Granatstein and Bothwell 1990; and Head and Trudeau 1995; Canada. Royal Commission on Conditions of Foreign Service 1981, p. 61. Trudeau's remark is quoted in Thordarson, p. 91. It also prompted a study by the Policy Analysis Group of DEA on "The Role of the Diplomat," circulated in March 1970.
21. At the time of the "integration," more than 20 government departments and agencies had personnel serving overseas (Andrew 1993, pp. 149-50; Canada. Royal Commission on Conditions of Foreign Service 1981, pp. 75-78).
22. For an oblique reply to Trudeau's criticisms see pp. 1-3.
23. On problems of morale in the foreign service, see Keenleyside 1976, pp. 208-26.

24. See Robertson 1987; Starnes 1987*a-c*; Manseau 1987; Lobsinger 1987; "Vignettes" 1988.
25. In 1990, when 80 positions had been available, there had been 6,013 applications (up from 5,165 the year before) as the only qualification was a BA (Hantel-Fraser 1993), p. 80.
26. Danielle Carignan (PSC) to Barry Koentges (University of Calgary), 31 August 1994.
27. Denys Vermette to Elvi Whittaker, 14 October 1994.
28. John English to Donald Barry, 21 October 1994. English cited a conversation with Gordon Smith "(Ph.D. in Political Science)."
29. Message to all posts from DFAIT/SPSS, 7 August 1996.
30. Message to Headquarters from DFAIT/SPSS, 3 September 1997.

9

Virtual Diplomacy

Richard Kohler

INTRODUCTION

Information is at the heart of diplomacy. The word itself comes from "diploma," the term the Romans used for certain sorts of official documents. Harold Nicolson recalls that "diplomacy" was long associated with "the preservation of archives, the analysis of past treaties and the study of the history of international negotiations" (Nicolson 1939/1988, pp. 11-12). The traditional list of diplomatic functions codified in Article 3 of the 1961 *Vienna Convention on Diplomatic Relations* includes "ascertaining by all lawful means conditions and developments in the receiving State, and reporting thereon to the Government of the sending State." A more modern task is to provide information about the sending country to citizens of the host country. Information remains at the heart of what we call "virtual diplomacy,"(Smith 1996*a)* but our craft has been transformed in the same ways that all knowledge work has been transformed by changes in information technology and telecommunications.

Looked at from my standpoint as chief information officer, a foreign ministry is comprised of people who collect information, people who analyze and interpret information, people who provide information to others in the form of reports and policy advice, and people who use information to provide services to the public. Some of this information is sensitive and private, but some of it is intended for the general public in Canada and abroad. Yet other information is administrative data, or immigration files, or commercial intelligence for exporters. Tying the whole enterprise together are the people on my staff who transmit that information from place to place and those who store it so that it can be retrieved by members of the department now, and by historians in the future. New technology changes all of these tasks, and many departmental structures change in consequence, but they do not affect the department's purpose. In this chapter I want first to describe the new technologies available to the Department of Foreign Affairs and International Trade (DFAIT) before discussing how they affect heads of mission abroad.

THE TECHNOLOGY OF VIRTUAL DIPLOMACY

New developments in transportation and communications have had a continuous impact on diplomacy. With the arrival of steam, diplomats could carry messages more quickly from country to country, but new letters of instructions could also reach them more quickly. Diplomats could more readily send letters back home with information on local developments, but the newspapers could also be carried back to capitals, occasioning questions about the need for expensive diplomats when journalists could do the job. Ambassadors used to rely on couriers carrying the "diplomatic bag," which is inviolate under the Vienna Conventions, to send confidential letters home, a process that became much easier when jet airplanes began to shrink the world. As telecommunications improved, ambassadors could report home by telegram and later by telex, although both methods were relatively slow, and coding sensitive information was cumbersome. It was possible to use the telephone for important conversations, but its utility was limited by considerations of costs and security. The technology of creating messages on paper, transmitting messages to Ottawa, and providing secure management of records on post required a relatively elaborate establishment. Missions abroad had a staff of Canadian secretaries, communications technicians, and file clerks whose major role was facilitating this process. Things are different now. Technology allows the creation of a "smart" foreign service, providing "just in time and place" intelligence. Officers can obtain information from their colleagues around the world and from electronic sources on the Internet. It allows the department to create "virtual work teams" with officers abroad and in Ottawa working together in real time on a single issue (Smith 1996*b*).

Transmitting and Storing Information

All of the people in the department who use information are dependent on the available means of transmission, the area where we have seen the greatest changes. Over the past 20 years, DFAIT has gradually built up a global network of leased telecommunications circuits that are now linked together in a state-of-the-art digital network that we call MITNET. The digital lines carry both voice and data transmissions. All of our missions and offices can be reached from anywhere on MITNET by dialing a seven-digit number, a feature that is unique among foreign ministries. Diplomats are now issued "call me" cards that can access MITNET from any telephone booth in the world. Sitting atop the MITNET system is SIGNET, the department's information management system, which is effectively one global network that links many local area networks. SIGNET links desktop computers (PCs) wherever they are in the world with departmental servers in one comprehensive electronic "Web." Today, every officer has a desktop PC with a standard package of software applications (to ensure compatibility and efficiency) and an electronic mail (email) system. For security reasons, SIGNET has built-in systems that prevents access from the Internet. Our officers can send and receive email with anyone on the Internet, however, and email between DFAIT and many other foreign ministries is possible.

The new system allows us to maintain a central electronic "information management" system to which SIGNET users can have access from any desktop. We do not use the term "filing" system anymore since the system is much broader because of the variety of media that have to be stored digitally and in hard copy, from voice messages to scanned material and video clips. Now that we have the technology, document management is one of our highest priorities. We have to ensure that information can be turned into knowledge: that is where the real productivity payoff comes from this investment in technology. But we have already seen a financial return.

These new means of transmitting and storing information not only let us do more things, they let us do it more cheaply. With all of our local networks linked, telex has disappeared, we have fewer secretaries, and communications technicians are rare. The diplomatic bag still exists, but many fewer leave Ottawa each week. While the new network is expensive, the savings from shutting down the old telecommunications system have paid for this significant investment in new technology. DFAIT now handles 24 million email messages per year on its network, something the previous system never could have supported. The network leases cost about $25 million per year to handle all voice and data communications; if we were to rely on private carriers instead, the cost would exceed $75 million per year for the same traffic load, a boon for taxpayers.

Changing Structures and Operations

Technology is having some effect on the structure of DFAIT, but less than you might think. In response to the creation of MITNET/SIGNET, all direct client service units were consolidated into one flexible and reliable client service division. The Information Management and Technology (IMT) unit includes elements of the library, the records-management service (the diplomatic archives of old), and the electronic "infocentre" that serves the public as well as system administration and user-training functions. The consolidation encouraged staff to look outward, focused on users, rather than looking inward, focused on our own process.

We have worked hard to ensure that technology supports but does not drive the department. What new forms of communication can do, however, is alter how we support the department's functions. We can keep more staff in Ottawa, or at regional posts. The small missions described in the chapter by Janet Graham in this volume, with their "hub-and-spoke" relations with regional support centres, are only possible because of new technology. The hardware and software combined in the MITNET/SIGNET network system have offered DFAIT capabilities that have never existed before. In the era of virtual diplomacy, every post in every location can be staffed 24 hours a day, seven days a week. During non-business hours, the telephones of more than 50 posts are forwarded to Ottawa for response to consular enquiries. Should the situation be an emergency that warrants the head of mission becoming involved, staff in Ottawa know how to reach him or her, or mission staff. A Canadian traveller is quite simply a phone call away from consular services anywhere in the world.

The SIGNET/MITNET system also allows for a "virtual" or instant mission to be established with a plane ticket, a portable computer, and a dial tone. The department can respond to a crisis anywhere, anytime. The head of mission can put up a brass plate outside a hotel room door and be operational almost immediately after arriving in a trouble spot, which has huge implications for the mobility of DFAIT operations. This approach was used to establish a new embassy in Zagreb, Croatia, at the height of the Bosnian conflict. This virtual mission faced many difficulties operating out of a hotel room, but it was operational within hours of staff landing in Croatia. We can now establish a small diplomatic mission in hours, a task that previously took weeks, even months. This flexibility both enhances our foreign policy and is cost effective, especially when we do not need a permanent mission.

The technology also allows a virtual team to be assembled to tackle any policy or operations issue without having to move people. The team members can be drawn entirely from within the department, anywhere in the world, but the team can also include officers of other departments in Canada, even other governments, as well as academics and civil society organizations. Team members may never have to meet face-to-face, which reduces the costs associated with travelling and hosting meetings. Perhaps in the future we will see hybrid, just-in-time virtual teams, drawn from throughout the diplomatic and non-governmental communities, as the operational norm, rather than the novelty that such teams are today (Smith 1996).

Collecting Information

A "wired" world in which information flows in real time and news is broadcast as it happens is a further step in the alteration of the diplomat's information gathering role. Desk officers in Ottawa can read the Australian budget speech off the Internet as it is delivered, or monitor discussions among non-governmental organizations (NGOs) active in the campaign to ban land mines. It is now CNN on television that is informed and in turn is informing diplomats as it informs the public. Data or information are not knowledge, however, even when repeated endlessly on the Internet. When CNN has the pictures, thereby influencing the political agenda in Ottawa, then selecting, filtering, and analyzing the information available from their own sources becomes an even more important role for the ambassador. Diplomats still have access to information not available to journalists, and they have the training, experience, and contacts to make judgements about that information. Technology helps our missions stay current with the latest news available to the Canadian public, and it lets our ambassador's views be available on the minister's desk as the CNN report appears on the TV screen. The ambassador is not in competition with CNN — understanding of the local context and an interpretation from a Canadian perspective turns CNN's information into useful knowledge.

Working with Information

SIGNET supports any application or business process that may be needed, including financial services, the personnel system, and property management. Now that missions can communicate quickly with headquarters, much of the work in these areas has been centralized. Payments for services provided locally to missions can be made from a central processing centre, eliminating the need for staff to be deployed abroad for such purposes. This organizational change is not only more efficient because duplication and overlap have been eliminated, but accountability is enhanced through greater supervision of expenditures, given the inclusion of headquarters staff in the daily business. In the past, routine audits would uncover questionable expenditures, but this back-end process is often late and ineffective in preventing monies from being improperly disbursed. Property-management staff located at headquarters can develop greater expertise — the knowledge they gain through comparison of procedures and decisions in the management of several missions is not available to an officer working at only one mission. For example, a post in one European city may discover a more cost-effective means of maintaining the Chancery premises by hiring firms on a retainer fee, rather than through a tender process. Given the similarity of business practices throughout Western Europe, a supervisor at headquarters may be able to implement a similar process at other posts in the region, capturing an efficiency that might otherwise have been missed.

Separate SIGNET applications provide shared global databases of information about Canadian exporters, about the status of immigration files and about outstanding consular cases. Trade commissioners, immigration officers and consuls can collaborate with colleagues in Ottawa and at other posts, allowing staff to provide more services to Canadians, at lower cost.

Providing Information

We have seen a revolution in how we provide information in the last three years because of the Web. We are proud of a recent press review of Canadian government Web sites that awarded ours four stars. The reviewer wrote: "Stunning graphics and an index that's a pleasure to cruise — I actually enjoyed going through the many parts of this site to see what new nugget of info I could come up with." He went on to give his readers:

> a sample of the sorts of things you can learn more about: Canada's relations with just about every country in the world, what you need to know about working in or visiting the United States, Canada's role in the recent international land mine treaty, the phone numbers and addresses of all Canadian embassies and consulates abroad, how to set up a business in Canada if you're an international company, travel advisories for tourists visiting troublesome areas of the world, and the complete text of the Foreign Service Exam that's given to all applicants in the Foreign Service" (Brown 1998).

The Web can also serve people in other countries. The minister of foreign affairs has proclaimed a vision of a "Canadian International Information Strategy" using the tools of "electronic diplomacy" to use posts as electronic kiosks for the local diffusion of electronic information about Canada (Axworthy 1996). We now have Web sites at a growing number of missions that offer a window on Canada by providing local information and links to the major Canadian government sites. The public can get this information at their convenience. Business hours or proximity to a library are no longer a constraint on access to information. Abroad, routine requests for information can in effect be handled from Ottawa. This new power does not mean that the ambassador is no longer responsible for the dissemination of information. The ambassador will still be called upon to provide the press or government officials with information about Canada or Canadian policy. Since the Web is a passive source, ambassadors must develop an appropriate strategy to ensure that Canada's story is told in their countries of accreditation, but the new means of collecting and disseminating information should free them to spend more time trying to shape local opinion.

IMPLICATIONS OF VIRTUAL DIPLOMACY

The implementation of a new communications network enhances the operating capabilities of the department by offering new sources of flexibility and efficiency. New information technologies will not replace missions abroad, but the work conducted at missions has evolved, and the number of people posted abroad has declined as some work is centralized in Ottawa. The technology allows a mission to be the "single window" for Canadian government services discussed in the chapter by Lucie Edwards. Small offices can provide a great many services. Any ambassador, with any staff size, can inform themselves about anything happening in Canada that is relevant to the post, and the ambassador can draw on the whole foreign service for support, instantly. This brave new world is not unambiguously a positive development, however, as we discovered at the workshop that gave rise to this volume.

Don Hilliker mentioned, for example, that the Historical Section undertook a study of the Zaire crisis of 1996 due to concern that the record might not be well preserved in the light of technological change. They found that it was at least as well documented if not better than a good many long-ago and far-away events. The records came from the Central Registry files, they came from "working files" (the files officers keep in their own filing cabinets), and they came from electronic storage. Hilliker identified two problems, however. One is that officers must have confidence that a system of records exists, because a great deal of what they found came from working files and not from Central Registry files — building the record, in consequence, was enormously time consuming. The second is that it is obviously important that electronic storage be stable: if the system is superseded most of the material that exists only in electronic form will be lost. It may have been printed out for working files, but the working files themselves are ephemeral — if the material does not go to central storage then it becomes lost.

In my view, a third problem exists: the record is uneven. We were lucky to find a wealth of paper on the Zaire issue, but will another manager have the zeal or the diligence or the good luck, on another issue, to leave the same paper or electronic trail? We need to develop an easy-to-use records and information document management architecture — one of the traditional and still vital tasks of a foreign ministry — that will give all of our employees the confidence that will allow them, some day, to throw away the paper. Right now paper costs in the department have gone up exponentially because of the ease with which technology allows copies of everything we do. But more paper does not equal better records.

Email has enhanced the ability of members of the department to communicate more quickly and effectively in a secure format. Email is flexible, and it does not require the communicating parties to be connected simultaneously, unlike personal meetings or telephone calls. Furthermore, an individual's weight in an organization is less evident on email, as contact is direct from desktop to desktop free from filtration of (administrative) support staff. Headquarters can consult the head of mission on many more policy issues in ways that were not practical in the past. But this boon is also a threat, and not only because desk officers in Ottawa as well as officers abroad can collapse under the weight of information, or never have time to respond to the hundreds of email messages piling up in their virtual in-basket, now that everybody can communicate with everybody else all the time, about the weather in Miami as well as the latest crisis in Iraq.

Information technology flattens hierarchies and empowers staff at all levels. The creative corridor conversations that have always been important for the department are now global in scope. At the workshop, however, some former ambassadors expressed concerns about the ease with which exchanges can now take place among desk officers in Ottawa and at posts on policy issues, discussions that are not cleared with program managers, or necessarily conducted on links with a high level of security. J.H. Taylor, a former ambassador and under-secretary, observed considerable tension between the structures that exist and technologically-driven developments. The ambassador is still responsible, and the deputy minister is still responsible, and the minister is still responsible, in ways that the users of the system are not aware of very often. In the end this phenomenon even raises constitutional issues about how the parliamentary system functions. Taylor said that he would worry about developments that moved entirely in the direction of instantaneous communications at the desk level without any controls because that would mean that in effect there is no responsibility in the system, or that if anybody was responsible it was an individual desk officer and everyone else would be in a position of saying that you "cannot in fairness hold me responsible."

I do not disagree that new technology challenges managers at all levels to create objectives and structures in which officers are both empowered and accountable. Of course, that was true many years ago when it became possible for people abroad to phone Ottawa. Managers still have the capacity to develop procedures to ensure that they remain accountable in practice as well as in law for policy decisions. Security is more complex. The department is responsible to Parliament for protecting the integrity and the security of our information. Allies will stop sharing with us if they suspect that we do not give appropriate protection to their information. We do have very high grade processes that allow us to communicate the most precious information with all the security we want, but it is not as easy to use or as ubiquitous as we would like, because the technology is very expensive.

And more complex still, especially now, is fundamental system integrity: when we are this dependent on technology, we have to be sure that all elements of the system are still working at 12:01 am 1 January 2000. Our Year 2000 Project is my highest priority.

CONCLUSION

Arthur Andrew wrote nearly 30 years ago that if you thought the diplomat was merely a transmitter of messages, then he would be obsolete. He thought, however, that the representative of a smaller power is much more important as an interpreter of information available from other sources (Andrew 1970, p. 69). I agree. Diplomacy is still about information — getting it, interpreting it, passing it on to other governments, providing advice to the minister, and helping Canadians understand the world. Information, however, is not neutral. It does not just appear, and it matters who has it, and who interprets it. And it matters now more than ever. Modern news-gathering techniques mean not only that Ottawa has multiple sources of information on events, as they are happening, but that anything an ambassador says abroad can suddenly appear in Canadian living rooms. Ambassadors are much more engaged in policy discussions with Ottawa than their predecessors, but this enhanced visibility comes at a price: Ottawa is now much more involved with the post, from administrative minutiae to questions of strategy. The information sharing facilitated by electronics allows for much better unity of focus, of message, across our foreign service; it underpins collective clarity; and it allows mandarins to focus on pure foreign policy. Technology has replaced many of our staff abroad as their functions are taken over by machines, or staff are moved back to headquarters. The irony is that the more we know about the world, the more we want to have our own people abroad, obtaining first-hand information, and putting forward a Canadian view. We know that human communication is comprised of 8 percent words and 92 percent tone of voice and body language. No matter how hard Nicholas Negroponte pushes his students at the Media Lab, they will not get a PC to tilt and inflect. In the end, virtual diplomacy — enhanced and turbo-charged as it is by fast breeder servers, allowing DFAIT to comfortably compete in the global marketplace — equates to traditional diplomacy. Technology does not alter the centrality of the ambassador in the conduct of foreign relations, because it cannot replace experience, local contacts, and judgement, even as it alters everything around.

10

The Ambassador as Senior Trade Commissioner

Anthony T. Eyton

INTRODUCTION

Canada had trade commissioners long before it had ambassadors. The search for new markets for Canadian goods prompted the appointment of part-time commercial agents in 1892, and two years later, what became the trade commissioner service (TCS) began when John Larke was sent to Australia as Canada's first full-time commercial agent (Knowles and Mackenzie 1994, pp. 15-17; Hill 1977, pp. 45-51). Within 17 years, there were 21 trade commissioners in 16 countries, with 5 additional part-time commercial agents working in what was known as the Commercial Intelligence Service (CIS). It took a long time for them to be seen as integral parts of Canadian missions. Separately administered, the trade-commercial function, political relations, immigration, and foreign aid worked independently for many years, often in conflict. Today the ambassador embodies the "single window" that is the motivating principle behind most of the reorganization that infects Ottawa today (see Edwards, this volume). The ambassador is responsible for everything that happens at the post. He or she is the senior political officer, the chief trade commissioner, and the visible communicator of Canadian culture and values. The ambassador is the leader of the trade team in the modern embassy, on whom depends the effectiveness of government efforts to facilitate increased exports and inward investment. In this chapter I discuss how this centrality of trade emerged before I look ahead to the growing importance of trade in the role of the head of mission.[1]

THE GOOD OLD DAYS?

Thirty years ago, Canada appeared to be "blessed" with four apparently independent foreign services. There was the tradition-bound and highly intellectual Department of External Affairs. The TCS had its own foreign operations which were managed by the Department of Trade and Commerce. The Immigration Foreign Service, the oldest of all the foreign services, was a branch of the Department of Manpower and Immigration, and the Foreign Aid Office was agitating to separate from External Affairs to become the Canadian International Development Agency (CIDA).

When I was first assigned to Lima, Peru in 1965 as a third secretary (commercial), I entered the murky world of bureaucratic warfare. The ambassador, first secretary and their locally engaged staff occupied one-half of the space at the Canadian embassy, and the commercial counsellor, our locally engaged staff and I occupied the remaining space. The only shared resource was the receptionist. On the trade side we had our own accountant, our own telephone lines, a separate communications link back to Ottawa, and separate authority and budgets for everything from leasing residences to providing for hospitality. The relationship between the ambassador and the commercial counsellor was strained, I think primarily because the ambassador wished to exercise some power of coordination over post programs, and the commercial counsellor resisted any entreaties from the other side. In the power struggle that ensued, the Department of External Affairs firmly supported their man in Lima, and three commercial counsellors succeeded one another over the next four years as the TCS tried fruitlessly to find someone who could co-exist with the ambassador. Our embassy in Peru did not operate in an optimal manner, and our efforts in the trade and economic areas were somewhat splintered as a result. The trade team simply did what it could in the circumstances, and deemed the ambassador a bloody nuisance.

I cannot say if other posts were as fractious, but sadly, the relations between the departments in Ottawa appeared to be. Each department ran a separate foreign service bureaucracy, with some limited consultation in the appointment of trade commissioners to head-of-post positions at consulates in the United States, Europe, Brazil, and Australia because trade was the raison d'être of these posts. There was also reasonably close consultation on trade policy questions, with the departments of Trade and Commerce and Finance playing the lead roles, and External Affairs playing a useful support role in the Ottawa trade policy triad.

After spending the 1960s fretting about government reorganization, the first major evolutionary step came in 1971 when the government established the Interdepartmental Committee on External Relations (ICER), chaired by the undersecretary of state for external affairs. This innovation clearly reflected the wish of ministers and the senior bureaucracy for improved coordination and more effective foreign policy formulation and program delivery. In other words, people in positions of authority lost patience with the internecine warfare between the foreign service departments and their separate foreign services abroad. ICER agreed that the head of mission abroad was to have a coordinating role over all post programs, reinforced by changes in the personnel management systems to give the head of mission primary responsibility for completing performance assessments on all staff, including the counsellors responsible for trade, immigration, and CIDA programs. In turn, the ICER departments were asked to contribute to the appraisal of all ambassadors. The creation of ICER and the decision to make one person responsible for the full range of Canadian interests certainly led to improved coordination of programs and personnel at posts abroad.

I believe it took more time for perceptions to change in Ottawa than at posts abroad. Trade policy was still dominated by the departments of Finance and of Industry, Trade and Commerce. Trade development programs, including the scheduling of trade fair participation and trade missions, were seen as the exclusive responsibility of the Department of Industry, Trade and Commerce. CIDA yearned for complete independence from External Affairs, and the Immigration Foreign Service by choice remained largely insulated, and even managed to convince the government that their personnel requirements could be determined by a mathematical formula related to the number of visas issued and immigrants processed in the preceding year.

In the late 1970s I was the director general of the trade commissioner service and, therefore, an active participant in the ICER process. In my recollection, the External Affairs' strategic plan stressed the "peace and security" themes that had guided departmental priorities since the Second World War. It made reference to the consular program, and to the CIDA programs in developing countries. International economic relations were important but little was said about the trade and investment programs that, by that time, had become a top priority of the government. The External Affairs' strategic plan devoted attention to Canada's broad foreign policy priorities while the TCS concentrated on programs and marketing/investment priorities in the United States, Japan, and the European Economic Community.

While the head of mission became clearly responsible for all post programs during the 1970s, ordering overall priorities and funding foreign operations and programs remained split between the four departments. Coordination of foreign policies/programs in Ottawa was weak, and interdepartmental struggles continued. In late 1981, the government decided, on the advice of senior officials, to integrate the four foreign services into a new department, later renamed the Department of Foreign Affairs and International Trade (DFAIT). With that decision, ownership of all of the positions in the Immigration Foreign Service and the trade positions of the Department of Industry, Trade and Commerce was transferred to a restructured Department of External Affairs.

The reorganization dramatically changed the Ottawa landscape. Now, the strategic plan encompassed all foreign policy priorities, and funding and staffing of operations in Ottawa and posts abroad were determined based on priorities across the full range of departmental activities. And although there have been subsequent reorganizations of the department, the role of the ambassador has essentially remained unchanged since 1981. Since then, the ambassador or head of post has been considered the senior trade commissioner at the post, and is responsible to DFAIT, as well as to the other economic departments, for providing the trade program with dynamic leadership.

Recent initiatives taken by the department's International Business Development Branch have addressed remaining problems of strategic coordination. Cabinet assigned DFAIT leadership in the development of an annual international business strategy that now largely determines how resources are deployed. The new process engages all of the federal departments and agencies with international programs, and equally significant, all provinces. An interdepartmental committee on trade and investment has been established representing some 22 different departments and agencies. An executive committee comprising the deputy ministers of Industry Canada, Agriculture Canada, and International Trade leads the effort to coordinate, in Ottawa, all of the government's trade and economic activities. In addition, each of these deputies has been assigned geographic responsibilities for coordinating investment development in the more promising of the advanced economies. With these important developments, it seems to me that the machinery is in place, both in Ottawa and at posts abroad, to assist our ambassadors in achieving optimal effectiveness in their strategic direction and leadership of trade and investment development programs.

THE AMBASSADOR AS CHIEF TRADE COMMISSIONER

In the so-called "golden age" of Canadian diplomacy following World War II, many ambassadors played only a limited role in providing commercial intelligence to Canadian exporters, promoting tourism, or encouraging foreign investment in Canada. As pointed out, the Department of Trade and Commerce ran its own foreign service, and worked through the trade commissioners in the field rather than the ambassadors. As well, some ambassadors may have been reluctant to become involved in the mundane world of commerce. In their view, such activities were unlikely to change the course of the world, and were better left to trade commissioners educated and trained to do that sort of thing. Ambassadors were required to spend a considerable amount of time drafting exquisite political reports, and reputations were in some measure based on the quality of such reporting. There was always frenzied activity before the diplomatic courier arrived to ensure that the always-confidential reports were completed for delivery back to the desk officer in Ottawa. Today with CNN and instant communications with Ottawa, the ambassador's political role has been transformed.

The "ICERization" of posts in the 1970s and the reorganization of 1981 dramatically changed ambassadorial self-perception. Freed of departmental constraints, most ambassadors largely welcomed the expanded trade role. Working with their trade staffs, they became deeply involved in all major trade, tourism, and investment events. Able to open doors at the highest level in government and in business, ambassadorial efforts complement those of senior trade staff in furthering Canadian economic interests. Ambassadors meet senior Canadian businessmen visiting their countries of accreditation, and speak on bilateral economic issues to business groups at posts and to business conferences on trips back to Canada.

The role is satisfying, but it is also a challenge, especially for officers whose earlier career was in a different branch of the service. The ambassador must have a reasonably good grasp of the trade and economic file. He or she must understand the nature of the host country economy and know the commodities Canada exports to determine if some Canadian companies might find local niches. Equally important is fluency in the host-country language. If these essential attributes are missing, and the ambassador fumbles through a presentation on the Canadian economy before an audience of businessmen, or is unable to respond to straightforward inquiries from senior interlocuteurs, Canadian trade and economic interests may well be damaged rather than facilitated. Some posts have a higher trade orientation than others, but the ability to communicate effectively with a business audience and to provide dynamic leadership to the trade and economic programs of the embassy is central to the role of all heads of mission today. In those posts where export interests are paramount, ambassadors must devote the greater part of their time and energy to the trade program. For example, our ambassador in Washington is expected to devote considerable time and attention to informing the administration, Congress, lobbyists, academics, and the media on trade issues of importance to Canada. Even the cultural affairs program in Washington is seen as a useful tool to improve access to decisionmakers who shape Washington's trade policy environment.

The ambassador as chief trade commissioner works with the provinces to support their individual trade and economic interests. I think it is true that provincial officials and politicians are more likely to accept the advice and support of ambassadors and consuls general than the direct assistance of the director general of an Ottawa geographic bureau. This partly reflects the touchiness of federal-provincial relations, but mainly it is because the ambassador can provide direct information and assistance and is seen as the representative of all Canadians rather than of a specific federal department. As Kim Nossal indicates in this volume, the provinces have had difficulty deciding whether and where to maintain representatives abroad. In those cities where embassies and provincial delegations are both present, the ambassador clearly has an important coordinating job. I do not think anyone would argue with the proposition that provinces have important interests in promoting trade and investment, and in informing financial markets of recent and prospective developments. Indeed, ambassadors generally welcome the visits of provincial leaders and provincial trade missions since they serve to expand the Canadian presence. Budgetary pressures have forced all provinces to scale back or eliminate their foreign services, and consequently have increased the ambassador's role of supporting provincial trade and economic interests abroad. One can also argue that the ambassador, by directly assisting and counselling the provinces, improves federal-provincial relations and helps to bind the nation together.

THE FUTURE COMMERCIAL ROLE OF THE AMBASSADOR

Shortly before the workshop that gave rise to this volume, the Liberal government won reelection, and the party platform would seem to be a useful guide to the government's intentions. The 1997 Liberal *Red Book* attaches priority to creating jobs through exports, implicitly endorsing a DFAIT analysis that estimates that 14,000 jobs are created with each increment of $1 billion in export sales. Indeed, if one measures relative priorities by column inches, trade and investment are the most important elements of Canadian foreign policy and operations, since relatively little attention was devoted to other DFAIT programs in the *Red Book*. Trade and investment are meant to be priority activities for the current government, for DFAIT and for our ambassadors abroad.

It was stated in Chapter 3 of the *Red Book*, that "we will explore new forms of trade promotion, learning from what has worked so well thus far. A new Liberal government will create a Trade Promotion Agency that builds on the Team Canada approach to promoting international business. The agency will integrate trade promotion functions across various government departments to provide better service to Canadian businesses." The activities of the proposed Trade Promotion Agency, including its role in coordinating federal and provincial trade/investment promotion strategies, are then described. The Trade Promotion Agency will not be a policy-making body. Rather "it will serve as an information resource centre for Canadian firms and as a marketing agency to help sell Canadian goods and services around the world. Tapping the federal government's international network of trade officials, it will make information more available to Canadian businesses. The agency will actively promote Canadian products to foreign buyers and encourage foreign direct investment in Canada." One must assume that the Liberal Party was thinking of creating the Trade Promotion Agency out of the trade development resources of DFAIT, along with a transfer of commodity specialists from Industry Canada. It is not clear whether the new agency would "own" the trade positions at posts abroad, nor how it would become involved in the decisions related to resource allocations abroad, performance measurement, promotion processes and assignments.[2] Even less clear is how the role of the ambassador would change in the new equation.

My suspicion is that this proposal had its origins in the never-ending debate about the efficacy of the 1981 decision to move trade from the Department of Industry, Trade and Commerce, and to the Department of External Affairs. Some bureaucrats still believe that trade should either have its own department or be rejoined with Industry Canada, though few in the business community support this view. Others in Ottawa have felt that trade development was an activity better left to the private sector. Noting that other OECD countries, in particular Australia, Sweden, and Britain have partially "privatized" their trade development agencies, some have argued that we should do the same, again notwithstanding the mixed results that these agencies have achieved, and the very limited savings they have brought to the public purse. From a Canadian perspective, a privatized trade development agency would, in some measure, be separated from the ambassador who, as outlined above, is the government official best placed to open doors at the highest levels and who, in our present structure, provides strategic leadership to the trade and investment program.

My own view is that the government should not tinker with a structure that seems to be working well. To the extent that some of the pressures for change reflect a need to reduce federal expenditures, the user-fee principle can undoubtedly be extended to cover market studies and other services offered by our trade posts. Now, most costs in respect of trade missions and trade-fair participation are recovered through user fees. But it seems unlikely to me that a new Trade Promotion Agency would improve the overall coordination of trade and investment activities, since the machinery is now in place to ensure optimal coordination. At any rate, the government has thus far shown little inclination to move ahead on that particular *Red Book* promise, preferring instead to use existing machinery and proven trade promotion vehicles, such as the Team Canada trade missions led by the prime minister.

CONCLUSION

From a trade and investment point of view, I believe that Canada's interests in strong relationships with selected multinational companies are more important than Canada's bilateral relationships with many independent countries.[3] If one can accept this proposition, then Canada should put as much effort into working with those companies as we put into developing bilateral relations with many countries where we have full-fledged embassies. In this effort, the ambassador's role is critical. Only an ambassador can gain access to the most senior decisionmakers, whether in government or in business. The ambassador is uniquely placed to promote both a Canadian trade policy position and a major export contract, to persuade a multinational company to invest in Canada, or alternatively to consider the benefits of assigning world product-production mandates to existing Canadian branch plants. In taking any initiatives in these areas, the ambassador again is best positioned to coordinate the various players, including the Canadian subsidiary, and the provincial and federal government departments and agencies. An ambassador can open doors that even the president or chief executive officer (CEO) of a company cannot. Obviously you do not necessarily want to have your ambassador accompany a Canadian export manager from a food products firm on visits to supermarkets, but to involve a head of mission, even in developing countries, to reach those groups and individuals that only the head of mission can access by very reason of the title. I think that it is particularly important in pursuing capital projects to ensure that Canadian companies are on a competitive level, that our ambassadors are making the presentations to host-country governments just as the Japanese and the Germans and the Americans are.

Governments in all advanced economies have been getting more involved in trade promotion. Prime Minister Chrétien's Team Canada missions follow a model practised by many other countries, as does the trade role of the head of mission. Should governments do this sort of thing? *The Economist* argued in February 1997 that

> One sort of export promotion does no particular harm and (depending on the cost) may even do some good. That is general marketing of a country, carefully insulated from particular contracts and particular companies, in a way analogous to the work done by an industry association for its members: drum-beating, information-gathering, information-disseminating. Beyond that, there are two other legitimate roles for governments. One is that for some longer-term export contracts, as for inward investments, reassurances about the stability of regulatory and macroeconomic policy can be important. This is no truer of a foreign buyer than a domestic one, but the foreigner may have less information or understanding of policy trends

than the resident does. Even more important, of course, is actually maintaining that stability. The other legitimate role is that in the defence business governments do typically have to deal with governments. There, if you want to be in the business, you have to get into the fray ("Don't be Salesmen" and "Thoroughly Modern" 1997).

I think that is right. The government must be involved in trade development, and ambassadors must be involved in the program. The ambassador is obviously a key member of the Team Canada mission, and is deeply involved in designing the visit program, selecting the Canadian businessmen who should participate, making the arrangements for the visit, attending to the requirements of the prime minister and provincial premiers, and ensuring follow-up of all leads and loose ends after the departure of the mission. The role of the ambassador in trade development should be strategic, dealing only with the high points of the trade program — the senior trade commissioner on post should deal with everything else. As consul general in New York, I had access to the senior management of major multinational companies. In the case of one that has perhaps six or seven factories in Canada, the president of their Canadian operations is a mid-level company officer not necessarily in a position to influence investment decisions by the board. But because of my title, I could meet with the chairman of the board and with the president and CEO of the parent company, who would fly the Canadian president in for the meetings. We learned what they were thinking about and whether or not they planned to maintain or expand their Canadian investments, and were in a position to develop a follow-up strategy. If we had left the ambassador or the consul general entirely out of the equation, the company may have decided these issues based on its rather imperfect knowledge of the political and economic situation in Canada.

John Cleghorn, CEO of the Royal Bank, recently said that Canada, despite its standing internationally, and although it has inflation under control and is an excellent place to invest money, still does not get anywhere close to its reasonable fair share of international investment because Canada remains a very well-kept secret. Our heads of mission have work to do to convince multinational companies that Canada is a great place in which to do business and a great place in which to invest their shareholders' money. Left to its own devices, a globalized market will not necessarily produce enough jobs, and enough good jobs, for Canadians. I still believe that the state has a role in promoting economic growth in our country, and in the future more than ever, our heads of mission abroad will have an increasing part in that enterprise.

NOTES

1. For a more comprehensive history and an analysis of future challenges, see Griffith (1992/93).
2. I note that DFAIT is developing a performance measurement initiative for the trade commissioner service, which should make it possible to deploy our trade team and determine priorities more effectively. The initiative, which will be completed before summer 1998, will have six components: client and service definition, employee surveys, client surveys, workload indicators, service standards, and a service-charge option.
3. For an academic discussion of a related set of ideas, see Stopford *et al.* (1991).

PART III

DIPLOMATIC PARTNERS

11

A New Diplomacy?
How Ambassadors (Should) Deal with
Civil Society Organizations

Alison Van Rooy

OVERVIEW

Canadian diplomats now work with non-diplomats to get diplomatic jobs done. This intervention is not a *new* kind of diplomacy, of course; it is simply a diplomacy with a changed set of actors. Ambassadors have always had complex relationships with their official and non-official counterparts abroad and the ambassadorial mandate in reality has never been restricted solely to state-to-state communication. Today, however, that mandate is even larger, as more people want — and rightly believe they should get — access, services, voice, influence. What does that proliferation of actors and their demands mean for tomorrow's ambassadors?

In this chapter I try to explain both the push and pull factors that have expanded the ambassadorial mandates to include interaction with more people and organizations. Push factors include the growing demand for services from missions as Canadians increase their interaction with citizens of other countries; demands at home on headquarters and missions to consult with Canadians on policy matters; and pressure from like-minded countries to pursue in-depth relationships with civil society organizations (CSOs). Factors which pull mission staff toward more interaction with CSOs are practical: the "instrumentalist" need for CSOs to help missions undertake their wider, if shallower, mandates; and "essentialist": foreign policy itself is developing goals of supporting civil society, part of Canada's good governance and democratic development mandate.[1]

But first, let me say something about these groups and sketch some of the other factors that affect this "new" diplomacy before addressing problems raised within that relationship. I will then turn my attention to some practical tools for guiding interaction with this body of increasingly important actors.

WHO?

Canadians who work abroad are used to the idea of non-governmental development organizations (NGOs or NGDOs) as intermediaries in the development process, whether based in Canada or in a host country. Indeed, Canadian foreign service officers, particularly if posted in the south, have probably had more to do with the Canadian NGO community than any other population of Canadians living abroad. They have probably met a wide variety of NGOs from other northern countries and an even wider variety of local organizations.

This constellation of NGOs is only a part of a wider category of civil society organizations, however. What, then, is civil society? The battle over definitions is certainly a vibrant industry these days.[2] The term is used in political speeches, project proposals, academic treatises, and activist language alike, sometimes to contradictory ends. The definition used in The North-South Institute's research on civil society sifts through the debate and produces two important components. One is organizational: civil society encompasses organizations and the "space" they occupy in society. The second is civil society as a "political project." In the first sense, civil society encompasses those organizations formed for collective purposes primarily of the state and marketplace. They therefore include NGOs, but encompass labour unions, professional associations, organized religion, community self-help groups, and even recreational groups. In Canada, over 20,000 organizations qualify as civil society organizations — and only some 350 of them work in countries of the south.[3]

Of course, not all the purposes of civil society organizations are for the collective good, and not all necessarily improve the quality of public life — civil society organizations may be racist, elitist, or predatory. However, what is considered important is that civil organizations *can* exist, they have the political, social, economic, and regulatory space to exist, and they *can* fulfil important goals for society. This part of the definition leads to the second sense in which civil society is commonly used, in the sense of a political project. In this aspect, civil society organizations are valuable because they can promote a certain kind of society, compensating for the failures of the state or the market to fulfil human aspirations. The idea assumes that a third sector is necessary to guarantee a just society, and that the formation of civil society itself — a population of groups and the enabling environment necessary for their survival — is therefore a good thing.

WHY NOW?

These debates are not just academic. Discussion about the role of civil society has been resurrected out of its lonely existence in political philosophy in order to explain some of the rapid changes characteristic of the late twentieth century. In particular, civil society has come to our attention because of the changes in the past decade throughout Eastern Europe. Western observers trying to explain the rapidity of that transformation listened to what the underground intelligentsia were saying. Well versed in Gramscian and Hegelian philosophy, and borrowing from Latin American interpretations of social protest, East and Central European academics explained that civil society, forced underground by distortions in socialism, was bursting forth to rectify the political and social order.

Northern Malaise

Of course, the civil society debate rang bells in northern countries as well, lending momentum to the discussion: civil society might also rectify political and social disorder at home. Remarkably, in a rather rosy view, civil society is now thought by some to promise salvation for a range of societal woes. Some of those woes, only jotted here, include:

Concern about the welfare state. North Americans and northern Europeans alike have been worried about the welfare state. Concern about the ability of the state to provide an ever-widening array of public goods has turned attention to voluntary organizations which are now to step in (Salamon and Anheier 1994). While this "replacement philosophy" is a contentious (and arguable) proposition, it has redirected attention to the voluntary or third sector, now being rechristened as civil society.

Social capital at home. A related concern, albeit fanned more in the United States (where communitarian political discourse is comparatively influential than in Canada), is the idea that society is breaking apart. Social capital, that invisible glue of community trust and solidarity, is supposedly on the wane. Again, while debatable, this fear of the possible consequences of diminished social capital has redirected attention to the creator of social capital: civil society (Putnam 1993; 1995).

Crisis in aid. These thoughts carry over into our aid programs as well. Throughout the donor community, whose Overseas Development Assistance (ODA) contributions have dipped markedly in recent years, talk of a crisis in aid is common.

There is some question whether there actually is a drop in public confidence in aid — Canadian polls show support for the idea has remained rock solid for 30 consecutive years — but aid bureaucrats are certainly anxious (Clark and Van Rooy 1997). Talk of crisis has led to a search for alternatives: the off-loading of aid jobs (and dollars) to NGOs and CSOs is an increasing phenomenon.

Free marketeering. A final factor is the rush to liberal market systems. The collapse of the Berlin Wall indicated to many in the northern hemisphere that centralized economies were no longer viable, and the push for market liberalization in quasi- or fully-centralized developing countries accelerated, a move that was often fueled by conditions placed on aid. In some instances, requirements to downsize the bureaucracy have been accompanied by recommendations to have the voluntary sector provide some services. Just as the debate on the welfare state at home prompted renewed interest in civil society, the voluntary or civil society sector in other countries has been vested with new importance by moves to create free-market conditions (Anheier and Salamon, forthcoming).

All of these points are familiar ones. What is new, however, is what the changes imply for the work of ambassadors and their staff. Why would CSOs therefore become more relevant in the conduct of international relations? A number of push and pull arguments are offered below.

Growing Demand

Both Canadian and host-country organizations are demanding more of Canadian posts. These demands will not be limited to claims on the restricted discretionary funds available to Canadian missions (last year, amounting to less than $40 million worldwide; see Figure 1), but will include requests for political and other interventions as well. Such demands are not new for Canadian missions, of course — Canada has long been involved in behind-the-scenes efforts to shape the political and social environment, especially for organizations within civil society that support Canadian values. A recent example was Canada's use of mission funds to support a year-long roundtable of Salvadoran and other experts to discuss El Salvador's proposed legislation on NGOs. Formulated by the governing party, the initially draconian bill would have put power to decide on the "existence" of NGOs into the hands of the minister of the interior — whose office was responsible for the death squads of the 1980s that terrorized many of the groups now working in civil society. The bill was eventually passed into law, albeit with important amendments, and Salvadoran NGOs have organized to bring a constitutional case against the law to the courts.

FIGURE 1: Trends in Mission Fund Spending

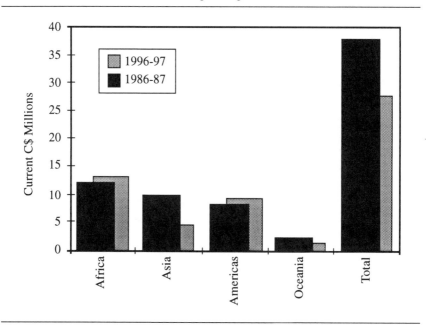

Source: Table M, Total Net Disbursements by Country, CIDA, *Statistical Report on Official Development Assistance,* Fiscal Year 1996-97 and *Annual Report, 1986-1987,* 1987.

The Consultation Imperative

Another push factor is the imperative, spread across the public service, to consult more broadly with Canadians. The Department of Foreign Affairs and International Trade (DFAIT) will press mission staff, and will in turn be pressed by the Privy Council Office, for greater interaction on foreign policy in particular, spurred in part by the 1994-95 government foreign policy review process that solicited hundreds of briefs and presentations by members of the public across the country. Some parts of the department have long had formal consultative relationships, as illustrated by the annual consultations with the Canadian human rights community prior to Canada's attendance at the UN Human Rights Commission meeting in New York. Other examples include the now defunct ITAC-SAGIT process, where a central International Trade Advisory Committee and its subcommittees of Sectoral Advisory Groups on International Trade joined DFAIT officials, business leaders, and some union and environmental group representatives to discuss policy directions. There was also the important one-off process of consultation around the UN Conference on Environment and Development, where NGOs and others worked with DFAIT and Canadian International Development Agency (CIDA) officials to draft Canada's policy at the world meeting in Rio (Van Rooy 1997a).

Until 1994, however, those consultations were the exception rather than the rule (Van Rooy 1993). The resistance to more widespread efforts was based on an explicit opinion within the department that foreign policy should be undertaken by foreign policy professionals. The public was seen, and continues to be seen in many circles, as a mass of uninformed or deeply partisan interest groups, without a capacity for balancing Canadian interests. The mood has begun to change, particularly in areas where the policy dilemmas seem unresolvable: Kurdish Iraq, Burma, post-conflict rehabilitation in Guatemala, the Balkans, Russian social disintegration, Rwanda, and China are raising difficult questions. Now, meetings are more regularly held in both formal and informal venues, paid for out of the public purse, to debate foreign policy issues with the Canadian public. The John Holmes Fund at DFAIT sponsors debates on issues of ongoing or upcoming foreign policy, and the department's annual National Forum is designed to give the foreign minister pointed advice on current policy issues.

The imperative passes on to the work of ambassadors, as well. Business leaders have always had access, of course, and their participation is growing particularly as missions focus more heavily on trade promotion, but other Canadians also count. In countries where prominent NGOs like Development & Peace or Oxfam are active and where the post supervises a great deal of development work, as in Sri Lanka or India, there is more interaction. More broadening of the diplomatic circuit could and should happen, however. Heads of mission are primarily information brokers, dependent on sound analyses of a country's political, economic, and social events in order to undertake their work. Any analysis of Indonesia, for example, would be deeply skewed if it focused on the trade implications of the Southeast Asian financial crisis alone; rising ethnic tensions and violence, the continuing outrage at the occupation of East Timor, and the intractibility of President Suharto are also crucial. The broader the range of voices heard, the better is the ambassador's hope for a balanced analysis and a better rendition of what Canada's and Canadians' interests may really be.

The Jones' Effect

A further push factor is the weight of peer pressure. Other missions and foreign ministries are setting a trend that will affect Canadian behaviour: Sweden has an NGO ambassador, responsible for formally meeting with, gathering information from, and developing policy with the community of NGOs in Sweden involved in foreign relations issues. In the United States, the Agency for International Development's New Core Initiative has promised that fully 40 percent of American aid is to be channelled through NGOs in coming years — probably a tripling of that agency's spending. Canada now spends about 14 percent. That volume of spending will involve Americans working in CSOs very closely in developing responses to development issues abroad. Canada has itself long been a promoter of NGOs within its international dealings, most notably, during the 1992 Earth Summit, and has used language about civil society in more recent meetings, even if CIDA and DFAIT have yet to elaborate what the shift in terminology may mean for their work. The Development Assistance Committee of the OECD, of which Canada is an active member, has also spent much time and energy on NGO and, increasingly, civil society issues: all these factors contribute to more, rather than less, Canadian attention on the topic.

Instrumentalism

Working with CSOs also has certain attractions, or pull factors. One, in crass terms, is the *utility* of CSOs in helping Canada undertake the broadening range of tasks now considered part of the diplomatic workload. I call this the pull of instrumentalism. This broadening has happened in part because of changes in the distinction between "low" and "high" policy. The shift in attention to one-time low policy issues — environment, development, social policy, governance — from the high policy concerns of security, territory, and monetary policy means that different people and organizations now have relevant information that diplomats need. Prior to the Earth Summit, for example, many governments had no policy to deal with indigenous people's management of their own environment — an area on which governments were now asked to pass judgement and spend dollars.

In contrast, some low policy issues that involve CSO activity have become high ones in the post-Cold War world: human rights, democratization, and the strengthening of civil society itself. Many of these issues involve CSOs at their very core; and for foreign missions, the labour intensity and knowledge required to deal intelligently with these new areas demands outside help, especially in a world of small, understaffed missions. This instrumental interest lies in the ability of CSOs to provide services, generate leverage and information, and legitimize activity.

Providing services. CSOs can provide key diplomatic services for Canada. One illustrative case was the role of Canadian, Eritrean, and Tigrayan NGOs in helping Canada fulfil its humanitarian obligations in Ethiopia in the mid-1980s. The diplomatic tensions were high: direct assistance to groups in the region had been strictly forbidden by the secretary of state for external affairs on the grounds that relief assistance might imply recognition of rebel groups, thereby seriously jeopardizing the peace process. Yet the Canadian government and CIDA continued to be concerned with the worsening situation. After long discussions, the Canadian coalition, African Emergency Aid, was allowed to provide aid for distribution through local NGOs.

Generating leverage. Working with CSOs can leverage Canada's shrinking aid budget and Canada's influence. The central component of our relations with a great many of the poorest countries, especially in Africa, is the aid we give them. Worldwide, Canada spent over 22 percent of her bilateral aid through NGOs in 1995-96.[4] In many developing countries, therefore, the most visible representatives of Canada are members of the voluntary sector, not diplomats. Even when the dollar figures are low, CSOs allow the aid budget to be spread further, and the potential foreign policy leverage can be significant. As we see in Table 1, the

TABLE 1: Who Is Dependent on Canadian Aid?

	Total Canadian Aid in C$ millions (all sources) 1995-96	Rank of Canada Among Bilateral Donors in Recipient Country (1995)	Rank of Recipient Country for Total Canadian Aid* 1995-96
St. Lucia	6.61	1	
Trinidad & Tobago	2.06	2	
Guyana	7.69	3	48
Dominica	2.47	3	
Cameroon	30.12	3	12
Saint Kitts and Nevis	0.88	4	
Jamaica	9.57	4	43
Haiti	35.77	4	8
Equatorial Guinea	0.40	4	
Venezuela	1.55	5	
St. Vincent /Grenadines	0.87	5	
Seychelles	1.62	5	
Niger	8.62	5	44
Malaysia	5.31	5	
Egypt	93.20	5	5
Cote d'Ivoire	67.49	5	6
Comoros	1.15	5	
Afghanistan	10.45	5	41

Note: * Includes multilateral aid. Only countries ranking in the top 50 are listed.
Source: North-South Institute, 1997.

dollar numbers may be small for Canada (columns 1 and 3), but the relative importance of Canada's aid to the host country can be enormous.

Generating information. The CSO community in Canada has also provided DFAIT with key pieces of information in generating policy — such as the participation of environmental and labour representatives on the International Trade Advisory Committee, once an exclusively business-focused roundtable. As the importance of the environment rose on the public agenda — rating the highest Canadian concern in polls early this decade (Runnalls 1991) — information about the environmental consequences of international trade policy became critical. The environmentalists' presence became a necessity from then on, both in generating information and legitimizing the process.

Legitimizing activity. As Canadian CSOs and NGOs have pressured their own government on a host of policy issues, it has become politically impossible to develop many areas of foreign policy without some reference to civil groups. A recent example is the work by DFAIT to include Canadian organizations in the lead-up to the November 1997 APEC Summit, hosted by Canada in a bitter public opinion environment. Organizations that opppose Asia Pacific Economic Cooperation's (APEC) economic agenda and the human rights abuses of some of its members were included in policy conversations around the meeting, leading to Canada's initial steps to open APEC to CSOs in other countires as well (Van Rooy 1997*b*).

Essentialism

While debates on the instrumentalist arguments that seem to have pulled Canada's foreign policy machine toward greater interaction with CSOs continue, an additional pull factor is the goal of "civil society strengthening" itself. This factor is "essentialist" in that civil society has become interesting not only for what it can *do*, but for what it *is,* its essence. The topic of civil society has taken a central role in today's diplomatic tasks as "promoting good governance" rises on the foreign policy agenda. We are interested in civil society organizations because of their overall role in society, not just because of how they may make diplomatic tasks easier. Canada's work in Kenya as the leader of the Donor Coordination group in the early 1990s is a good example of this emphasis: concerned with the restrictions on civil organizing, wide-scale violence promulgated by the regime, and its insistence on a single-party system, Canada was key in convincing like-minded states to impose a moratorium on aid, instead supporting organizations working toward constitutional, social, and political reform. Allied unofficially with CSOs in a country straining for change, Canada was able to make a strong diplomatic mark.

COUNTER FORCES AND A RESPONSE

This trend toward greater interaction with CSOs is not met with warm responses everywhere in the diplomatic community. Some argue that involving CSOs simply adds more work for overworked diplomats and their staff, that CSOs focus too narrowly on special interests and that time and attention should not be diverted from trade promotion.

An additional task. Some heads of small missions, who may have few other Canadians on their staff, may believe that they cannot afford to take time from properly "diplomatic" tasks to consult with CSOs. The notion of adding *yet* another burden to an overweighted agenda is a genuine disincentive. However, while consultation can be time-consuming, it also can improve the effectiveness of the mission by generating broader information from more diverse sources, and by surveying the field of Canadian activity and representations. As mentioned earlier, Canada is often most visible through the unofficial ambassadors of the Canadian voluntary sector.

Special interests. Another counterpoint frequently made is that CSOs represent special interests versus the public interest. As one commentator in the workshop that led to this volume mentioned, "it is not their job to put together a coherent foreign policy. They represent one particular policy concern to the exclusion or even to the detriment of a range of others." I agree; it is indeed not the job of CSOs to make coherent foreign policy, nor should anyone rightly expect that of them. Of course, even interests within government are "special"; different departments, divisions, and agencies are continually advocating particular policy choices, sometimes in opposition to existing policy. I think questions of legitimacy are important, as I discuss below. An alternative perspective, however, is to rephrase the objection in a way that acknowledges that these voices are *all* presenting particular views; now, there are simply more voices. The ambassador, as always, plays a coordinating role in the country of accreditation, trying to project a coherent view of Canada.

Widget selling. Another point often made is that an emphasis on civil society distracts from the real business of promoting Canadian trade abroad. The rhetorical shift, even in Canada's relationship with the poorest countries, to a trade- (versus aid-) based relationship has only added fuel to that argument. After all, many posts are losing political and economic officers in favour of those trained in trade issues (and immigration). In this view, what is the relevance of dealing with non-trade actors like CSOs? My response is that interaction with CSOs is not only about the "soft" side of foreign relations. CSOs are *also* involved in trying to shape the international trade regime. Pointed recent examples include Common Frontiers, an anti-NAFTA Canadian-Mexican-American NGO coalition that fought the initial agreement, and the People's Summit at APEC held in Vancouver in November 1997. In both cases, CSOs were legitimately pushing the widget-selling agenda in another direction. Ambassadors should expect to hear more from such CSOs in future.

The backlash. A final point is that Canada needs to be wary: in many countries, anti-NGO sentiments have grown large in the political arena.[5] This is also true in some parts of the CSO-government relationship in Canada, of course: in 1994, backbench MP John Bryden tabled a report that suggested dramatic curtailing of the rights of Canadian organizations entrusted with public money (Bryden 1994).

Yet in Canada, we have always thought it important to fund the social infrastructure, just as we funded the railways. The Canadian policy stance has always been clearly to favour, or at least not to oppose, the articulation of views from non-elected members of society. Canada's position on APEC is a good example. In its turn as chair of that forum, one of Canada's key goals has been to increase the involvement of civil society organizations in the forum's process — a difficult task indeed.

PRACTICAL TOOLS

Based on material developed for the UNDP (Van Rooy 1996), this section of the chapter suggests ideas for dealing with questions about legitimacy and capacity on both sides of the diplomatic fence. These ideas are not meant as recipes, but rather as ways of thinking about relationships with new kinds of organizations.

Mutual Legitimacy Assessment

Key to the role of the ambassador is the art of juggling with legitimacy claims. Civil society organizations on the whole are a legitimate part of the democratic system and can sometimes be *more* legitimate than their governments, but we have no simple electoral yardstick to measure them. Many CSOs will visit heads of mission to share information, seek support for political projects, or raise funds. In each case, questions of legitimacy about the organization itself arise, but also about the proposed Canadian intervention.

TABLE 2: Legitimacy Assessment

Criteria	Legitimacy of Organization	Legitimacy of Post
Stakehold*	• Who might be affected (positively or negatively) by the concern to be addressed? • Who are the "voiceless" for whom special efforts may have to be made? • Who are the representatives of those likely to be affected? • Who is responsible for what is intended? • Who is likely to mobilize for or against what is intended? • Who can make what is intended more effective through their participation or less effective by their non-participation or outright opposition? • Who can contribute financial and technical resources? • Whose behaviour has to change for the effort to succeed?	What stake does the post have in the process? Does the post's intervention affect how the organization represents or serves its members? negatively or positively? (i.e., how onerous are its reporting require-ments?)
Election/ Selection	• Is there a process whereby leaders in an organization are chosen which satisfies the membership? • Does the organization respond to the needs of its constituency or mem-bership?	How will the post's involvement affect the perceived legitimacy of the proposed partners?
Comprehensive membership	• Does the organization represent all those who *could* be members? Are there competing forces? If so, does that division help or hinder the chances for desired change?	Has the post reviewed the work of others in this field? Has a coordinated approach been tried?
Multi-sectoral respect	• Does the organization have the respect of key players in other sectors or issue-areas, even if they hold opposing views? • Is it relevant whether the organiza-tion holds registered status? If so, does it hold that status? If not, why?	

Note: *Some of these questions are excerpted from World Bank 1996.

Too often, in assessing the political lay of the land and the role of CSOs, we focus on organizational types or names that appear to be similar to organizations we are familiar with in Canada. Yet CSOs occupy a politically complex ground, distinct from country to country. Kenyan Girl Guides, for example, play a much larger role in community service and in promoting political and gender awareness than their Canadian counterparts — a role we might not notice if we looked at organizational type alone.

One way of getting out of those conventions is to walk methodically through a list of questions about legitimacy. There are questions of voice and representation, about the politics of an organization's existence, about the nature of governance, about Canada's own policies and their legitimacy, and about intended and unintended consequences of action. The key in dealing with CSOs is to begin with the post's own role and legitimacy within the host country and to begin to ask questions of the organization from that vantage point. Table 2 suggests one way of organizing those inquiries.

In the end, ambassadors do not judge the legitimacy of the new organizations arriving on their doorstep very differently than they evaluate other, more traditional interlocutors. The difference is that the criteria for legitimacy *outside* an elected, governmental system or the marketplace require more research. The stake a new organization has in a particular political outcome, its own representative function and membership, as well as the respect accorded it by other players are not as immediately obvious to foreign mission staff as they might be for a visiting official or businessperson. The point, however, is that the task is not different in kind, but simply in degree.

Mutual Capacity Assessment

Only after questions of legitimacy have been broached do questions about capacity to undertake joint work become relevant. Too often, we consider whether or not an organization *can* do something before deciding whether or not it *should*. Similarly, we often neglect to examine the capacity of the Canadian post: Given the mandates and mix of abilities on site, what is possible? Table 3 looks at some criteria derived for donors in examining capacity questions. The point here is that capacity assessment is also not a mysterious undertaking — ethical and politically sensitive standards are applicable and practical.

As in the section on legitimacy, these questions are standard ones, applicable across sectors although tuned to the work undertaken by CSOs. For representatives from other governments and for private sector actors, many of the answers are probably already known by diplomatic actors, but they are always *implicitly* asked. The kind of checklist indicated in Table 2 simply illustrates that working

TABLE 3: Capacity Assessment

Criteria	Organization Capacities	Post Capacities
Experience	• Has the group done exactly this kind of work before? How have they managed the work? the administrative load? the financial load? • Has the group undertaken similar work before?	• Do the relevant post staff members have experience in the area? • Are they able to draw from experience elsewhere?
Recommendation	• What do other peer organizations say about their work? about their stake in the project? • What do other donors say about their work? about their stake?	• Is the post able to gather peer assessments?
Qualifications	• Are formal qualifications necessary to the project? If so, are they held by the group's members? Can they be acquired? • What informal qualifications seem necessary? Are they held by the group's members? Can they be acquired?	• Does the post have the appropriate skills to transfer? to learn from the organization concerned?
Longevity	• How long has the organization been doing the kind of work envisaged? What was it doing before? Does the work envisaged build on previous experiences?	• How long has the post been involved in the host country? What networks has it developed?
Sustainability	• How has the group managed to stay together to date? 1. Financially (noting that reliance on external funding is not necessarily a sign of weakness.) 2. Organizationally (how has the organization changed to reflect its needs? niche?) 3. Within the sector (how does the organization fit within its network – is it likely to remain an important component?)	• What commitments is the post able to make to the given problem? its individual project-solutions? the organizations which are broaching them?

relationships with CSOs can be of the same type, but require more research to develop. Again, diplomatic interaction with non-diplomats is nothing new; the cast has simply been altered. These kinds of schemas illustrate how the same rules can be applied to the newcomers.

CONCLUDING THOUGHTS

These matrices of questions are meant to help heads of mission understand and deal with the growing population of civil society organizations they will meet and watch in their work abroad. As the number of organizations grows, it may help to think of CSOs as organized evidence of the values of a wider society, in their aggregate, vital to the construction of public interest and good governance. This civil organizing is, of course, critical for our own democracy and for the quality of policy and practice undertaken by our representatives abroad. One participant in our workshop, for example, rightly called civil society "the fundamental fabric" of our country.

The growing importance of CSOs does not indicate a waning of the relevance of the state, however; nor in turn does it mark a waning of the role of the ambassador as representative of the state. In day-to-day mission life, the state is personified in the head of mission who, like everyone else in the foreign service, is meeting private individuals, bureaucrats, diplomats, and a range of groups promoting different points of view. The job of the ambassador and staff is to continue to walk a diplomatic tightrope. Decisions still rest formally, and finally, with Parliament and the state's representatives, but the process of coming to a decision has been — happily, I argue — complicated by a changing cast of characters.

NOTES

1. The North-South Institute will co-publish with Earthscan a study on this topic in 1998, titled *Civil Society and the Aid Industry,* with chapters on civil societies and donors in Kenya, Sri Lanka, Peru, and Hungary.
2. See Kumar 1993; Chandhoke 1995; Keane 1988; Cohen and Arato 1992; Hall 1995.
3. The *Directory of Associations in Canada, 1993-94* (Micromedia Ltd., 1994) lists some 20,000 voluntary, non-profit associations in Canada formed to promote particular causes, especially in the public interest. Groups concentrate on issues as diverse as abortion, work safety, cross-cultural education, dance, business promotion, ornithology, and literacy. About 60, including the Heart and Stroke Foundation, have budgets of over $5 million, but the majority work with budgets under $100,000. The 350 figure is an estimate drawn from Van Rooy 1994.

4. Calculated on a cash basis, minus debt relief, from figures prepared by the Policy Unit of the Canadian Council for International Cooperation.
5. In Eastern Europe, in many "countries in transition," the movement to enlarge the space for civil society has met with mixed success. In 1995, US philanthropist George Soros criticized developments in Slovakia, calling for the development of the third sector as a base for an open civil society. His comments sparked a campaign by the government coalition not only against Soros' Open Society Foundation, but also other foreign foundations supporting politically active, non-governmental organizations. According to local activists, "the final target of the campaign, however, were Slovak citizens' organizations that have never been and never will be ready to accept the totalitarian practices of the current government coalition," (Zamkovsky and Mesik 1996). In the spring of 1996, the government of V. Meciar put into place laws to curtail civil society (the law on foundations, an amendment of the Act on Civic Associations), freedom of speech (the press law), and legislation designed to conserve the governing coalition's power over the long term (changes in the system of territorial administration and in the election system, among others).

12

An Ambassador by any Other Name?
Provincial Representatives Abroad

Kim Richard Nossal

> *Legatus provincialis est vir bonus peregre*
> *missus qui erogat nimiam pecuniam respublicae.*
>
> With apologies to Sir Henry Wooton

> *Oh, I didn't know that.*
>
> Ontario minister responsible for international relations,
> when asked if he knew that the provincial
> offices abroad he had just ordered closed
> had been opened and closed three times before

INTRODUCTION

The popular tag has it that an ambassador is a good person sent abroad to lie for the commonwealth; it would seem that the popular view of those individuals who are sent abroad by Canada's provincial governments to represent the province is that they are good people sent abroad — who spend too much of the commonwealth's money. This view has resulted in what might be best described as a "banging door" policy of openings and closings of Canadian provincial missions abroad. Provincial governments are constantly opening new offices abroad (as they are allowed to do under section 92.4 of the *Constitution Act, 1867*, which provides provincial governments with authority over "establishment and tenure of provincial offices"); they are constantly despatching new provincial agents to represent the province in other jurisdictions. With equal consistency, however, the provincial

governments also close these offices and recall their representatives. Like annoy-
ing doors banging in the wind, these offices are forever opening and then slam-
ming shut, often with an apparent randomness. Moreover, there appears to be
little learning curve evident in the process: the provincial ministers who preside
over the openings and closings of offices abroad are seemingly oblivious to the
persistence in the longer-term pattern of their behaviour (as the comment from
the Ontario minister quoted above suggests).

The purpose of this chapter is to examine why provincial governments send
provincial representatives (who are known by various titles, such as agent general
or *délégué générale*) to other jurisdictions, and why they open and close missions
abroad as frequently as they do. I will argue that there are good reasons for non-
central governments like Canada's provinces to maintain permanent representatives with all the trappings of official missions in other countries. And, once in a
while, Canadian provincial governments catch the wave of such reasoning and
seek to put their person in place. But I will also argue that there is a contrary
dynamic — a deeply ingrained propensity to close these offices by those who
manage provincial finances. Often seen as expensive extravagances that produce
no visible "deliverables," provincial offices abroad offer the most inviting targets
for budget-cutters.

I will suggest that much of this willingness to recall representatives and close
offices abroad — and in the process throw away not only the sunk costs of opening the mission in the first place, but also the human capital invested in this enterprise — comes from a fundamental misunderstanding of the function of these
representatives abroad by those who manage provincial finances. The representatives of provincial governments may not have the formal diplomatic credentials
necessary for participation in the "society" that sovereign states have created for
themselves.[1] They may not enjoy the symbolic perks of diplomatic immunity, and
they certainly do not get to participate in the world of sovereign diplomacy on an
equal footing with the ambassadors of sovereign states. But a great deal of the
activity of provincial agents abroad — and that of the permanent missions that
sustain them — is activity that is fundamentally generic. In particular, provincial
representatives share with their federal counterparts a task that all "external" representatives of all institutions (governments, firms, organizations) engage in:
diplomacy, or the effort to manage a bilateral relationship smoothly.

This, however, does not tend to be the perspective from provincial capitals.
Rather, the view from provincial capitals tends to be — what else? — provincial.
The functions of the resident agent abroad tend to be interpreted in ways that lead
provincial officials to believe that diplomatic functions are not important to the
interests of the province — at least not as important as saving several million
dollars here and there. As a result, those who manage public finances for the

province also tend to find the target offered by the overseas representative simply too tempting for budget-cutting.

THE BANGING DOOR OF PROVINCIAL REPRESENTATION ABROAD

From the earliest days of Confederation, the idea of providing the province with a permanent overseas representative has been attractive to many provincial governments. In 1882, Quebec sent Hector Fabre as its agent general to Paris; in 1911 it opened a commercial office in Britain; and in 1915 a Quebec agency was opened in Brussels. Commercial offices were opened in Britain — by Ontario in 1908 and by Quebec in 1911. In addition, Quebec opened an agency in Brussels in 1915 (see Hilliker 1990; also Beaudoin 1977, p. 447; Hamelin 1969, pp. 19-26; Keith 1912, vol. 1, p. 343; Balthazar 1993, pp. 140-52).

But this early activity was relatively short-lived. The Quebec government closed the provincial agency in Paris in 1912, because the French business community was so uninterested in Quebec. Both the missions in Brussels and London were closed in the early 1930s in an effort to trim provincial expenditures during the Great Depression. And when the Union Nationale under Maurice Duplessis came to power in 1936, he ordered all of Quebec's representatives abroad to be withdrawn; not content merely to decree the closure administratively, the premier sought to entrench the closure by passing a law against the maintenance of overseas representation (Beaudoin 1977, p. 461).

The end of both the Great Depression and the Second World War saw a rapid increase in the social welfare function of the state in Canada at both the federal and provincial levels. This increased the burden on the provinces to provide social and other services, and created in turn a need for provincial governments to promote the growth of their economies to provide the funds necessary for the provision of expanded provincial services — an imperative that, of course, had an implicit electoral connection. Thus, the expansion of provincial trade, the maintenance and expansion of a provincial infrastructure, and the raising of capital in foreign markets assumed increased importance in the post-1945 period. This economic imperative was one reason for the rapid growth of provincial representation abroad, particularly in financial centres.

Thus, for example, Ontario reopened its London office in 1945; it opened a number of missions in the United States: Chicago in 1953, New York in 1956, and Los Angeles and Cleveland in 1967. Five Ontario missions were opened on the European continent in the 1960s: Milan in 1963, Stockholm in 1968, Brussels and Vienna in 1969, and Frankfurt in 1970. Ontario missions were opened in Tokyo in 1969 and Mexico City in 1973.

Quebec followed a similar pattern. It established a mission in New York as early as 1943, but the major expansion in its external representation did not come until the 1960s, when, in a few short years, missions were opened in Paris (1961), London (1962), Chicago and Milan (1965), Dusseldorf, Los Angeles, Boston, Dallas, and Lafayette (1970), Brussels (1972), and Tokyo (1973).

The other provinces demonstrated a different pattern. Alberta, which had had an office in London since 1948, opened one in Los Angeles in 1964 and a mission in Tokyo in 1970. Some provinces — Prince Edward Island, Newfoundland, New Brunswick, Manitoba, and Saskatchewan — tended either to avoid overseas representation altogether or to keep an office in London open. Patterns were idiosyncratic: New Brunswick tried an office in London from 1970 but closed it in 1975; perhaps not surprisingly given north-south flows, Manitoba opened an office in Minneapolis in 1975; somewhat more improbably, Nova Scotia operated a tourism office in Wisconsin for some years in the 1970s. British Columbia's contacts were primarily on the west coast. By the early 1980s, seven provinces were operating over 35 agencies on three continents (Blanchette 1980, p. 302); by 1990, eight were operating 40 offices abroad, 23 of which were in the United States (Fry 1989).

At the same time, however, the pattern of opening and closing was rather sporadic and not at all predictable. Between 1967 and 1977, for example, both Ontario and Quebec had each opened three offices; but both provincial governments had also each closed three offices as economy measures. Other provinces followed suit. Indeed, throughout this period, openings and closings occurred with such frequency that mapping them becomes the only way to get a sense of who has an office where.[2]

Ontario offers an interesting case study of the banging-door syndrome at work. In the past 25 years, it has gone through the opening/closing cycle three times. In the boom years of the late 1960s and early 1970s, the Ontario government opened offices around the world, only to close many of them in the middle of the 1970s as a cost-cutting measure. In the early 1980s, the number of offices grew again, and then contracted by the middle of the decade, and then grew once again under the Liberal government of David Peterson. And, then, once again, they were closed by the New Democratic Party government of Bob Rae in the early 1990s. The pattern has been particularly pronounced in the case of Ontario's offices in the United States. At one time or another, Ontario has opened offices in ten American cities, it has closed five, and reopened two. The Ontario offices in Boston and Atlanta are indicative: both offices were opened in 1968, and both were closed in 1975; Atlanta was opened again in 1980 and Boston in 1985; both were closed in 1991.

THE IMPETUS FOR OPENING

What prompts a provincial government to open an office abroad? A generalized answer is that all Canadian provinces are propelled abroad by economic interests. As has been noted above, the expanding welfare role of the provincial state after the Second World War gave larger provinces considerable impetus to extend themselves well beyond the geographic bounds of neighbourhood. But the increasingly global reach of some provinces more recently reflects the increasing globalization of the world economy over the last 50 years — a process marked by the growing integration of international financial markets, the internationalization of trade and investment, and the growing importance of tourism. Provincial governments, eager to maintain the economic competitiveness of the provincial economy in a changing international division of labour, and hence the economic security of their citizens, have sought to respond to the processes of globalization by extending the reach of their activities out into the international sphere, in search of new markets for the products of provincial industry, and new sources of investment. To be sure, the overwhelming pull tends not to be truly "international," but hemispheric and continental, as the focus of much provincial activity in this sphere remains fixed on the United States. But as the American economy itself became increasingly globalized in the 1980s and 1990s, the challenges of the global economy became greater (Nossal 1996, pp. 503-18).

There are also political reasons. Most obviously, provincial governments can treat the appointment of representatives abroad as a form of patronage. Unlike the federal prime minister, who can appoint party faithful to the Senate to trough undisturbed into their dotage, provincial premiers have a harder time finding comparable rewards for their faithful. And just as the federal government has used some diplomatic missions abroad for patronage appointments, so too have provincial premiers been attracted to the idea of using missions abroad for similar purposes. But sometimes the political reasoning is not as base, though perhaps just as idiosyncratic. For example, the Ontario Liberal government of David Peterson was seized with the idea, fashionable in the late 1980s, that many national economies were propelled by vibrant regional economies, known colloquially as "motors." The idea was that focusing Ontario's economic activity on a "motor" was more effective than diffusing that activity within a broader national economy. Thus, much of Ontario's new overseas activity during the Peterson government can be attributed to what one federal official disparagingly called that government's "obsession" with the "four motors" of Europe — Baden-Württemberg in Germany, Rhône-Alps in France, Lombardy in Italy, and Catalonia in Spain — even to the point of becoming an associate member of the Four Motors grouping (see Dyment 1993, pp. 162-63).

In addition, one province has an additional and distinct set of motivations for international activity and maintaining representation abroad. Whether the province is governed by a federalist-oriented party such as the Liberals or a sovereigntist party such as the Parti Québécois, the impetus for the Quebec government is to maintain representatives abroad for the political purpose of projecting a sense of the province's distinct status into the international system. In addition, Quebec's overseas representatives are responsible for implementing the province's immigration policy, encouraging immigration to the province. Thus, while Quebec is propelled outwards like every other province for economic reasons, it also has additional political motivations.[3]

Whether the impetus is primarily political or primarily economic, the search for a local and resident anchor for this international provincial activity flows naturally. If one looks at the stated reasons for office openings, one can readily see the degree to which the rationalization for such representation is deeply grounded in geoeconomic location. (Note, however, that these rationalizations are distinctly *ex post facto*: provincial governments rarely explain why they *didn't* establish a representative in a particular city.) Many of Quebec's offices have more obviously political rather than geoeconomic rationalizations.

TABLE 1: Stated Reasons for Selected Office Locations

Province	Foreign Office	Stated Reason
British Columbia	Seattle	Easy launch point for BC exporters
	Irvine	Industry sectors targeted by BC government centred there
Ontario	Atlanta	Main centre for southeast
	Chicago	Centre of US investment in Ontario; prime destination of Ontario exports
	Hong Kong	Centre of Asia Pacific trade; HK Chinese link with Toronto
Saskatchewan	Minneapolis	Centre for half of Saskatchewan's exports and imports
Nova Scotia	Boston	Historical destination of Nova Scotia exports
Quebec	New York	Centre of financial investment; centre of international organizations
	Paris	Centre of francophone activities
	Hong Kong	Centre of Asia Pacific trade
	All US offices except Louisiana	Regional economic trading centres

Source: Adapted from McNiven and Cann, 1993, table 6.4, p. 174.

Because of the close connection with the economic purpose of these offices, one might think that their opening and closing would be connected in some fashion to fluctuations in the business cycle. One can see some elements of this dynamic at work. Provincial representatives do tend to be sent abroad in larger numbers when the provincial economy is expanding — and recalled when the provincial economy shrinks and budgets are tightened. This trend has been seen, particularly in Ontario: offices were closed during the 1930s, opened in the boom years of the 1960s, closed in the recession of the mid-1970s, opened again in the 1980s, and closed again in the recession of the early 1990s.

It might be thought that it would be precisely during periods of recession that provinces would expand rather than contract foreign representation, in order to encourage increased international economic activity. Only in one turn of the cycle have we seen this logic at work: the spate of provincial office openings in the early 1980s appears to have been driven by the desire to increase economic activity — this round of openings occurred at the very time when recession was hitting the economy of all provinces particularly hard.

The idea of despatching a provincial representative to other jurisdictions has considerable attractiveness, largely because a resident can perform so many functions and fulfil so many purposes that a non-resident simply could not. McNiven and Cann outline briefly the various functions of a resident representative (1993, pp. 178-81). The primary function of most provincial representatives abroad is unabashedly economic: to promote trade and investment between the province and the foreign jurisdiction; to promote provincial products and services in the foreign market; to identify local trade and investment opportunities for provincial businesses (and of course the obverse: to identify provincial trade and investment opportunities for local businesses). This means getting to know the local economic scene — its structure, the personalities of local businesspeople, its opportunities, where doors can be opened and where they will remain resolutely closed. The economic intelligence gathered, and the economic links established, cultivated, and maintained by the provincial representative, will be crucial for the success of higher level visits or trade missions.

But there are other functions that are not so obviously economic but nonetheless have considerable material benefits. For example, monitoring legislation and policy being considered by the foreign government that might have an impact on provincial interests — or acting as the first line for lobbying foreign governments when necessary are two related roles. Now it is true that lobbying is something that one could, in theory, leave to locally-engaged lobbyists or the diplomats of the federal Canadian government. However, it can be argued that there is little percentage in hiring foreign lawyers to work on the province's behalf. The structure of interests is all wrong: no one has an incentive to listen to, much less buy, the arguments put on the province's behalf by a locally-engaged lawyer in a foreign jurisdiction. Indeed, it can be argued that the only ones who clearly profit from such lobbying are the locally-engaged lawyers, suggesting that it is a mug's game. Leaving provincial interests in the hands of the Canadian federal government and its diplomats in the Department of Foreign Affairs and International Trade (DFAIT) makes somewhat more sense. DFAIT has an institutional store of knowledge and intelligence in dealing with the foreign jurisdiction that can be useful. On the other hand, because the central government, by definition, has bigger fish to fry, there is a persistent concern that provincial interests may get massaged in the service of a broader national interest.

Likewise, there is a range of other possibilities. For example, the promotion of provincial tourism could be left entirely to TV advertising, slick brochures, and toll-free phone numbers. But the high visibility of a glad-handing provincial representative can be equally as effective an advertisement for the delights of a province's tourist attractions. Provincial representatives can also be important facilitators of "twinning" relations between the province and the local jurisdiction, a "people-to-people" activity that can pay off in benefits, even if these tend to be somewhat unpredictable. Provincial representatives also assist in the negotiation of international agreements, network with consulates of other countries, and develop educational exchanges.[4]

Finally, provincial representatives, like their federal counterparts, play an important and necessary travel-agent role. They are responsible for managing local visits for provincial politicians, ensuring that the keynote speech is given to crowded ballrooms, arranging for appropriate local and Canadian news coverage, making sure that the visiting politicians meet the appropriate people. (It should be noted that provincial representatives often expect the local Canadian embassy or consulate to undertake these tasks on behalf of the province, adding considerably to the burdens of the federal mission.) In short, these are functions that a non-resident advance person, sent in cold by the provincial government, simply could not engage in. "Being there," in other words, makes all the difference.

THE IMPETUS FOR CLOSING

Provincial governments might be attracted by the benefits of operating in the international system. But they are rarely happy when the bills for external operations come rolling in. After all, maintaining permanent representatives in other countries is a highly expensive proposition, and considerable resources are needed to play the game properly.

First, maintaining provincial offices in the major financial and/or political centres of the international system by definition involves major expenses. The high prices that come from high demand is, after all, a reflection of why these cities are international centres and why one wants to be there in the first place rather than located in some cheaper city. And there can be no doubt that the expenses that come with high demand can be daunting. Space must be rented in an appropriate part of town, and that usually means the high-priced financial district. It is true that one could "slum it" by locating one's office in more remote (and thus cheaper) parts of the city. For example, one does not need to locate one's office in Exchange Square in Hong Kong's Central District, or the City in London, or in Manhattan; one could as readily find office space in a nine-floor office building in Shatin in the New Territories, or Richmond-upon-Thames in London's southwest, or a walk-up in Queen's. But one pays heavily for not being accessible. Such accessibility is not only defined in a physical (i.e., it is easy for people to visit you, easy for you to get to them), but also in a metaphysical sense: choosing not to locate in a central, accessible, and yes, highly expensive, location sends important messages about how seriously one's government is taking the exercise.

Second, resident diplomacy requires entertaining, which is the ritualized method in international affairs for meeting people, getting to know individuals, exchanging gossip and intelligence, making one's presence felt, seeing and being seen. Again, there is no absolute need for this facet of diplomatic behaviour: a cocktail party is no more necessary to conclude a trade deal than a wedding reception is to marry two people, but trying to do it another way that runs against dominant norms is a hazardous exercise. When one is in Rome — or Hong Kong, or New York, or Tokyo — it makes little sense to behave as one would in the Mowat Block. But there can be no doubt: buying into the entertainment game adds significantly to the costs of the overall operation. It means housing for the agent that is appropriate for hosting sizeable parties — for surely it would be *infra dig* to have them at a commercial location rented for the occasion. And it means an appropriate budget, usually for servants, perhaps even for a car and driver. It means memberships at posh clubs and memberships at golf courses where initiation fees are priced at levels that can be afforded only by those operating on tabs paid for by shareholders or taxpayers.

Then there are the provincial representatives themselves. They and their families must be relocated, and housed in accommodations that are at least comparable to suburban middle-class Canada, but which in most international centres will run at prices akin to Marine Drive, Rosedale, Rockcliffe, or Mont Royal. And the normal package usually available to expatriate employees must also be provided: "comparable" schooling for the children, annual home leaves back to Canada, and special medical insurance. In short, setting up a permanent provincial representative in a major international centre involves not only considerable start-up costs, but also a major annual outlay. And even if one runs a frugal operation, the costs involved invariably stand out.

Moreover, the "returns" or "deliverables" are not always immediately visible. The careful cultivation of a local group of investors or entrepreneurs or dealmakers may not yield a payoff for a while. The benefits of having someone on the scene in a location who can interpret local conditions and provide decisionmakers back in the provincial capital with some more relevant advice than they are going to read in the *Wall Street Journal* or *The Globe and Mail* or pull off the WorldWideWeb may not often be apparent, particularly in those jurisdictions where one has to spend not only energy but time developing relationships, such as the Asia Pacific.

The problem is that deliverables are what jaundiced-eyed provincial officials in management boards back home want; time is what the provincial agent abroad does not have. The expense reports coming in every quarter from New York, or London, or Hong Kong, or Los Angeles, or Tokyo, or Brussels will jump off the print-outs at provincial officials who, it must be remembered, are stuck in the drab confines of the average provincial office block in the average provincial capital; they are constrained to eat plain lunches, play their golf on public courses, and drive themselves home at night to a house where the servants still haven't done the breakfast dishes — again. It is little wonder that such officials ask themselves what the province is getting out of what is invariably seen as an extravagance.

This dynamic — which pits an understandable parochialism (and perhaps even envy) against the exceedingly high costs of running an appropriate representative mission abroad — means that provincial offices abroad are a highly visible and attractive target for budget-cutting exercises. It is hardly surprising that provincial governments look at the costs, look at the clearly observable concrete returns, and conclude that there must be a cheaper way.

FRUGALITY: COSTS AND CURES

But there are costs to letting the door bang open and closed. For hinging provincial representation abroad to the mood swings of the capitalist economy inexorably produces an endless procession of openings and closings. There are two types of obvious costs. The first are the financial costs of starting up an operation (getting the leases, or purchasing the property, paying all the lawyers, setting up the offices, hiring the locally-engaged staff), and then some years later wrapping it, and then, a few years after that, doing it all again.

The other cost is the human capital that is wasted by opening and closing offices abroad. Instead of developing an institutionalized expertise that can be brought to bear, a revolving-door approach to missions abroad encourages a certain dilettantism and lack of professionalism among the one-off representatives that happen to luck out during a boom period of provincial office expansion. In other words, because of the lack of institutional continuity, extending over a number of decades, most provinces have not been able to develop the provincial bureaucratic equivalent of the federal foreign service, which is able to draw on a huge pool of officials who have been schooled and socialized in the ways of interstate diplomacy. (Here Quebec is once again the exception: since the 1960s, all Quebec governments, sovereigntist and non-sovereigntist alike, have put a premium on maintaining a highly professional permanent bureaucratic unit, the *Ministère des Affaires internationales*, that the province tries to make as indistinguishable as possible from the foreign ministry of a sovereign state.)

There are obvious ways to avoid the huge waste involved in opening and closing offices. One solution is to eschew such exercises altogether, and simply refuse to engage in personal diplomacy. Let locally-engaged advertising/marketing firms flog the province's delights as a tourist destination; let central government diplomats handle whatever political problem may arise; let the Canadian embassy or consulate or mission arrange logistics for a visiting provincial dignitary; let private firms, organizations, and individuals seek each other out, by themselves and without assistance from the state. In short, one could simply take the provincial government out of the international relations sphere altogether.

This may sound elegantly simple, and, when presented alongside the budget figures for foreign operations, may appear convincing to some provincial decisionmakers. But it would not be at all an attractive option to Quebec officials, who have well-entrenched political reasons for keeping the provincial government as deeply engaged in international relations as possible. And while Canada's other provinces lack Quebec's particular impetus for international activity, the pressure for diplomacy with a human link seems inexorable, and only the poorest provinces have been prone to resist the logic of having a provincial representative physically located in important financial or political centres abroad.

The key is to achieve the benefits of a resident presence without sending bean-counters back home into envious orbit. One solution being tried by provincial governments is "co-location" — renting space in the Canadian embassy, high commission, or consulate. This saves money, allows the province to maintain a presence abroad, sustains a modicum of institutionalized memory, and avoids having to spend large amounts on start-up costs. Another is a practice copied from Britain: the Ontario Ambassadors program hires corporate executives for $1 per year to act as part-time business ambassadors abroad (*The Globe and Mail*, 5 February 1996).

A third option is the possibility of privatizing some of the diplomatic functions, contracting them out. This latter option may offer some superficial attractiveness, but just because an operation is privatized will not, *ipso facto*, reduce the expenses of operating abroad. Moreover, unless numerous other jurisdictions also move to privatized diplomatic operations at the same time, there is a real possibility that privatized operations will be shunned, and shut out of the regular circuit. By contrast, if cost-cutting by numerous jurisdictions results in a transformation, and increasing numbers of jurisdictions are represented abroad by private companies, then it is possible that we will see a small transformation in diplomatic practice.

CONCLUSIONS

I have argued in this chapter that provincial representatives abroad, if they are doing what their governments pay them to do, are often engaged in activities that are not markedly different from their central government and sovereign counterparts. The form may be different — provincial representatives are not concerned with the rituals of the sovereign state system — but the essence of their *diplomatic* purpose does not change. The key functions associated with the diplomats of sovereign states — representation, communication, promotion of their political community's interests, negotiation, public diplomacy, intelligence gathering, and providing advice to one's home government — are also performed by the resident representatives of provinces.

The one major difference is that there is a more entrenched willingness to recognize the importance of these kinds of functions at the federal level, and lay out significant sums to support resident representatives abroad. Federal diplomats may grumble about the degree to which a cost-cutting culture cuts into the ability to advance Canadian interests in the international system; the federal government may be engaged in downsizing and even closing missions; it may be experimenting with such innovations as co-location with other countries or single-person missions. But there is no question about the federal government's commitment to the *idea* of resident representation abroad.

At the provincial level, by contrast, the recognition of the worth of provincial diplomacy tends to be more scattered, less deeply ingrained, and more ephemeral. As a consequence, the *idea* of provincial representation abroad is not well rooted in provinces other than Quebec; and fresh cohorts of representatives despatched abroad during the periodic fits of enthusiasm of provincial governments rarely survive the razor of a determined cost-cutter — until the next time, that is, when the wheel is discovered once again, and, with much fanfare, an enthusiastic minister opens an expensive provincial mission abroad.

NOTES

1. Here I follow Hedley Bull (1977) in assuming that the various governments in the international system which are deemed to be endowed with sovereignty constitute a kind of society separate from the non-sovereign actors in world politics.
2. For such a list of openings and closings of provincial offices in the United States, see McNiven and Cann (1993) table 6.3, p. 172.
3. For discussion, see Balthazar (1993); also Nossal (1997, chap. 12).
4. McNiven and Cann (1993, pp. 178-81); for a discussion of "twinning" with China, see MacLean and Nossal (1993, pp. 170-89).

13

Many Masters: How Others See the Head of Mission

Alan B. Nymark, Jean-Marc Métivier, David Lee,
Peter Sutherland and Michael Pearson

Heads of missions all have similar responsibilities, but how they do their work differs as much as the circumstances of Canada's 157 missions and offices abroad. Any attempt to draw the diffuse threads of this book together in a summary would therefore be misleading. The difficulty is compounded because the head of mission, rather than being simply the servant of the minister of foreign affairs, is in fact responsible to the entire government, and to all Canadians.[1] In lieu of a conclusion, since no single perspective on diplomatic missions would suffice, this chapter allows a representative group of the ambassador's diverse masters to describe how they see diplomatic missions.[2] They write from the perspective of other government departments (Health Canada); another agency of the Foreign Affairs portfolio (the Canadian International Development Agency); the multilateral side of Foreign Affairs (since the focus of the volume is on the resident ambassador, whose working environment is quite distinct from that of the permanent representative to an international organization); the business community; and a minister's office.

"HEALTH POLICY IS FOREIGN POLICY... "

Alan Nymark

Discussing the role of Canadian missions from a domestic department's perspective is no longer possible. I do not accept the premise that there is a purely domestic point of view to consider. We have long since passed the point where any major department at the federal level operates in anything other than a global context. A survey for the Canadian Foreign Service Institute discovered that 4,500 people outside the Department of Foreign Affairs and International Trade (DFAIT) and the Canadian International Development Agency (CIDA) claimed to be spending at least 50 percent of their time on international issues. That figure may understate matters. My department, for example, in one branch now has 2,800 scientists who operate at the global level in that their expertise is intellectual and their network is international — but they do not rely on DFAIT. Globalization is far more than the exchange of goods and services — it is about the transmission of ideas; it is about culture and the human predicament. The international dimension of many departments, but notably Health Canada, has grown incrementally in response to globalization in travel, trade, and immigration. Foreign policy, in consequence, increasingly has a human dimension. Therefore, I want to describe why we think we are not a domestic department and, conversely, why DFAIT is not merely the *foreign* ministry. All international issues must relate either to the government's agenda or to the welfare of Canadians. Most so-called domestic departments have large foreign policy agendas, and only a small part of those foreign policy agendas come through DFAIT. The biggest challenge for the foreign ministry is articulating how it relates to the domestic agenda.

I would like to address how we see diplomatic missions in terms of our expectations, which are probably common to many departments, then, to illustrate those expectations, to briefly describe some issues in which Health Canada is engaged with our missions. I think of our expectations in three categories. First, in a strategic context, all departments need to know what Canada's relationship is with another country, in its political, institutional, security, social, or an economic dimension, and whether particular foreign policy considerations impinge on our interest in developing a more specialized relationship with someone in that society.

Second, we expect missions to be knowledge brokers, whether by acquiring, generating, or disseminating knowledge. To take one example, Canada spends a great deal of public money on health — we are anxious to share information and to learn from the policy experiences of comparable societies. Talking about this aspect of foreign relations now may be fashionable, but we probably do rely on our foreign missions primarily in their role as knowledge brokers, and it is a role that we have not thought through as carefully as we should from a client perspective.

Third, we expect operational support from missions. Operational in the context of health obviously means the immigration process, but health is also part of development assistance, and health is part of trade relations. For example, increasingly food, medical devices, and pharmaceuticals are being imported from non-traditional partners. Such things as alternative and herbal medicines are huge areas of international commerce not now subject to traditional regulation. Health Canada has to move into this area, even if some people in DFAIT worry about potential trade barriers. We want to ensure that new regulations are not protectionist, but we have to ensure the health and safety of Canadians who consume these products. We rely on our missions to help us understand the context in which potentially alternative medicines are used in their host countries. Many other trade issues arise from the role of governments as major producers and consumers of health-related goods and services.

A different kind of operational support is relevant at multilateral missions. As a department we spend $35 million a year on international health organizations. Of course, we have a direct relationship with these organizations, but we count on the head of mission to help us manage the relationship to maximize the return on our investment. One of the oldest areas in modern international cooperation among states is disease surveillance. New diseases, like ebola, are arising, while old diseases such as plague, are gaining new vigour. Diseases ignore borders; they can now be transmitted within 24 hours; and many new diseases have no known sources and no cures. Protecting the health and safety of Canadians starts in foreign countries, not at the border. The first line of defence is often our embassy in an affected country, where our head of mission must be familiar with these issues, and the second is international cooperation, either with international organizations like the World Health Organization, or with national organizations, like the US Centers for Disease Control in Atlanta. In both cases, our missions play a role.

I like Louis Delvoie's suggestion that perhaps all health policy is foreign policy, and all foreign policy is health policy. We, along with most modern countries, do not view health as the treatment of sickness and disease. The size of the Canadian health system, big as it is (accounting for 10 percent of GDP and 9.6 percent of all the jobs in the country) is only one determinant of the health of the population. Trying to reduce smoking can have a bigger impact on health than increased spending on hospitals. Poverty is a primary determinant of health. In Aboriginal communities, the quality of the health system available is probably the factor that affects the health of the population the least. International peace and security, or trade and investment promotion can be viewed as health policy, even if the only "domestic" department engaged on the issue is the foreign ministry. Nuclear war, or a failure to participate in the global economy could certainly be seen as determinants of health. Of course much of what Health Canada does is not "foreign policy" in this sense, but much of foreign affairs is in our domain in some way.

"INTERNATIONAL DEVELOPMENT IS FOREIGN POLICY..."

Jean-Marc Métivier

In its major review of foreign policy (Canada 1995), the Chrétien government said international assistance is a vital tool for the achievement of its central foreign policy objectives. When the Canadian International Development Agency was young, Canada's relationship with developing countries was largely contained within the area of development assistance, especially in Africa. Over the last 15 years, the relationship has become much more complex — security issues, environmental issues, trade issues, and political issues have become, in many cases, more important than the development relationship alone. The current mandate of CIDA as clarified in the foreign policy review is to promote sustainable development in developing countries to reduce poverty and contribute to a more secure, equitable, and prosperous world. The review also established priorities for development assistance: basic human needs, infrastructure, environment, the role of women in development, the role of the private sector, and finally, human rights, governance, and democratic institutions.

In the past, relations between CIDA and the Department of Foreign Affairs were marked by controversy and conflict as the two departments tried to pursue different policy agendas. Some people in CIDA saw poverty reduction as the only objective, believing that we should not weaken the mandate of the agency by considering trade or political issues. That point of view is no longer in the forefront; now the more commonly held view is that development can only be sustained in a secure, prosperous environment. There is no contradiction in pursuing development objectives and, at the same time, contributing to broader Canadian foreign policy directions.

The new CIDA mandate may take us into the realm of foreign policy, but CIDA cannot fulfill its responsibilities without the active engagement of heads of mission. Cooperation begins in Ottawa where we have what we call a shared agenda with DFAIT. We encourage officials in both departments to work closely to develop broad program objectives in a region and then define specific activities that should emerge from this vision. Sharing the agenda is even more important at posts — it is essential for the heads of each program to work together. The leadership role of the ambassador is crucial.

Our first expectation of heads of mission is sound analysis. In each country in which CIDA programs are active, we depend on mission staff to help us understand the social, economic, and political situation and the strategic issues in the relationship between the host country and Canada. We also expect to learn about the effectiveness of our programs and our projects. This is not to say that we expect the ambassador to undertake micro-level assessments of our programs; rather, CIDA establishes a broad strategic direction for its programs with the head of post who then is in the best position to monitor progress toward achievement of the general goals of the project. A second important, if traditional, role for heads of post is the establishment of contacts with key decisionmakers. From our perspective, we see a need to broaden this network beyond government circles and the business community to include academics and non-governmental institutions. In many countries, as Alison Van Rooy argues in this volume, issues related to governance are largely dealt with through civil society organizations.

"FOREIGN POLICY SUPPORTS MULTILATERALISM..."

David Lee

What do we expect of our bilateral ambassadors from a multilateral point of view? My point of departure is that all heads of mission must understand the place of multilateral institutions and multilateral diplomacy at the core of Canadian foreign policy, whether seen from a trade and economic perspective or from the political and security side. As that reality is unlikely to change, part of representing Canada will be reflecting the multilateral dimension of our policy. The second point I would make is that multilateral issues will not have the same importance at every post. Heads of mission must ask if multilateral relationships are important in their host country. Are there points of convergence between Canadian policy in the multilateral area and that of the country concerned? I am thinking here not just at the government level but also at the civil society level where work and reflection on multilateral activities take place.

My third point is again perhaps an obvious one: for some posts at some times, the multilateral dimension will be particularly important. At times the posts in G7 countries prepare for summit meetings, as do posts in the countries of la francophonie or NATO or the Commonwealth. The role is sometimes direct, in the traditional sense of passing messages between the Canadian and host governments. However, even in the absence of direct tasking, posts must be aware of host-country views on multilateral issues, they must know who the key officials are, and they must be reporting to Ottawa. In this domain as in so many others, the head of mission is a vital source of information.

My fourth and final point is that this understanding of Canada's interests and of the host country's views on a multilateral issue come together when bilateral heads of mission must make representations on policy issues or support campaigns for election to senior positions in international organizations. Whether it is a campaign for election to the United Nations security council or a campaign for a Canadian to be chosen as head of a particular international organization, it is important to the government that our bilateral posts have the capacity to know the decisionmakers and the ability to make our case at a senior level.

"THE AMBASSADOR IS A MEMBER OF TEAM CANADA..."

Peter Sutherland

The expectations placed on heads of post by the business community go back more than 100 years, to the time when the first officials serving abroad were trade commissioners. In effect, businesspeople have always looked to ambassadors to support their efforts, but in recent years they have come to expect even more of them.

I believe heads of mission have become more central to business enterprise in Canada for three reasons. The role of trade and investment in the Canadian economy now, quite justifiably, has a higher public profile. In the first half of the 1990s more than 40 percent of the new jobs created in Canada came from trade and investment. Such statistics have attracted attention from the media, from the business community, and from politicians — the phenomenon of Team Canada missions led by the prime minister is a clear demonstration of the importance the government attaches to this part of our foreign policy operations. Those in the business community understand the signals the government is sending, they recognize that trade is a priority, and in consequence they expect a great deal from heads of mission.

As well, Canadian firms must now relate to the world in more varied and complex ways, and the demands they make on missions abroad are correspondingly more varied and complex. In addition to the comparatively straightforward task of establishing relationships to sell goods, today the economic dimension also includes investment, the foreign dimension of science and technology, and a complex array of economic- and information-related activities.

The nature of the clientele has also changed. People in business now tend to be much better informed when they are dealing with our posts overseas. In part, this is because the export community is very small — roughly 50 firms account for 50 percent of our total exports and something like 5,000 firms account for 95 percent. The men and women running these firms are experienced exporters who know their business and are no longer content with rudimentary information that is available to the public from other, often electronic sources. They want value-added advice and counselling from heads of mission.

What do they look for specifically? Recently our new heads of posts were briefed by a panel of businesspeople that included representatives of large multi-million dollar corporations as well as much smaller companies, firms with under $5 million turnover and 25 to 50 employees. The range of views expressed indicates that businesspeople expect market intelligence, advice, access to a network of contacts, advocacy, leadership, and coordinating skills from heads of mission.

Intelligence is required in both senses of the word. Businesspeople want heads of mission to give them a feel for the environment in the market. They want to know about the political and economic situation, and about the country's relationship with Canada. They want relevant information about the playing field — will they be able to repatriate invested capital, for example — before they decide to do business in that market. Ambassadors are in the best position to gather this type of information, and businesspeople expect them to provide it.

The advice the business community requests from heads of mission can be relatively elementary or require more expertise. For example, it can range from suggesting potential partners or providing lists of the key people to deal with to ensure the success of an investment, to providing informed reaction to proposed strategy for entering a specific market.

Businesspeople expect ambassadors to develop a network of accessible and useful contacts in their host country. The head of mission who does not have access to key people in the political sphere, as well as to business leaders, bankers, and cultural leaders, may be asked to explain to those he represents why he does not have such access. When a team from a major exporter is negotiating a huge contract, they expect mission personnel to provide access to the right minister at the right time.

Ambassadors are the businessperson's advocate in the host country. That role may include escorting Canadians to meetings with important customers in both the public and private sector, and then working to ensure that the playing field remains level — not an easy task when other large G7 countries are using their political influence to tilt important negotiations.

Finally, business people look to a head of mission to be a team leader, a coordinator. They recognize the value of the tools at the ambassador's disposal — all the different programs that can be marshalled to support a particular objective. The leadership role includes setting an example for the rest of the mission. Businesspeople on the panel observed that it is the head of mission who determines the nature of the response they receive from others in the mission. If the ambassador is available to and interested in the needs of the business community then the people who work for the ambassador are going to be equally responsive. Consequently, they look to ambassadors to be the real leaders setting the tone and indicating the critical importance of the trade and investment portfolio to staff members.

As Tony Eyton stresses in this volume, business really does expect the ambassador to be Canada's chief trade commissioner.

"GOOD AMBASSADORS MAKE FOR GOOD MINISTERS..."

Michael Pearson

One of the recurrent myths of diplomacy is that greater ease of travel allows ministers to conduct foreign relations, diminishing the role of the head of mission. It is not true. In my experience as a senior policy adviser to two ministers, I have found that the ambassador remains central to diplomacy. Canada's heads of mission and their staff do an outstanding job supporting their minister. The foreign minister relies on advice from heads of mission when setting priorities, and even more when travelling abroad.

On the question of setting priorities, feedback from the field about what the minister is trying to do is vital. Ambassadors have to try to explain the policy, or to implement it. Some complex issues may serve a headquarters agenda, but may make less sense to people in the field. I think knowing what heads of mission and their staff understand a policy to mean in the context of their own experience can be invaluable to a minister.

Second, I want to say something about mandate letters. (Louis Delvoie discusses his letter in this volume, and excerpts from recent letters appear in Appendix B.) I have spent a lot of time, more time than I really should have, looking over mandate letters for heads of mission before the minister signed them and sent them to the prime minister for approval. There is a tendency for these mass-produced letters to be statements of a generic set of priorities into which are plugged the little things that seem to be relevant to a particular post. But I have often felt that the mandate letter was not an adequate expression of what the head of mission should be thinking about. I suppose many heads of mission even think they are, to some extent, superfluous because the letters say things they already know or fail to say what they want to know. I found that the statement of the policy objectives that any head of mission should pursue — beyond questions of management, beyond the narrowly defined bilateral relationship — are not there. I think that a clearer sense of direction should be given our ambassadors as they take up their posts.

A final point about setting priorities, and this will lead into my discussion of ministerial travel, is the issue of where a minister should go and, as important, why the minister should go there. Ministers are incredibly pressed for time as they pursue multiple agendas and interests. Every head of mission wants a visit from a minister. I remember one meeting with heads of mission from a certain region where each expressed their view about what was going on in their particular area of responsibility, and almost without exception, they all emphasized how important it was for the minister to travel to their location. I know how valuable the presence of the minister of foreign affairs can be to a mission, but there are many other ministers who may, at a particular time, be able to advance certain policy objectives more effectively than the foreign minister.

I would like to make two more mundane, but, I believe important, comments about ministerial travel abroad. The first is what I call the Vaughan Johnston rule, named for the long-serving protocol officer who has accompanied more ministers on more foreign trips than any other Canadian official. Personnel at missions who have not recently had a ministerial visit may believe that the minister can do 25 things in three hours having just been on an airplane for 15 hours. If you want to have a happy, productive minister, Johnston says, never schedule a briefing upon his or her arrival. As well, he advises, do not assume a minister needs to have his or her hand held at all times and expect the unexpected in terms of ministerial desires or interests. I would add a fourth element to the rule: concentrate on the reasons for the minister's trip, not on who pays for or attends dinner in a local restaurant. The devil is in the details, as we have all learned to our cost, and ministers have their own reasons for travel, but mostly they are in the host country to advance the head of mission's agenda. Ambassadors must be sure that they have identified the highest priorities for the use of the minister's time, and that the rest of the program supports the minister's ability to be effective.

The second and more important thing that heads of mission can do reduces to one word: follow-up. A minister may articulate a position with his or her counterpart and six months later we in Ottawa are wondering if anything has happened, or we see no evolution in the issue. Policy stagnation can have many explanations, but if I was going to ask a head of mission to do one thing it would be this. Having sat in on the minister's meetings, of the six things the minister said, the ambassador should identify the three that need high-level follow-up. The ambassador should then report back to the minister about what happened on those issues. I think this sort of interaction with the head of mission is crucial for the development and the successful implementation of policy.

Finally, the late John Halstead reminded us that if ministers want effective ambassadors, the responsibility begins in the minister's office. If ambassadors are to be effective advisors, Halstead said, they require more insight into the minister's thinking than can be gleaned from official statements, which do not always adequately outline the intention or ideas of the minister, of other ministers, or of the prime minister. Ambassadors also have a right to expect to be kept informed of the minister's direct contacts with his counterparts in other countries. Modern ministers frequently speak to each other by telephone and they are regularly at meetings together, and, happily, they sometimes ask each other questions much more important than "how's the weather in Ottawa?" or "how's the weather in Bonn?" It takes an extra effort to report to missions both on the substantive questions and the answers. The effort pays off if it avoids those embarrassing moments when an ambassador is told by a good friend in the foreign ministry that the two ministers had an interesting conversation and such and such was planned and — and the Canadian ambassador is left to nod sagely, as if he or she knew what was what in Ottawa.

In short, good ambassadors make for good ministers and vice versa. Ambassadors must be well-informed about their host country, sophisticated advisors on Canadian policy, and good hosts. I think all of the participants in this project would agree with that summary, but I think that my father and my grandfather, both of whom were Canadian ambassadors, would also agree. Technological, commercial, and political change have altered how the ambassador does the job, but the task in its main outlines endures.

NOTES

1. The *Department of Foreign Affairs and International Trade Act* provides that "the head of mission shall have ... the supervision of the official activities of the departments and agencies of the Government of Canada in the country or portion of the country or at the international organization to which he is appointed." (R.S., 1985, c. E-22, s. 1; 1995, c.5, s.2, section 13(2).)
2. This chapter was prepared by the editor from the transcripts of the concluding session at the workshop that gave rise to this volume.

References

Andrew, A. (1970), *Defence by Other Means: Diplomacy for the Underdog.* Toronto: Canadian Institute for International Affairs.

—— (1974/75), "The Diplomat and the Manager," *External Affairs*, XXX (1):45-56.

—— (1993), *The Rise and Fall of a Middle Power: Canadian Diplomacy from King to Mulroney.* Toronto: J. Lorimer.

Anheier, H.K. and L.M. Salamon, eds. (Forthcoming), *The Nonprofit Sector in the Developing World: A Comparative Analysis.* Manchester: Manchester University Press.

Axworthy, Hon. L. (1996), "Foreign Policy in the Information Age," notes for address, Department of Foreign affairs and International Trade, December.

Azmi, M.R. (1982), *Pakistan-Canada Relations, 1947-1982.* Islamabad:Qaid-I-Azam University.

Bailey, G. (1995), "Canadian Diplomacy as Advocacy: The Case of Chile and the NAFTA," *Canadian Foreign Policy*, 3 (3):97-112.

Balthazar, L. (1993), "Quebec's International Relations: A Response to Needs and Necessities," in *Foreign Relations and Federal States*, ed. B. Hocking. London: Leicester University Press.

Beaudoin, L. (1977), "Origines et développement du rôle international du gouvernement du Québec," in *Le Canada et le Québec sur la scène internationale*, ed. P. Painchaud. Québec: Centre québécois de relations internationales.

Berridge, G.R. (1995), *Diplomacy: Theory and Practice.* London: Prentice Hall/Harvester Wheatsheaf.

Bertrab, H. von (1997), *Negotiating NAFTA: A Mexican Envoy's Account.* Westport, CT: Praeger.

Bissell, C. (1981), *The Young Vincent Massey.* Toronto: University of Toronto Press.

Blair, A. (1998), "Permanent Representatives to the European Union," *Diplomatic Studies Programme Newsletter*, 4 (May):17-19.

Blanchette, A.E., ed. (1989), *Canadian Foreign Policy, 1966-1976: Selected Speeches and Documents.* Ottawa: Institute of Canadian Studies, Carleton University.

Bothwell, R. (1988), *Loring Christie: The Failure of Bureaucratic Imperialism.* New York: Garland.

Bourgon, J. (1997), *Fourth Annual Report to the Prime Minister on the Public Service of Canada*. Ottawa: Clerk of the Privy Council and Secretary to the Cabinet.

Boyce, R., ed. (1998), *The Communications Revolution at Work: British and Canadian Perspectives on the Social and Economic Impact of Recent Innovations in Communications Technology*. Kingston: School of Policy Studies, Queen's University.

Brown, M. (1998), "Rating the Government's Sites: The First-Ever Review of the Canadian Government's Web Sites," *C/NET Briefs Canada*, http://canada.cnet.com/Briefs/News/local/mitch/mitch 980202c.html, 2 February.

Bryden, J. (1994), "Special Interest Group Funding: MP's Report," November.

Bruchési, J. (1976), *Souvenirs d'ambassade: Mémoires 1959-1972*. Montreal: Fides.

Bull, H. (1977), *The Anarchical Society*. New York: Columbia University Press.

—— (1995), *The Anarchical Society: A Study of Order in World Politics*, 2d ed. New York: Columbia University Press.

Cadieux, M. (1949), *Le Ministère des Affaires extérieures: Conseils aux étudiants qui se destinent à la carrière*. Montreal: Dussault et Peladeau.

—— (1963), *The Canadian Diplomat: An Essay in Definition*. Toronto: University of Toronto Press.

Caldwell, G. (1965), "The Participation of French-Canadians in the Department of External Affairs: A Comparative Study of English-Speaking and French-Canadian Participation in the Career Foreign Service of the Department of External Affairs." MA thesis, Université Laval.

Canada (1962/63), Royal Commission on Government Organization, Glassco Commission. *Report of the Royal Commission on Government Organization*, 5 Vols. Ottawa: The Queen's Printer.

—— (1963), Royal Commission on Government Organization, Glassco Commission. *Report*, Volume 4: *Special Areas of Administration*. Ottawa: The Queen's Printer.

—— (1969), Department of Supply and Services, Personnel Consulting Division, Bureau of Management Consulting Services. *Manpower Planning & Development for Foreign Service Officers in the Department of External Affairs*, Volume 1, *Summary and Recommendations* and Volume 2, *Detailed Report*. Ottawa: Supply and Services Canada.

—— (1970), Department of External Affairs. *Foreign Policy for Canadians*. Ottawa: Department of External Affairs.

—— (1981), Royal Commission on Conditions of Foreign Service. *Report*. Ottawa: Supply and Services Canada.

—— (1988), Department of External Affairs. "The Secretary of State for External Affairs Invites Canadians from all Backgrounds to Apply for the Foreign Service," *News Release* No. 204, 22 September.

—— (1995), Department of Foreign Affairs and International Trade. *Canada in the World: Government Statement*. Ottawa: DFAIT.

—— (1997), Department of Foreign Affairs and International Trade. *1997-98 Estimates*, Part III: *Expenditure Plan*. Ottawa: DFAIT.

Chandhoke, N. (1995), *State and Civil Society: Explorations in Political Theory*. New Delhi/Thousand Oaks, CA/London: Sage Publications.

Chrétien, Amb. R. (1996), "One Year into a Revolution," *Queen's Quarterly*, 103(1):137.

Clark, A. and A. Van Rooy (1997), *A Dormant Revival? The Future of Aid to the Sahel*, study prepared for the Club du Sahel, Paris. Ottawa: The North-South Institute.

Cohen, A. (1994), "The Diplomats Make a Comeback," *The Globe and Mail*, 19 November.

Cohen, J.L. and A. Arato (1992), *Civil Society and Political Theory*. Cambridge, MA/ London: MIT Press.

Cooper, A.F., ed. (1985), *Canadian Culture: International Dimensions*. Waterloo, ON: Canadian Institute of International Affairs.

Cooper, A.F. (1989), "Playing by New Rules: Alan Gotlieb, Public Diplomacy, and the Management of Canada-US Relations," *The Fletcher Forum*, (Fall):93-110.

—— (1995), "In Search of Niches: Saying 'Yes' and Saying 'No' in Canada's Relations," *Canadian Foreign Policy*, III (3):1-13.

—— (1997), *Canadian Foreign Policy: Old Habits and New Directions*. Scarborough: Prentice-Hall Allyn and Bacon Canada.

Cooper, A.F. and G. Hayes, eds. (1998), *Worthwhile Initiatives? Canadian Mission-Oriented Diplomacy*. Toronto: Irwin Publishing.

Copeland, D. (1997), "Foreign Policy, Foreign Service and the 21st Century: The Challenges of Globalization," *Canadian Foreign Policy*, IV (3):105-12.

Dawson, R.M. (1958), *William Lyon Mackenzie King: A Political Biography,* Volume 1, *1874-1923*. Toronto: University of Toronto Press.

Delvoie, L.A. (1995), *Hesitant Engagement: Canada and South Asian Security*. Martello Paper No. 11. Kingston: Centre for International Relations, Queen's University.

Der Derian, J. (1987), *On Diplomacy: A Genealogy of Western Estrangement*. Oxford: Basil Blackwell.

Dobell, P.C. (1972), *Canada's Search for New Roles: Foreign Policy in the Trudeau Era*. London: Oxford University Press.

Dobell, W.M. (1989), "Canadian Relations with South Asia," in *From Mackenzie King to Pierre Trudeau: Forty Years of Canadian Diplomacy*, ed. P. Painchaud. Quebec: Presses de l'Université Laval.

"Don't be Salesmen," (1997), *The Economist,* 1 February.

Dunn, D., ed. (1996), *Diplomacy at the Highest Level: The Evolution of International Summitry*. London and New York: St. Martin's Press.

Dyment, D.K.M. (1993), "Substate Paradiplomacy: The Case of the Ontario Government," in *Foreign Relations and Federal States*, ed. B. Hocking. London: Leicester University Press.

Eagleburger, L.S. and R.L. Barry (1996), "Dollars and Sense Diplomacy: A Better Foreign Policy for Less Money," *Foreign Affairs*, 75 (4):2-8.

Eayrs, J. (1960a), "The Origins of Canada's Department of External Affairs," in *The Growth of Canadian Policies in External Affairs,* ed. H.L. Keenleyside *et al.*

—— (1960b), " 'A Low Dishonest Decade': Aspects of Canadian External Policy. 1931- 39," in *The Growth of Canadian Policies in External Affairs*, ed. H.L. Keenleyside *et al.*

—— (1961), *The Art of the Possible: Government and Foreign Policy in Canada*. Toronto: University of Toronto Press.

—— (1971), *Diplomacy and Its Discontents*. Toronto: University of Toronto Press.

—— (1982), "Canada: The Department of External Affairs," in *The Times Survey of Foreign Ministries of the World*, ed. Z. Steiner.

English, J. (1989), *Shadow of Heaven: The Life of Lester Pearson*, Volume 1, *1897-1948*. London: Vintage UK.

—— (1992), *The Worldly Years: The Life of Lester Pearson 1949-1972*. Toronto: Alfred Knopf.

Enloe, C. (1989), *Bananas, Beaches and Bases: Making Feminist Sense of International Politics*. London: Pandora.

Evans, G. and B. Grant (1991), *Australia's Foreign Relations in the World of the 1990s*. Melbourne: Melbourne University Press.

Evans, P.B., H.K. Jacobson and R.D. Putnam, eds. (1993), *Double-edged Diplomacy: International Bargaining and Domestic Politics*. Berkeley, CA: University of California Press.

Farrell, R.B. (1969), *The Making of Canadian Foreign Policy*. Scarborough: Prentice-Hall.

Ford, R.A.D. (1989), *Our Man in Moscow: A Diplomat's Reflections on the Soviet Union*. Toronto: University of Toronto Press.

"Foreign Policy Review and the Foreign Service," (1986), *bout de papier*, II (4):32-34.

"Foreign Service Officer Examinations," (1949), *External Affairs*, 1(11):35.

"Foreign Service Officer Competition," (1953), *External Affairs*, V (7):218-22.

"Foreign Services Officer Competition,"(1958), *External Affairs*, X (9):225-29.

Freifeld, S. (1990), *Undiplomatic Notes: Tales from the Canadian Foreign Service*. Willowdale: Hounslow Press.

—— (1993), "Chester Ronning: A Canadian Diplomat," *bout de papier*, X (3):22.

Fry, E.H. (1989), "The New International Cities Era: The Global Linkages of North American Cities," in *The New International Cities Era*, ed. E.H. Fry, L.H. Radebaugh and P. Soldatos. Provo: Brigham Young University.

[Gelber, N.] [1980], *Canada in London: An Unofficial Glimpse of Canada's Sixteen High Commissioners, 1880-1980*. London: Canada House.

Gibson, J.A. (1987), "Coal Fires and Candlesticks: Joining External Affairs Fifty Years Ago," *bout de papier*, V(4):12-14.

Gotlieb, A. (1979), *Canadian Diplomacy in the 1980s*. Toronto: Centre for International Studies, University of Toronto.

—— (1991), *"I'll Be With You in a Minute, Mr. Ambassador": The Education of a Canadian Diplomat in Washington*. Toronto: University of Toronto Press.

Gowing, N. (1997), *Media Coverage: Help or Hindrance for Conflict Prevention?* Washington, DC: Carnegie Commission.

Granatstein, J.L. (1981), *A Man of Influence: Norman A. Robertson and Canadian Statecraft 1929-68*. Ottawa: Deneau Publishers.

—— (1982), *The Ottawa Men: The Civil Service Mandarins, 1935-1957*. Toronto: Oxford University Press.

——, ed. (1986), *Canadian Foreign Policy: Historical Readings*. Toronto: Copp Clark Pitman Ltd.

Granatstein, J.L. and R. Bothwell (1990), *Pirouette: Pierre Trudeau and Canadian Foreign Policy*. Toronto: University of Toronto Press.

Griffith, A. (1992/93), "Straight Talk on Why Canada Needs to Reform its Trade Development Systems," *Canadian Foreign Policy*, 1 (1):61-86.

Hall, J., ed. (1995), *Civil Society: Theory, History, Comparison*. Cambridge: Polity Press.

Halstead, J.G.H. (1983), "Today's Ambassador," in *The Modern Ambassador: The Challenge and the Search*, ed. M.F. Herz.

Hamelin, J. (1969), "Québec et le monde extérieur," *Annuaire statistique du Québec, 1968-69*.

Hamilton, K. and R. Langhorne (1995), *The Practice of Diplomacy: Its Evolution, Theory and Administration*. London and New York: Routledge.

Hampson, F.O. (1989/90), "Climate Change: Building International Coalitions of the Like-Minded," *International Journal*, 45 (Winter):36-74.

—— (1990), "Pollution Across Borders: Canada's International Environmental Agenda," in *Canada Among Nations, 1989: The Challenge of Change*, ed. M.A. Molot and F.O. Hampson. Ottawa: Carleton University Press.

Hancock, P. (1997), "The Diplomacy of Recognition: Canadian Representation in Post-Communist Eurasia," paper presented to Workshop on the Role of Canadian Heads of Mission, Ottawa, July.

Hantel-Fraser, C. (1993), *No Fixed Address: Life in the Foreign Service*. Toronto: University of Toronto Press.

Haskel, B.G. (1980), "Access to Society: A Neglected Dimension of Power," *International Organization*, 34 (1):89-120.

Head, I. and P. Trudeau (1995), *The Canadian Way: Shaping Canada's Foreign Policy, 19681984*. Toronto: McClelland & Stewart.

Healy, T. and M. Neufeld (1997), "International Relations in Canada: Critical Reflections of a Discipline," *The Canadian Political Science Association Bulletin*, XXVI (1).

Heeney, A.D.P. (1972), "Independence and Partnership: The Search for Principles," *International Journal*, 27 (Spring):149-71.

Herz, M.F. ed. (1983), *The Modern Ambassador: The Challenge and the Search*. Washington: Institute for the Study of Diplomacy, Georgetown University.

Hill, O.M. (1977), *Canada's Salesman to the World: The Department of Trade and Commerce, 1892-1939*. Montreal and Kingston: McGill-Queen's University Press.

Hilliker, J. (1990), *Canada's Department of External Affairs, Volume 1, The Early Years, 19091946*. Montreal and Kingston: McGill-Queen's University Press for the Institute of Public Administration of Canada.

Hilliker, J. and D. Barry (1995), *Canada's Department of External Affairs, Volume 2, Coming of Age, 1946-1968*. Montreal and Kingston: McGill-Queen's University Press for the Institute of Public Administration of Canada.

Hillmer, N. (1985), "The Canadian Diplomatic Tradition," in *Canadian Culture: International Dimensions*, ed. A.F. Cooper. Waterloo, ON: Canadian Institute of International Affairs.

—— (1992), "The Canadian Diplomatic Tradition," in *Towards a New World: Readings in the History of Canadian Foreign Policy*, ed. J.L. Granatstein. Toronto: Copp Clark Pitman Ltd.

Hocking, B. (1995), "Beyond 'Newness' and 'Decline': The Development of Catalytic Diplomacy," Discussion Papers in Diplomacy No. 10. Leicester: University of Leicester.

Holmes, J.W. (1970), *The Better Part of Valour: Essays on Canadian Diplomacy*. Toronto: McClelland & Stewart.

—— (1973), "The Study of Diplomacy: A Sermon," in *The Changing Role of the Diplomatic Function in the Making of Foreign Policy*. Halifax, NS: Centre for Foreign Policy, Dalhousie University.

—— (1979, 1982), *The Shaping of Peace: Canada and the Search for World Order, 1943-1957*, 2 vols. Toronto: University of Toronto Press.

Ignatieff, G. (1985), *The Making of a Peacemonger*. Toronto: University of Toronto Press.

Jackson, Sir G., Lord Garner, R.Z. Smith, M.F. Herz and J.L. Granatstein, (1982), "Canada's Royal Commission on Terms of Foreign Service,"*International Journal*, XXXVII (3):378-412.

Jackson, R.H. (1990), *Quasi-States: Sovereignty, International Relations and the Third World*. Cambridge: Cambridge University Press.

Jamieson, D. (1979), transcript of interview for CBC program "The Internationalists," 27 November.

Karvonen, L. and B. Sundelius (1987), *Internationalization and Foreign Policy Management*. Aldershot: Gower.

Kaufman, J. (1988), *Conference Diplomacy: An Introductory Analysis*. Dordrecht: Marinus Nijhoff.

Keane, J., ed. (1988), *Civil Society and the State: New European Perspectives*. London: Verso.

Keenleyside, H.L. (1981), *Memoirs of Hugh L. Keenleyside,* Volume 1, *Hammer the Golden Day*. Toronto: McClelland & Stewart.

—— (1982), *Memoirs of Hugh L. Keenleyside,* Volume 2, *On the Bridge of Time*. Toronto: McClelland & Stewart.

Keenleyside, H.L. *et al.*, eds. (1960), *The Growth of Canadian Policies in External Affairs*. Durham, NC: Duke University Press.

Keenleyside, T.A. (1976), "Career Attitudes of Canadian Foreign Service Officers,"*Canadian Public Administration*, XIX (2):208-26.

—— (1979), "The Generalist versus the Specialist: The Department of External Affairs," *Canadian Public Administration*, XXII (Spring):51-71.

—— (1980/81), "Lament for a Foreign Service: The Decline of Canadian Idealism," *Journal of Canadian Studies*, XV (4):75-84.

Keith, A.B. (1912), *Responsible Governments in the Dominions*. Oxford: Oxford University Press.

Keohane, R.O. (1995), "Hobbes' Dilemma and Institutional Change in World Politics: Sovereignty in International Society," in *Whose World Order: Uneven Globalization and the End of the Cold War*, ed. H.-H. Holm and G. Sorensen. Boulder: Westview Press.

Kirton, J. (1985), "Managing Canadian Foreign Policy," in *Canada Among Nations – 1984: A Time of Transition*, ed. B. Tomlin and M. Molot.

—— (1988), "The New Internationalism: Implications for Canada's Foreign Policy and Foreign Service," *bout de papier*, VI (4):27-30.

Knowles, D. and H. Mackenzie (1994), "John Short Larke, the First Trade Commissioner," *bout de papier*, XI (3):15-16.

Kumar, K. (1993), "Civil Society: An Inquiry into the Usefulness of an Historical Term," *British Journal of Sociology*, 44(3):375-95.

Lalande, G. (1969), *The Department of External Affairs and Biculturalism. Diplomatic Personnel (1945-1965) and Language Use (1964-1965)*. Studies of the Royal Commission on Bilingualism and Biculturalism, No. 3. Ottawa: Supply and Services Canada.

Langhorne, R. (1996), *"Who Are the Diplomats Now? Current Developments in Diplomatic Services*. Wilton Park Paper No. 117. London: HMSO.

Lee, J. (1987), "The Reorganization of Canada's Department of External Affairs 1980-83: A Case Study," unpublished MA thesis, Carleton University.

Leyton-Brown, D. (1987), "External Affairs and Defence," in *Canadian Annual Review of Politics and Public Affairs, 1984*. Toronto: University of Toronto Press.

Lloyd, L. (1998), "What's in a Name? The Curious Tale of the Office of High Commissioner," mimeo, March.

Lobsinger, J. (1987), "From the President's Desk," *bout de papier*, V (3):54.

Locke, M. and C.A. Yost, eds. (1997), *Who Needs Embassies? How U.S. Missions Abroad Help Shape our World*. Washington: Institute for the Study of Diplomacy, Georgetown University.

Lyon, P.V. (1963), *The Policy Question: A Critical Appraisal of Canada's Role in World Affairs*. Toronto: McClelland & Stewart.

MacDermot, T.W.L. (1948/49), "Training for the Foreign Service,"*International Journal*, IV (1):24-32.

MacKay, R.A., ed. (1970), *Canadian Foreign Policy, 1945-1954: Selected Speeches and Documents*. Toronto: McClelland & Stewart.

[Mackenzie, H.] (1995), "William Dixon, Canada's First Immigration Agent," *bout de papier*, XII (3):17.

MacLean, G. and K.R. Nossal (1993), "Triangular Dynamics: Australian States, Canadian Provinces, and Relations with China," in *Foreign Relations and Federal States*, ed. B. Hocking. London: Leicester University Press.

Manion, J.P. (1960), *A Canadian Errant: Twenty-Five Years in the Canadian Foreign Service*. Toronto: Ryerson Press.

Manseau, C. (1987), "PAFSO News," *bout de papier*, V (3):50-54.

Marler, H. (1987), *Marler: Four Generations of a Quebec Family*. Montreal: Price-Patterson.

Martin, J. (1995), "Charm and the Embassy," *Financial Times*, 2 October, p. 2.

Massey, V. (1963), *What's Past is Prologue: The Memoirs of the Right Honourable Vincent Massey, C.H.* Toronto: Macmillan.

Mattingly, G. (1962), *Renaissance Diplomacy*. London: Jonathan Cape.

McDougall, P.A. with J. Hutson (1983), "Role of the Diplomat Today: Myth and Reality," *Diplomatic Post*, October.

McNiven, J.D. and D. Cann (1993), "Canadian Provincial Trade Offices in the United States," in *States and Provinces in the International Economy*, ed. D.M. Brown and E.H. Fry. Berkeley: Institute of Governmental Studies Press, University of California.

McRae, R. (1997), *Resistance and Revolution: Vaclav Havel's Czechoslovakia*. Ottawa: Carleton University Press.

Melissen, J., ed. (1998), *Innovation in Diplomatic Practice*. London: Macmillan.

Micromedia Ltd. (1994), *Directory of Associations in Canada, 1993-94*, 14ed. Toronto: Micromedia Ltd.

Miller, R.H. with S. Bosworth *et al.* (1992), *Inside an Embassy: The Political Role of Diplomats Abroad*. Washington: Institute for the Study of Diplomacy, Georgetown University.

Molot, M.A. (1990), "Where Do We, Should We, or Can We Sit? A Review of Canadian Foreign Policy Literature," *International Journal of Canadian Studies*, 1 (2):77-96.

Moon, C.-I. (1988), "Complex Interdependence and Transnational Lobbying: South Korea in the United States," *International Studies Quarterly*, 32 (1):67-89.

Morrison, B.M. (1976), "Canada and South Asia," in *Canada and the Third World*, ed. P. Lyon and T. Ismael. Toronto: Macmillan.

Neatby, H.B. (1963), *William Lyon Mackenzie King*, Volume 2, *1924-1932, The Lonely Heights*. Toronto: University of Toronto Press.

Nicolson, Sir H.G. (1962), *The Evolution of Diplomacy*. New York: Collier Books.

—— (1939, 1988), *Diplomacy*. Washington, DC: Institute for the Study of Diplomacy, Georgetown University.

Nierop, T. (1994), *Systems and Regions in Global Politics: An Empirical Study of Diplomacy, International Organization, and Trade 1950-1991*. Chichester and New York: John Wiley & Sons.

North-South Institute (1997), *Canadian Development Report 1996-97*. Ottawa: North-South Institute.

Nossal, K.R. (1993), "Contending Explanations for the Amalgamation of External Affairs," in *The Canadian Foreign Service in Transition*, ed. D.C. Story.

—— (1996), "Anything but Provincial: The Provinces and Foreign Affairs," in *Provinces: Canadian Provincial Politics*, ed. C. Dunn. Peterborough: Broadview Press.

—— (1997), *The Politics of Canadian Foreign Policy*, 3d ed. Scarborough: Prentice-Hall Canada.

Nye, J.S., jr. (1990), *Bound to Lead: The Changing Nature of American Power.* New York: Basic Books.

—— (1992), "What New World Order?" *Foreign Affairs,* 71(2):83-96.

Osbaldeston, G. (1982), "Reorganizing Canada's Department of External Affairs," *International Journal*, XXXVII, (3):453-66.

Pearson, L.B. (1972), *Mike: The Memoirs of the Right Honourable Lester B. Pearson, Volume 1, 1948-1957.* Toronto: University of Toronto Press.

Plumptre, A.W.F. (1973), "Diplomacy: Obsolete or Essential?" *Queen's Quarterly*, 18 (4):503-20.

Pollins, B.M. (1989), "Does Trade still Follow the Flag?" *American Political Science Review*, 83 (2):465-80.

Potter, E.H. (1996), "Redesigning Canadian Diplomacy in an Age of Fiscal Austerity," in *Big Enough to be Heard: Canada Among Nations*, ed. F.O. Hampson and M.A. Molot. Ottawa: Carleton University.

Putnam, R.D. (1988), "Diplomacy and Domestic Politics: The Logic of Two-Level Games," *International Organization,* 42 (Summer):427-60.

—— (1993), *Making Democracy Work: Civic Traditions in Modern Italy.* Princeton: Princeton University Press.

—— (1995), "Bowling Alone: America's Declining Social Capital," *Journal of Democracy,* 6(1): 65-78.

Queller, D.E. (1967), *The Office of the Ambassador in the Middle Ages.* Princeton, NJ: Princeton University Press.

"Recruitment of University Graduates," (1996), *External Affairs*, XVIII (8):344-49.

Reece, D.C. (1993), *A Rich Broth: Memoirs of a Canadian Diplomat.* Ottawa: Carleton University Press.

—— (1996), *'Special Trust and Confidence': Envoy Essays in Canadian Diplomacy.* Ottawa: Carleton University.

Reid, E. (1981), *Envoy to Nehru.* Delji, Toronto, Oxford: Oxford University Press.

—— (1989), *Radical Mandarin: The Memoirs of Escott Reid.* Toronto: University of Toronto Press.

Riddell, W.A. (1947), *World Security by Conference.* Toronto: Ryerson Press.

Ritchie, C. (1974), *The Siren Years: A Canadian Diplomat Abroad, 1937-1945.* Toronto: Macmillan Canada.

—— (1977), *An Appetite for Life: The Education of a Young Diarist, 1924-1927.* Toronto: Macmillan Canada.

—— (1978), "Views from the Pin-Striped Foxhole," transcript of interview by Bruce Little for CBC series, "The Internationalists," 13 November. Ottawa: Press Office, Department of External Affairs.

—— (1981), *Diplomatic Passport: More Undiplomatic Diaries, 1946-1962.* Toronto: Macmillan Canada.

—— (1983), *Storm Signals: More Undiplomatic Diaries, 1962-1971.* Toronto: Macmillan.

Robertson, C. (1987), "Dépêche d'Adieu: Or Three and a Half Years Later, the Self-Indulgent Farewell," *bout de papier*, V (3):46-49.

Rogers, B. (1976), "Canadian Representation Abroad," unpublished manuscript. Copy in Jules Leger Library, Department of Foreign Affairs and International Trade, Ottawa.

—— (1989), "Things Remembered: External Affairs in 1939," *bout de papier*, VII (2):20-22.

Rosenau, J.N. (1990), *Turbulence in World Politics: A Theory of Change and Continuity*. Hemel Hemstead: Harvester.

Ruggie, J.G. (1993), "Territoriality and Beyond: Problematizing Modernity in International Relations," *International Organization*, 47(1):139-74.

Runnalls, D. (1991), "What Should be Said at UNCED? Institutional Choices for the Rio Conference," in *From Stockholm to Rio, 1972-92*. Ottawa: Department of External Affairs and International Trade and Department of the Environment.

St. Laurent, Rt. Hon. L.S. (1947), "The Foundation of Canadian Policy in World Affairs," an address inaugurating the Gray Foundation Lectureship, University of Toronto, 13 January. Reference in Granatstein (1986).

Salamon, L.M. and H.K. Anheier (1994), *The Emerging Sector, an Overview*. Baltimore: The Johns Hopkins Comparative Nonprofit Sector Project Studies.

Scholte, J.-A. (1993), *International Relations of Social Change*. Buckingham: Open University Press.

Sharp, M. (1994), *Which Reminds Me: A Memoir.* Toronto: University of Toronto Press.

Sharp, P. (1997), "Who Needs Diplomats? The Problem of Diplomatic Representation," *International Journal*, LII (4):609.

Skilling, H.G. (1945), *Canadian Representation Abroad: From Agency to Embassy.* Toronto: Ryerson Press.

Smith, D.E. (1994), "From the President — Le mot du président," *CPSA Newsletter* November.

Smith, G. (1996*a*), "The Challenge of Virtual Diplomacy," speaking notes, Department of Foreign Affairs and International Trade, December.

—— (1996*b*), "Cyber-Diplomacy," speaking notes, Department of Foreign Affairs and International Trade, September.

—— (1996*c*), "Must Diplomacy Always Be on the Endangered Species List?" speech delivered at Harvard University, 12 April. Ottawa: Department of Foreign Affairs and International Trade, mimeo.

Speaight, R. (1970), *Vanier: Soldier, Diplomat and Governor General, A Biography.* Toronto: Collins.

Stairs, D. (1982), "The Political Culture of Canadian Foreign Policy," *Canadian Journal of Political Science*, 15 (4):667-90.

Stanbury, W.T. and I.B. Vertinsky (1994/95), "Information Technologies and Transnational Interest Groups: The Challenge for Diplomacy," *Canadian Foreign Policy*, 2 (3):87-100.

Starnes, J. (1987*a*), "Sunday Morning," *bout de papier*, V (1):9.

—— (1987*b*), "In Case You Missed It," *bout de papier*, V (1):9-11.

—— (1987*c*), "PAFSO News," *bout de papier,* V (1):35.

Steiner, Z. (1982), "Foreign Ministries Old and New," *International Journal*, XXXVII (3):349-77.

——, ed. (1982), *The Times Survey of Foreign Ministries of the World*. London: Times Books.

Stoner, G. (1998), "Golden Memories: A Glimpse of Life in Ottawa 50 Years Ago," *bout de papier*, XV (1):14-17.

Stopford, J., S. Strange and J.S. Henley (1991), *Rival States, Rival Firms: Competition for World Market Shares*. Cambridge: Cambridge University Press.

Story, D.C., ed. (1993), *The Canadian Foreign Service in Transition*. Toronto: Canadian Scholars Press.

Strange, S. (1992), "States, Firms and Diplomacy," *International Affairs*, 68 (January):10.

Strobel, W.P. (1997), *Late Breaking Foreign Policy: The News Media's Influence on Peace Operations*. Washington, DC: Endowment of the US Institute for Peace.

Swainson, R.F. (1975), "Canadian Diplomatic Representation in the United States," *Canadian Public Administration*, 18 (3):366-98.

Takach, G. (1989), "Clark and the Jerusalem Embassy Affair," in *The Domestic Battleground: Canada and the Arab-Israeli Conflict*, ed. D. Taras and D.H. Goldberg. Kingston, Montreal, London: McGill-Queen's University Press.

Taylor, J.H. (1997), Remarks at Workshop on the Role of Canadian Heads of Missions, transcripts, Ottawa, July.

Thibault, J.E. and C. Moreau (1991), *Canadian Heads of Post Abroad, 1880-1989*. Ottawa: Department of External Affairs and International Trade.

Thordarson, B. (1972), *Trudeau and Foreign Policy: A Study in Decision-Making*. Toronto: Oxford University Press. (Original quote in *Mclean's*, December 1969, p. 15).

"Throughly Modern Mercantilists," (1997), *The Economist*, 1 February.

Tomlin, B. and M. Molot, eds. (1985), *Canada Among Nations - 1984: A Time of Transition*. Toronto: J. Lorimer.

Tucker, M. (1980), *Canadian Foreign Policy: Contemporary Issues and Themes*. Toronto: McGraw-Hill Ryerson.

United Kingdom. Review Committee on Overseas Representation (1969), *Report of the Review Committee on Overseas Representation*. London: HMSO.

United States Advisory Commission on Public Diplomacy (1996), "A New Diplomacy for the Information Age," http://www.usia.gov/abtusia/ac, November.

Van Rooy, A. (1993), "Debating the New Imperative: Public Consultation and the Department of External Affairs," reference paper for Department of External Affairs and International Trade, March.

—— (1994), "The Altruistic Lobbyist? The Influence of Non-Governmental Organizations on Development Policy in Canada and Britain," D.Phil. thesis Oxford University.

—— (1996), "Integrating Civil Society Ideas into the World of the UNDP: Recommendations for Policy and Practice," policy paper commissioned by the UNDP's Bureau for Policy and Programme Support, November.

—— (1997*a*), "Frontiers of Influence: NGO Lobbying at the 1974 World Food Conference in Rome, the 1992 Rio Summit, and Beyond," *World Development*, 25(1): 93-114.

—— (1997*b*), "Engagement with Civil Society Organizations by Multilateral Organizations," document commissioned by DFAIT and presented at the Senior Officials Meeting of APEC member economies, August.

Veatch, R. (1975), *Canada and the League of Nations*. Toronto: University of Toronto Press.

"Vignettes - The Press on Patronage and the Foreign Service," (1988), *bout de papier, VI (1):33-34*.

Wallace, W. (1997), "The Changing Nature of Foreign Policy," London, 6 February.

Weiers, M.K. (1995), *Envoys Extraordinary: Women of the Canadian Foreign Service*. Toronto: Dundurn.

Winham, G.R. (1977), "Negotiation as a Management Process," *World Politics*, 30 (October):87-114.

—— (1993), "The Impact of Social Change on International Diplomacy," paper presented to the annual meeting of the Canadian Political Science Association, Ottawa, June.

Wolfe, R. (1998), "*Still* Lying Abroad? On the Institution of the Resident Ambassador," *Diplomacy and Statecraft*, 9 (2):22-53.

World Bank (1996), *Participation Sourcebook*. Washington, DC: World Bank.

Zacher, M.W. (1992), "The Decaying Pillars of the Westphalian Temple: Implications for International Order and Governance," in *Governance Without Government: Order and Change in World Politics*, ed. J.N. Rosenau and E.O. Czempiel. Cambridge: Cambridge University Press.

Zamkovsky, J. and J. Mesik (1996), "Slovak Republic: The Civil Society in Jeopardy, Political and Social Context," topic 256 in <peacegen.ngo.news>, posted 8 May.

PART IV

APPENDICES

APPENDIX A: Missions and Offices Abroad (February 1997)

	MISSIONS[1]		OFFICES		
	Embassies (72) and High Commissions (22)	Consulates General (17) and Consulates (9)	Trade (14)	CIDA (6)	Other (9)
Africa and Middle East MISSIONS = 28 OFFICES = 8	Abidjan, Abu Dhabi, Accra, Addis Ababa, Algiers, Amman, Bamako, Beirut, Cairo, Conakry, Dakar, Damascus, Dar-es-Salaam, Harare, Kuwait, Lagos, Libreville, Lusaka, Nairobi, Niamey, Ouagadougou, Pretoria/Le Cap, Rabat, Riyadh, Tehran, Tel Aviv, Tunis, Yaounde		Dubai Jeddah Johannesburg	Kigali Maputo	Abuja Kinshasa Tripoli
Latin America and Caribbean MISSIONS = 19 OFFICES = 8	Bogota, Brasilia, Bridgetown, Buenos Aires, Caracas, Georgetown, Guatemala, Havana, Kingston, Lima, Mexico, Montevideo, Panama, Port au Prince, Port of Spain, Quito, San Jose, Santiago	São Paulo	Guadalajara Monterrey Rio de Janeiro	La Paz Managua Tegucigalpa	San Salvador Santo Domingo
Asia Pacific MISSIONS = 29 OFFICES = 6	Almaty, Ankara, Bangkok, Beijing, Brunei, Canberra, Colombo, Dhaka, Hanoi, Hong Kong,[2] Islamabad, Jakarta, Kuala Lumpur, Manila, New Delhi, Phnom Penh, Seoul, Singapore, Tokyo, Wellington	Auckland, Bombay, Fukuoka, Guangshou, Ho Chi Minh, Nagoya, Osaka, Shanghai, Sydney	Bangalore Chandigarh Karachi Pusan	Kathmandu	Taipei[3]
Europe MISSIONS = 32 OFFICES = 3	Athens, Belgrade, Berne, Bonn, Brussels, Bucharest, Budapest, Copenhagen, Dublin, Helsinki, Kiev, Lisbon, London, Madrid, Moscow, Oslo, Paris, Prague, Riga, Rome, Sarajevo, Stockholm, The Hague, Vatican, Vienna, Warsaw, Zagreb	Düsseldorf, Hamburg, Milan, Munich, St-Petersburg			Berlin Tallinn Vilnius
United States MISSIONS = 12 OFFICES = 4	Washington, DC	Atlanta, Boston, Buffalo, Chicago, Dallas, Detroit, Los Angeles, Miami, Minneapolis, New York, Seattle	Princeton San Diego San Francisco San Jose		

Notes: [1]These figures do not include the eight missions to international organizations; when they are included, the total comes to 157 missions and offices in 107 countries.
[2]Commission
[3]under the aegis of the Canadian Chamber of Commerce

APPENDIX B

The Letter of Instructions

The letter of instructions is a key element of political direction, sent by the minister of foreign affairs to heads of mission as they take up their assignment. It confirms the relationship between the head of mission and the minister and defines managerial links between the Department of Foreign Affairs and the mission. Overlying departmental preparations, including intensive briefings, formal training, and in-depth contacts with other government departments, the private sector, and the provinces, the letter of instructions completes the preparation of the head of mission for the assignment.

It is not always possible for each head of mission to review in detail and in person with the minister of foreign affairs all aspects of an upcoming assignment. The letter of instructions bridges this gap and provides the head of mission with a political framework for the assignment. The tone is set at the beginning:

> I congratulate you on your appointment as ... (head of mission). In that position your first duty is to ensure that you and, with your leadership, your mission serve Canada and Canadians with effectiveness, probity, and economy, and that you and your mission are a credit to the country you represent and to the government on whose behalf you serve. I wish you well in that and I want to provide you with the advice, guidelines, and priorities that should direct your activities to that end.

The minister outlines the broad priorities of the government in relation to the department's international activities and the goals of the post.

> ... my basic message is to stress the importance of promoting a strong, united Canada abroad in order to strengthen Canadian prosperity at home.

This appendix was prepared by Graham Mitchell. All quotations in the text are drawn from recent letters of instructions to Canadian heads of mission.

You should bear constantly in mind that the priority of the government is to assure and enhance Canadian prosperity.... I expect you and your staff to focus on promoting the strengths of Canada to your interlocutors ... you should provide high-quality trade and investment advice to Canadian and local firms.... You should also strive to ensure that, consistent with our pursuit of rules-based, liberalized international trade, barriers to the access of Canadian goods and services are reduced to the extent possible...

I also want to underscore the importance the government attaches to the promotion of peace and security, of democratic development, of human rights and good governance, and sustainable human and economic development.

Letters of instructions have often stressed national unity and federal-provincial relations.

... you should be forceful in assuring your interlocutors that Canada is committed to making the necessary changes, in consultation with all Canadians, to remain strong and united. In all your dealings you should ensure that your hosts understand the value of the contribution that a united Canada brings to the bilateral relationship and to the international community.

Marshalling the talents and resources of Canada will enhance our ability to meet international challenges and to promote prosperity for all Canadians. In that connection, there is an evident need for the federal government to continue to work closely in... (country/countries of accreditation).

Consular and managerial priorities are always strongly emphasized.

The face of Canada to Canadians away from home is often provided by the consular section of a mission. Canadians are entitled to be well-served by it. Mishandled consular matters are a denial of that entitlement.... I stress the importance of the provision to Canadians of prompt, courteous, efficient and bilingual service.

... the government is committed to delivering quality services to Canadians. I will expect you to apply the principles of quality service in the management of your mission.... Our clients can expect to receive service that is prompt, dependable and accurate, that is courteous, that respects individual rights and dignity, and that represents good value for money.

As Head of Mission you are responsible for ensuring that the Official Languages Programme at your mission is fully implemented ... Within the mission, you should foster and encourage a bilingual working environment.... The most demonstrable aspect of implementation, however, is the spontaneous and continuous availability of bilingual services to the public.

The ministerial instructions establish both general and specific accountabilities, while describing the managerial tone the minister expects of the head of mission.

> As Head of Mission, you are the leader of a team; I expect you to lead it well and to ensure that it is a credit to Canada in the eyes of Canadians as well as of the host country. At the same time, in that team you are the leader, not *primus inter pares*: your officers and staff are accountable to you. You, on the other hand, are responsible and accountable, through me to the Government of Canada as a whole, to the Prime Minister, to the Minister for International Trade, and to each and every Minister whose responsibilities and programmes are served by your mission.

> Your principal interlocutor in the Department is the Bureau responsible for your mission, which you should keep abreast of major developments in the country and the region. In the interest of coherence and coordination, you should also ensure that the Bureau is kept informed of communications between the Mission and other Canadian federal and provincial entities, private sector companies, institutions and individuals.

The letter of instructions underlines the ambassador's responsibility for both the human and financial resources of the post. In some areas accountability goes beyond what is expected in the private sector; for example, the head of post is expected to assume a "custodial" role in relation to Canadian resources abroad.

> I want to emphasize your responsibility for your staff's welfare, including the personal protection of Canada-based employees and their families. I also draw your attention to the vital need for sound management of the human and financial resources available to you.

> As we depend increasingly upon the contribution that is made in all our missions by the locally-engaged staff, I expect you to take a close interest in the effective management of that staff.

> I attach great importance to the sound management of our posts abroad and I expect you to be manager of the totality of resources at your mission. You should see yourself as custodian of these important Canadian resources.

The letter refers specifically to policy or administrative directives concerning those departments present in the mission and their links to the Department of Foreign Affairs. For example, regarding development assistance a recent letter states, "You will be expected to advise both Foreign Affairs and the Canadian International Development Agency on the feasibility and political appropriateness of the programme in ... (country or countries of accreditation) ..., including projects proposed by Canadian non-governmental organizations." And, regarding the immigration program, "You are also responsible to the Minister of Citizenship and Immigration for carrying out our immigration programmes in ... (country or countries of accreditation) ..." In those countries where a defence liaison program exists, the minister writes, "... you are ultimately responsible for the activities and programmes of the Canadian Forces Attaché."

The letter of instructions closes with an expression of confidence.

> You have my full confidence and that of the Government in your mandate to promote and defend the interests of Canada in ... (the country/countries of accreditation). I wish you every success in your appointment.

The letter strengthens the head of mission's authority at post, particularly in relation to other government department programs. It also becomes an important reference point for issues on which the ambassador must act without specific ministerial instructions. The head of mission can draw on the letter as an indication of ministerial concern thereby strengthening the impact of an intervention.

Contributors

Andrew F. Cooper, professor of political science, University of Waterloo, is a former Léger Fellow with the Department of Foreign Affairs and International Trade. He is the author of *Canadian Foreign Policy: Old Habits and New Directions*; and *Niche Diplomacy: Middle Powers After the Cold War* (forthcoming). He is co-author, with Kim Richard Nossal and Richard Higgott, of *Relocating Middle Powers: Australia and Canada in a Changing World Order*.

Louis A. Delvoie, Skelton-Clark fellow at Queen's University and adjunct professor, Royal Military College, joined the Department of External Affairs in 1965. He served abroad in Beirut (1966-67), Cairo (1967-69), Algiers (1971-73), and Brussels (1976-78). He was ambassador to Algeria (1980-82), deputy high commissioner to the United Kingdom (1985-89), and high commissioner to Pakistan (1991-94). He is the author of numerous articles on international relations, including "Canada and Egypt: From Antagonism to Partnership," *International Journal* (1997) and "Canada and India: A New Beginning?" *The Round Table* (1998).

Lucie Edwards, assistant deputy minister (corporate services), Department of Foreign Affairs and International Trade, joined the Department of External Affairs in 1976. She has served abroad in Tel Aviv (1977-80), and Pretoria (1986-89). She was high commissioner to Kenya (1993-95), concurrently serving as ambassador to Rwanda, Burundi, Somalia, and Uganda, and as permanent representative to the United Nations Environment Programme and Habitat.

Anthony T. Eyton, The ARA Consulting Group, joined the Department of Industry Trade and Commerce in (1964), serving abroad in Lima (1965-68) and New Delhi (1971-74). He was executive director for Canada of the Asian Development Bank in Manila (1975-77); ambassador to Brazil (1983-86); and consul general in New York (1989-91).

Affiliations were current at the time of the workshop in June 1997.

Paul Frazer, minister (public affairs), Canadian Embassy, Washington, DC, joined the Department of External Affairs in 1974 serving abroad in Warsaw (1975-77), New York (1979-83), and Washington (1994-). He was ambassador to the Czech and Slovak Republics (1992-94).

Janet L. Graham, Human Resources Policy and Operations Division, Department of Foreign Affairs and International Trade, joined the Department of External Affairs in 1977 serving abroad in Pretoria (1978-80), Port of Spain (1986-88), and Harare (1992-96). She was acting high commissioner in Nigeria (1996-97).

Paul Heinbecker, assistant deputy minister (Global Affairs and Security Policy), Department of Foreign Affairs and International Trade, joined the Department of External Affairs in 1965, serving abroad in Ankara (1966-70); Stockholm (1972-75); the Canadian Delegation to the Organisation for Economic Co-operation and Development in Paris (1975-79); and Washington (1985-89). He was ambassador to the Federal Republic of Germany (1992-96).

Richard Kohler, chief information officer and director-general, Information Management and Technology Bureau, Department of Foreign Affairs and International Trade, joined the Department of Industry Trade and Commerce in 1972, serving abroad in Paris (1973-76 and 1992-94), Sao Paolo (1976-78), Bucharest (1978-80), and Bangkok (1985-88). Kohler is the author of numerous articles on issues related to the foreign service.

David Lee, director-general, International Organizations Bureau, Department of Foreign Affairs and International Trade, joined the Department of External Affairs in 1961, serving abroad in Geneva (1963-66), Tehran (1966-69), Tokyo (1972-75), Brussels-EC (1975-79), and in the Permanent Mission of Canada to the United Nations, New York (1982-86).

Hector Mackenzie, senior departmental historian, Department of Foreign Affairs and International Trade, is the editor of two volumes (for 1948 and 1949) in the series, *Documents on Canadian External Relations*. He has published numerous articles on Canadian foreign, defence, and economic policies during World War II and the Cold War, and he has been a member of the editorial board of *bout de papier* since 1992.

Jean-Marc Métivier, vice-president, Asia Branch, Canadian International Development Agency, joined the Canadian International Development Agency in 1972. He was executive director for Canada to the Asian Development Bank in Manila (1986-90).

Kim Richard Nossal, professor of political science, McMaster University, is the author of *The Patterns of World Politics* (1998), *The Politics of Canadian Foreign*

Policy (1997), *Rain Dancing: Sanctions in Canadian and Australian Foreign Policy* (1994), and a number of other works.

Alan B. Nymark, associate deputy minister, Health Canada, joined the International Branch of the Department of Finance in 1972. He was director of policy for the Royal Commission on the Economic Union and Development Prospects for Canada (Macdonald Commission); assistant chief negotiator with the Trade Negotiations Office of the Canada/US Free Trade Agreement (1985-89); and assistant deputy minister, Industry and Science Policy, Industry Canada.

Michael Pearson, senior policy advisor to the minister of foreign affairs, Department of Foreign Affairs and International Trade, served as policy advisor to Opposition Critics for Foreign Affairs and Defence (1987-93), and senior policy advisor to the minister of foreign affairs (1993-97).

Peter Sutherland, director-general, Trade Commissioner Service, Planning and Policy, Department of Foreign Affairs and International Trade, joined the Department of Industry Trade and Commerce in 1971, serving abroad in New York (1972-73), Abidjan (1973-75), and at the Inter-American Development Bank in Washington (1975-77). He was ambassador to Saudi Arabia (1993-96).

Alison Van Rooy, senior researcher, The North-South Institute, is a former Norman Robertson Research Fellow at the Department of External Affairs and International Trade. She has written on social development policy, civil society issues, and non-governmental organizations. She is the author of *A Partial Promise? Canadian Support to Social Development in the South*, co-author with Andrew Clark of *A Dormant Revival? The Future of Aid to the Sahel*, and editor of *Civil Society and the Aid Industry*.

Robert Wolfe, assistant professor of policy studies and senior fellow, Centre for International Relations, Queen's University, joined the Department of External Affairs in 1976, serving abroad in Dhaka (1977-79) and in the Canadian Delegation to the Organisation for Economic Co-operation and Development in Paris (1981-85). He joined the faculty of the School of Policy Studies in 1995. He is the author of *Farm Wars: The Political Economy of Agriculture and the International Trade Regime* (1998) and of numerous articles on international economic relations and diplomacy.

Queen's Policy Studies
Recent Publications

The Queen's Policy Studies Series is dedicated to the exploration of major policy issues that confront governments in Canada and other western nations. McGill-Queen's University Press is the exclusive world representative and distributor of books in the series.

School of Policy Studies

Issues in Defence Management, Douglas L. Bland (ed.), 1998
Paper ISBN 0-88911-809-4 Cloth ISBN 0-88911-811-6

Diplomatic Missions: The Ambassador in Canadian Foreign Policy, Robert Wolfe (ed.), 1998
Paper ISBN 0-88911-801-9 Cloth ISBN 0-88911-803-5

Canada's National Defence, vol. 1, *Defence Policy,* Douglas L. Bland (ed.), 1997
Paper ISBN 0-88911-792-6 Cloth ISBN 0-88911-790-X

Lone-Parent Incomes and Social-Policy Outcomes: Canada in International Perspective,
Terrance Hunsley, 1997
Paper ISBN 0-88911-751-9 Cloth ISBN 0-88911-757-8

Social Partnerships for Training: Canada's Experiment with Labour Force Development Boards, Andrew Sharpe and Rodney Haddow (eds.), 1997
Paper ISBN 0-88911-753-5 Cloth ISBN 0-88911-755-1

Institute of Intergovernmental Relations

Canada: The State of the Federation 1997, vol. 12, *Non-Constitutional Renewal,*
Harvey Lazar (ed.), 1998
Paper ISBN 0-88911-765-9 Cloth ISBN 0-88911-767-5

Canadian Constitutional Dilemmas Revisited, Denis Magnusson (ed.), 1997
Paper ISBN 0-88911-593-1 Cloth ISBN 0-88911-595-8

Canada: The State of the Federation 1996, Patrick C. Fafard and Douglas M. Brown (eds.), 1997
Paper ISBN 0-88911-587-7 Cloth ISBN 0-88911-597-4

Comparing Federal Systems in the 1990s, Ronald Watts, 1997
Paper ISBN 0-88911-589-3 Cloth ISBN 0-88911-763-2

John Deutsch Institute for the Study of Economic Policy

The 1997 Federal Budget: Retrospect and Prospect, Thomas J. Courchene and Thomas A. Wilson (eds.), Policy Forum Series no. 35
Paper ISBN 0-88911-774-8 Cloth ISBN 0-88911-772-1

The Nation State in a Global/Information Era: Policy Challenges, Thomas J. Courchene (ed.), Bell Canada Papers no. 5, 1997
Paper ISBN 0-88911-770-5 Cloth ISBN 0-88911-766-7

Reforming the Canadian Financial Sector: Canada in a Global Perspective,
Thomas J. Courchene and Edwin H. Neave (eds.), 1997
Paper ISBN 0-88911-688-1 Cloth ISBN 0-88911-768-3

Available from:
McGill-Queen's University Press
http://www.mcgill.ca/mqup
Tel.: 1-514-398-3750